iTunes® and iCloud® for iPhone®, iPad®, & iPod® touch

ABSOLUTE BEGINNER'S GUIDE

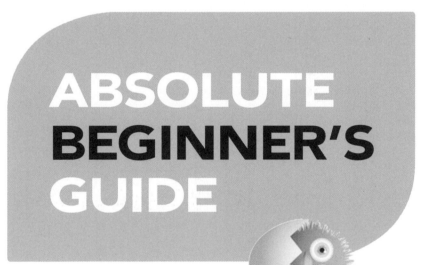

Brad Miser

800 East 96th Street,
Indianapolis, Indiana 46240

9030 00003 4331 2

iTunes® and iCloud® for iPhone®, iPad®, & iPod® touch Absolute Beginner's Guide

ISBN-13: 978-0-7897-5064-8
ISBN-10: 0-7897-5064-3

Library of Congress Control Number: 2013935264

Printed in the United States of America

First Printing: April 2013

Trademarks

Warning and Disclaimer

Bulk Sales

Que Publishing offers excellent discounts on this book when ordered in quantity for bulk purchases or special sales. For more information, please contact

U.S. Corporate and Government Sales
1-800-382-3419
corpsales@pearsontechgroup.com

For sales outside the United States, please contact

International Sales
international@pearsoned.com

Editor In Chief
Greg Weigand

Senior Acquisitions Editor
Laura Norman

Development Editor
Lisa Abbott

Managing Editor
Sandra Schroeder

Senior Project Editor
Tonya Simpson

Copy Editor
Barbara Hacha

Indexer
Lisa Stumpf

Proofreader
Jess DeGabriele

Technical Editor
Yvonne Johnson

Editorial Assistant
Cindy Teeters

Book Designer
Anne Jones

Compositor
Mary Sudul

Contents at a Glance

Table of Contents

About the Author

Brad Miser has written extensively about technology, with his favorite topics being Apple's amazing "i" technology—especially iTunes and the iPhones/iPod touches/iPads—that enable us to enjoy music, movies, TV shows, and other digital media wherever we are. In addition to *iTunes and iCloud for iPhone, iPad, & iPod touch Absolute Beginner's Guide*, Brad has written many other books, including *My iPhone*, 6th Edition; *My iPod touch*, 4th Edition; *Sams Teach Yourself Mac OS X Lion*; *Sams Teach Yourself iTunes 10 in 10 Minutes*; and *Sams Teach Yourself iCloud in 10 Minutes*. He has also been an author, development editor, or technical editor for more than 50 other titles.

Brad is or has been a sales support specialist, the director of product and customer services, and the manager of education and support services for several software development companies. Previously, he was the lead proposal specialist for an aircraft engine manufacturer, a development editor for a computer book publisher, and a civilian aviation test officer/engineer for the U.S. Army. Brad holds a Bachelor of Science degree in mechanical engineering from California Polytechnic State University at San Luis Obispo and has received advanced education in maintainability engineering, business, and other topics.

In addition to his passion for silicon-based technology, Brad is very active building and flying radio-controlled aircraft.

Originally from California, Brad now lives in Brownsburg, Indiana, with his wife, Amy; their three daughters, Jill, Emily, and Grace; a rabbit; and a sometimes-inside cat.

Brad would love to hear about your experiences with this book (the good, the bad, and the ugly). You can write to him at bradmiser@icloud.com.

Dedication

I leave you, hoping that the lamp of liberty will burn in your bosoms until there shall no longer be a doubt that all men are created free and equal.

—Abraham Lincoln

Acknowledgments

To the following people on the *iTunes and iCloud for iPhone, iPad, & iPod touch Absolute Beginner's Guide* project team, my sincere appreciation for your hard work on this book:

Laura Norman, my acquisitions editor, who made this project possible and who selected me to write it (thank you!). I've been privileged to work with Laura on many projects and really appreciate her professional, yet personal, approach.

Lisa Abbott, my development editor, who helped make the contents and organization of this book much better. Yvonne Johnson, my technical editor, who did a great job ensuring that the information in this book is both accurate and useful. Barbara Hacha, my copy editor, who corrected my many misspellings, poor grammar, and other problems. Tonya Simpson, my project editor, who skillfully managed the hundreds of files that it took to make this book into something real. Que's production and sales team for printing the book and getting it into your hands.

And now for some people who weren't on the project team but who were essential to me personally. Amy Miser, my wonderful wife, for supporting me while I wrote this book; living with an author under tight deadlines isn't always lots of fun, but Amy does so with grace, understanding, and acceptance of my need to write. Jill, Emily, and Grace Miser, my delightful daughters, for helping me stay focused on what is important in life. Although iTunes can play beautiful music, these precious people are beautiful music given form!

We Want to Hear from You!

As the reader of this book, *you* are our most important critic and commentator. We value your opinion and want to know what we're doing right, what we could do better, what areas you'd like to see us publish in, and any other words of wisdom you're willing to pass our way.

We welcome your comments. You can email or write to let us know what you did or didn't like about this book—as well as what we can do to make our books better.

Please note that we cannot help you with technical problems related to the topic of this book.

When you write, please be sure to include this book's title and author as well as your name and email address. We will carefully review your comments and share them with the author and editors who worked on the book.

Email: feedback@quepublishing.com

Mail: Que Publishing
ATTN: Reader Feedback
800 East 96th Street
Indianapolis, IN 46240 USA

Reader Services

Visit our website and register this book at quepublishing.com/register for convenient access to any updates, downloads, or errata that might be available for this book.

INTRODUCTION

- What this book is about
- How this book is organized
- Technology covered
- Conventions used in this book
- Let me know what you think

INTRODUCTION

Apple's "i" hardware and software revolutionized the ways people enjoy music, movies, TV shows, books, and other digital media both on computers (using the iTunes application) and, of course, on the incredibly popular iPads, iPhones, and iPod touches. This book is designed to help you get up to speed quickly and easily so that you can make the most of this great technology for yourself.

iTunes is the starting point for your digital media travels. That's because you can use iTunes to store and play all kinds of things, including music, audiobooks, movies, music videos, TV shows, and so on. You can build your content library using the iTunes Store, which is integrated into iTunes to make downloading new content simple. You can also add music, movies, and other media you already own almost as easily.

After you've stocked your digital shelves, you can use iTunes to enjoy your digital media on a computer. You can listen to music or watch an episode of a favorite TV show with just a few clicks of your mouse. And because iTunes is so useful, you'll likely end up with a large amount of music, movies, TV shows, podcasts, books, and the like in your iTunes Library. Fortunately, iTunes also includes many features to help you keep this content organized so that you can listen to or watch whatever you want easily and quickly.

iCloud is Apple's online service that enables you to store content in the Internet "cloud." This is useful because it enables you to access the same content from multiple devices. For example, you can start listening to a podcast on your computer and then move over to an iPad and pick it up right where you left off. Or you can quickly access and play any of your music, even if it isn't stored on your iOS device or computer.

Speaking of iOS devices, let me say that they are amazing. After you start using an iPad, iPhone, or iPod touch, you may wonder how you ever got along without one (at least, that is the case for me!). These powerful devices are outstanding digital media players. You can use their apps for music, video, podcasts, books, your own photos and video, and much more. Incredible! (iOS devices can also be used for a lot more than digital media, including email, texting, web surfing, running apps, and so on, but here we are focused on digital media.)

It is my hope that the *iTunes and iCloud for iPhone, iPad, & iPod touch Absolute Beginner's Guide* enhances your life by helping you get the most out of this fantastic technology with a minimum of fuss and absolutely no muss (whatever that is!).

How This Book Is Organized

This book contains several parts:

- **Part I, "iTunes,"** provides you with an in-depth explanation of the iTunes application. It starts with a detailed tour of the application followed by information you need to use the iTunes Store. From there, you learn how to add media to your iTunes Library, and then you explore how you can enjoy that content, which includes music and video. After the basics are covered, you learn how to add and edit information about your media, create and use playlists, enjoy podcasts, and play your iTunes content on other devices.

- **Part II, "iCloud,"** tells you how to connect iTunes and your iOS devices to Apple's iCloud service so that you can easily share your media among computers and iOS devices. You learn how to set up an iCloud account on each type of device and how to use iCloud with photos and music.

- **Part III, "iPads/iPhones/iPod touches,"** guides you through the many ways you can experience your iTunes media on iPads, iPhones, and iPod touches. You first learn how to put movies, TV shows, and other types of media onto these devices by downloading it directly or syncing the devices with iTunes.

Then, you learn how to use various apps, including Music, Podcasts, Videos, and iBooks. The part concludes with using iOS devices for your own photos and video.

Technology Covered

All three of the "i" topics explained in this book are applicable to people who use Windows PCs and for those who prefer Macintosh computers. In fact, most of the information is the same, no matter which type of computer you use. When differences exist, you see the information that applies to each, such as how to accomplish a specific task using the appropriate keyboard shortcut for each type of hardware.

For Windows users, the information in this book is based on Windows 7. If you use Windows 8, there may be some differences, but because we spend most of the time in the iTunes application, those differences shouldn't be significant.

For Mac users, this book is based on OS X Mountain Lion.

When this book was written, iTunes was on version 11, which was quite different from the previous versions, so make sure you are using the latest version, as explained in Part I.

Finally, the book was also based on iOS 6, which is the version of software that runs iPads, iPhone, and iPod touches as of the writing of this book.

Conventions Used in This Book

The following sections describe the conventions used throughout this book.

Commands

On a Mac or Windows PC, you tell the computer (or more specifically, the application you are using) what you want it to do by issuing commands. You do this by opening the menu on which the command is located and selecting it. The shorthand I use for choosing a menu command is **Menu**, **Command**. The name you should look for on each level is in bold, and each level is separated with a comma. For example, if you see "choose **View**, **View Options**," that means you should click the **View** menu and choose the **View Options** command. There can be more than one level in a menu, too, as in **File**, **New**, **Playlist**.

On iOS devices, you tap the screen to issue commands. For example, to open the Settings app, you tap the **Settings** icon. Similar to menu commands, there are levels of command; you may see something like, "Tap **Settings**, and then tap **General**." This indicates you should tap the **Settings** icon on the Home page and then tap the **General** command on the Settings screen.

Keyboard and Other Shortcuts

iTunes provides lots of keyboard shortcuts to make commands easier and faster to use; a keyboard shortcut is a combination of one or more special keys along with a letter or symbol that are joined with the + on a Windows computer or a - on a Mac to indicate that you should press the keys at the same time. For example, Shift-⌘-N tells you that you should press the Shift key, the Command key (on a Mac), and the letter N at the same time.

You don't have to use keyboard shortcuts because you can always make a menu selection to do the same thing. However, using a keyboard shortcut is faster and easier, so they are worth learning for the commands you use frequently.

There are also times when you perform a secondary click, which is also known as a right-click, on something on the screen to access commands on a contextual menu. It's called a secondary click (instead of a right-click) because many devices don't use a mouse. Instead, they have trackpads, on which you may use gestures to accomplish a secondary click rather than the "right button" on a mouse.

Special Elements

As you read through this book, you encounter special elements in the text. These are designed to enhance your experience with this book by providing additional information that doesn't necessarily belong in the main text. There are three types of special elements: Notes, Tips, and Cautions.

NOTE   Notes are tidbits of information that I think are useful, but not essential, for you to get the most from iTunes, iCloud, or iOS devices. You could skip the notes and still get the key information, but I hope you find them interesting as you move through this book.

TIP   Tips provide you with shortcuts or alternative ways of doing things. Tips are not essential, but in them you may discover information that enables you to get things done faster or easier.

CAUTION A caution calls your attention to things that may result in something happening that you probably won't want to happen. There aren't many of these in this book, but when you run across one, make sure you give it your attention to avoid an unpleasant outcome.

Let Me Know What You Think

I hope you have a great experience with this book, and that it helps you get a lot of enjoyment from iTunes, iCloud, and your iOS devices. I've tried to cover the topics that I think most people need. However, every reader is unique, so you may run into an issue or need information that isn't included. Or you may simply have a correction or suggestion that you'd like to share, which I always appreciate and use to improve future versions.

In any or all of these circumstances, I'd love to hear from you. You can reach me at bradmiser@icloud.com. I do my best to respond to each and every email I receive as quickly as possible, and I look forward to hearing from you!

GETTING STARTED WITH ITUNES

As you learned in the introduction, iTunes is an amazing application you can use to store, organize, and enjoy music, movies, TV shows, podcasts, audiobooks, and so on. It is also a great partner for your iOS device, whether you have an iPhone, iPad, or iPod touch—or one of each! You can also use iTunes to stream content, such as music or movies, to other devices including home theater systems, Apple TVs, or other AirPlay-enabled devices. In this chapter, you'll start to learn how to take advantage of all that iTunes offers.

In the first part of this chapter, you'll learn how to install and maintain iTunes on a Windows PC or maintain it on a Mac. The steps for using iTunes on a Windows PC and on a Macintosh are nearly identical; however, there are differences in how you maintain iTunes on each. Just read the section that is applicable to the type of computer you use.

From there, you'll take a tour of iTunes so that you get the "big picture" of what the application can do and how it works. You'll also learn about some key preferences you can set in iTunes and how to set up the iTunes window so that it matches the figures in this book.

Installing and Maintaining iTunes on a Windows PC

Computers that run the Windows operating system don't include iTunes by default, so you need to download and install it on your computer. Then you should configure iTunes so that it keeps itself current to ensure you are always running the latest (and hopefully greatest) version.

 NOTE   Many versions of Windows can run iTunes. This book is based on Windows 7. If you use a different version of Windows, what you experience may be a bit different from what the text and figures provided in this section describe. You should still be able to use this information to install iTunes. The good news is that using iTunes is very similar under all versions of Windows, so most of the information in this book will work for you as written, regardless of the version of Windows on your computer.

Downloading and Installing iTunes on a Windows PC

To see whether iTunes is already installed, open the Windows menu, choose All Programs, and look for the iTunes folder. If you don't see that folder, iTunes isn't installed and you need to complete these steps. If you do see the iTunes folder, iTunes is installed and you can skip to the next section.

 NOTE   To install iTunes on a Windows PC, it must be running Windows XP, Service Pack 2 or later, or 32-bit editions of Windows Vista, Windows 7, or Windows 8. The 64-bit versions of Windows Vista, Windows 7, or Windows 8 require the 64-bit iTunes Installer application. Does all this really matter? Not really, because your web browser should detect the version of Windows you are using and download the correct installer. Two things you need to keep in mind are that you need at least 400MB of available disk space and a broadband Internet connection (such as cable, DSL, or high-speed cellular), which is required to work with the iTunes Store.

To download and install iTunes, perform the following steps:

1. Open your favorite web browser, such as Internet Explorer.

2. Move to www.apple.com/itunes/download.

3. Uncheck the check boxes if you don't want to receive email from Apple (see Figure 1.1); if you want to receive email from Apple, leave the box for the type of information you want to receive checked.

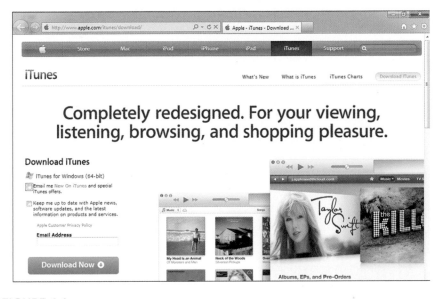

FIGURE 1.1

Downloading iTunes is easy and free; what could be better?

4. Enter your email address if you left either of the boxes checked; if you unchecked both of them in step 3, you don't need to enter your email address.

5. Click **Download Now**. What happens next depends on the specific version of Windows you are running, the brand and version of security software you are using, and whether some Apple software is already installed. The rest of these steps are for Windows 7 and assume some Apple software has been installed already. If you are using a different version of Windows or don't have any other Apple software, the specific dialogs and steps may be a bit different. That's okay, though, because Windows prompts you for any information you need to provide to download and install iTunes.

6. Click **Run**. The installer software is downloaded to your computer; when that is complete, it opens and starts the installation process. (You can click Save if you

want to just download the installer and run it later, but you might as well do both with one click.)

7. Read the information in the Installer window and click **Next**.

8. Using Figure 1.2 as a guide, check the following options to make them active, or uncheck them to make them inactive:

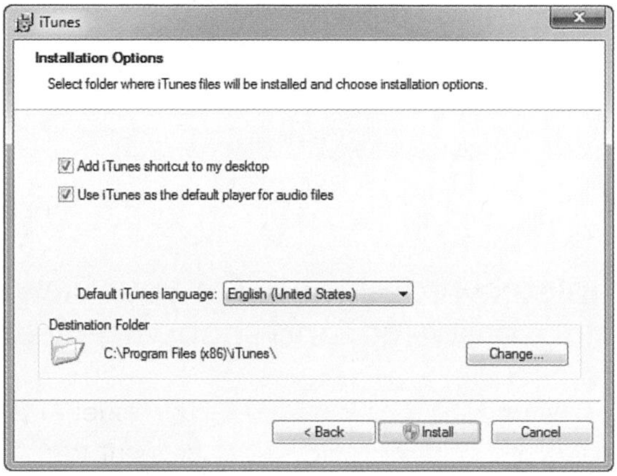

FIGURE 1.2

As you install iTunes, you have several options, such as whether you want iTunes to be the default player for audio files.

- **Add iTunes shortcut to my desktop**—This option places a shortcut to iTunes on your desktop. Unless you don't like desktop shortcuts for some reason, you should leave this option checked.

- **Use iTunes as the default player for audio files**—This option selects iTunes to be used to play most audio files you access on the Internet, your computer, CDs, and so on. If you prefer to use another application, such as Windows Media Player, uncheck this box. However, I recommend that you leave it checked for now. You can always change the default application to something else after you have become comfortable with iTunes.

- **Default iTunes language**—If you don't want iTunes to display the language shown on the drop-down list, select a different language.

- **Destination folder**—If you don't want iTunes to be installed in the default location, click **Change** and use the resulting dialog to choose a different location.

TIP You might be prompted to allow Apple software to be auto-matically updated. If so, you should enable automatic updates.

9. Click **Install**.

10. Click **Yes** in any security warnings you see, but make sure they are related to iTunes before you do! You'll likely have to do this at least a couple of times during the process. When the installation process is complete, you see the Congratulations screen.

11. Click **Finish**. Unless you uncheck the corresponding box in the Congratulations dialog, iTunes opens. The first time you use it, you must agree to the license terms and conditions, and after you do that, the application is ready for you to use.

Maintaining iTunes on a Windows PC

Apple is continually updating iTunes to address issues and enhance the way it works. You should keep your copy of iTunes current to ensure that you have the best experience possible. You can do this manually or configure iTunes to keep itself up-to-date.

If iTunes isn't running, you need to open it. To open iTunes, you can double-click its shortcut on the desktop or open the **Windows** menu, choose **All Programs**, open the **iTunes** folder, and click the **iTunes** icon.

NOTE By default, the iTunes menu bar is hidden. You can show it by pressing the Alt key. You need to show the menu to access some of iTunes' controls (though many have keyboard shortcuts).

You can check for an iTunes update manually at any time. If the menu bar isn't shown, press the Alt key so that the iTunes menu bar appears. With the menu bar shown, select **Help**, **Check for Updates**. iTunes connects to the Internet and checks for a newer version of the application. If a new version is available, you are prompted to download and install it. If a newer version is not available, you see a dialog box telling you that you are using the current version.

Setting up iTunes so that it keeps itself current automatically is good because you don't have to think about doing it yourself. To check to make sure automatic updates are enabled, choose **Edit**, **Preferences** (if the menu bar isn't shown, press the Alt key to see the Edit command) and click the **General** pane of the iTunes Preferences dialog box. Check the **Check for new software updates automatically** box and click **OK**.

When iTunes detects that a new version is available, you are prompted to download and install it.

Maintaining iTunes on a Macintosh

Because iTunes is developed by Apple, it is installed with OS X by default; unless you've removed it for some reason, you don't need to install the software on your Mac.

 TIP If iTunes isn't on your Mac, open your web browser and go to www.apple.com/itunes/download. Uncheck the two email check boxes, click the **Download Now** button, and follow the onscreen instructions to download and install iTunes.

Apple is continually updating iTunes to address issues and improve its functionality so you should make sure you are using the current version. You can do this manually or you can configure OS X to keep iTunes current for you automatically.

To check for updates manually, open the **Apple** menu and choose **Software Update**. The App Store application becomes active, and you move to the Updates tab. Here you see and can download and install any updates for your software that are available, including iTunes. If an update is available for iTunes, click its **Update** button to download and install it.

Although you can easily update iTunes manually, it's better to have OS X update iTunes for you automatically:

1. Open the **Apple** menu and choose **System Preferences**.

2. Click **Software Update**.

3. Check the **Automatically check for updates** box (see Figure 1.3).

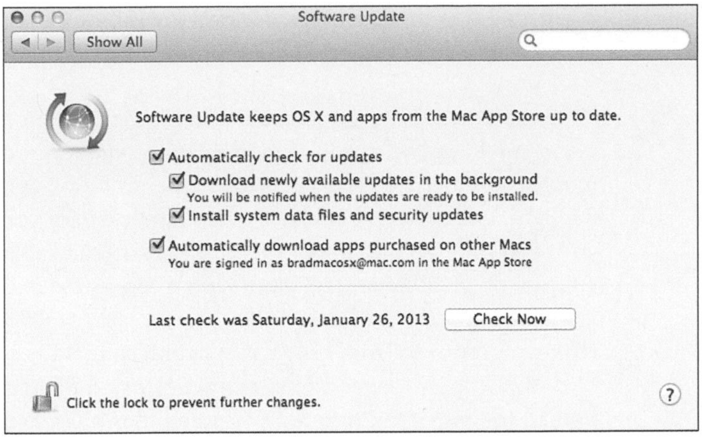

FIGURE 1.3

Configure Software Update to keep your software, including iTunes, updated automatically.

4. Check the **Download newly available updates in the background** box. OS X automatically checks for updates for iTunes, along with all the other software that is available in the Mac App Store on your Mac. When updates are available, they are automatically downloaded and installed through the App Store application.

> **TIP** It's a good idea to check the **Install system data files and security updates** box so that these important parts of OS X are kept current too.

Touring iTunes

iTunes is a very useful application; here are just some of the things you can do with it:

- Listen to music, podcasts, and audiobooks.

- Watch movies, TV shows, video podcasts, and music videos.

- Shop in the iTunes Store for music, video, iOS apps, and much more.

- Store and organize your video, audio, and other digital media.

- Create playlists to customize how you watch and listen to the content of your iTunes Library.

- Manage the content on your iOS devices (iPads, iPhones, and iPod touches).

- Stream your content so that it plays on other devices, such as a home theater system.

Fortunately, even with all this functionality, iTunes is well designed, and you'll get used to it quickly.

NOTE If you have very little or no content in your iTunes Library, when you open the application, the iTunes window may not look much like the figures you see in this chapter because they show a fully stocked iTunes Library. If that is the case for you, I suggest you read through the rest of this chapter without replicating what you see on your computer. When you're done, move to Chapter 2, "Working with the iTunes Store," and Chapter 3, "Building Your iTunes Library," to learn how to add content to your library. Then come back to this section to get practice using the iTunes window before you move to Chapter 4, "Listening to Music with iTunes."

Understanding the iTunes Window

When you open iTunes (on a Windows PC, click the iTunes desktop shortcut; on the OS X Dock, click the iTunes icon), you see the various elements of its window, as shown in Figure 1.4. (The specific elements you see depend on the type of content you are working with; more on that in the next section.)

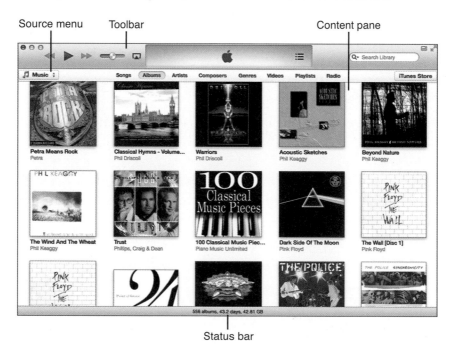

FIGURE 1.4

iTunes offers many tools you can use to enjoy different kinds of content.

On the toolbar at the top of the window, you see a set of tools you can use to work with your content. This toolbar looks a bit different on a Mac (see Figure 1.5) than it does on a Windows computer (see Figure 1.6), but both have similar features.

FIGURE 1.5

The toolbar on a Mac contains a number of useful buttons along with the Information window and Search tool.

FIGURE 1.6

The toolbar on a Windows PC looks a bit different than on a Mac, but it works similarly.

The toolbar includes the following features:

- **iTunes menu (Windows)**—Because the iTunes menu bar is hidden on a Windows computer by default, the application includes the iTunes menu that you can use to access more commonly used commands. On a Mac, the iTunes menu bar is always shown (except when you use Full Screen mode).

- **Window controls**—iTunes uses the standard window controls on both Macs and Windows computers. You can use these to close, minimize, or zoom/ maximize the iTunes window.

- **Playback controls**—Here you see the familiar Play/Stop, Fast Forward, and Rewind buttons along with the Volume Control slider. These work as you probably expect them to. What may not be as familiar to you is the AirPlay button that you can use to play iTunes content on other devices (you learn more about this in Chapter 9, "Streaming Music and Video Through an AirPlay Network").

- **Information window**—In the center of the top part of the iTunes window is the Information window. In this area, you see a variety of information about what you are doing at any point in time. For example, when you are playing music, you see information about the music currently being played. When you import music, you see information about the import process. When you download music from the iTunes Store, you see information about the download process. When you are syncing an iOS device, information about that process displays. It also contains the Up Next button that you can use to see what will play next and to control how music plays (more on this in Chapter 4).

- **Search tool**—You use the Search tool to search for content that you want to work with.

- **MiniPlayer button (OS X)**—Click this to put iTunes into the MiniPlayer view, which collapses the window to the "bare essentials" so it takes up less space on your desktop. On a Windows computer, you can switch to the MiniPlayer view by opening the **iTunes** menu and choosing **Switch to MiniPlayer**.

- **Full screen (OS X)**—This button, which appears only on the OS X version of iTunes, puts iTunes in Full Screen mode.

As mentioned previously, on a Windows PC the iTunes menu bar, which appears just below the toolbar, is hidden by default. There are a number of ways to show or hide this menu bar. If you press the Alt key or press Ctrl+B, the menu bar appears. To hide it again, press Ctrl+B. You can also show or hide the menu bar by opening the **iTunes** menu and choosing **Show Menu Bar** or **Hide Menu Bar**.

On a Mac, the iTunes menu bar appears in the normal location at the top of the screen, except when you put iTunes in Full Screen mode. In this mode, the iTunes window fills the screen and the iTunes menu bar is hidden. If you move the pointer to the top of the screen, the menu bar appears, and you can use its options. When you move off the menu, it is hidden again.

In the center part of the iTunes window are the Source menu and Content pane, which are explained in the next section.

Located at the bottom of the iTunes window, the Status bar provides information about the source of content with which you are working; the Status bar is hidden by default. If the Status bar doesn't appear, choose **View**, **Show Status Bar**. (On a Windows PC, you need to show the menu bar by pressing the Alt key to see the View menu.) The Status bar provides information you may find useful, such as the playback time and storage required for the source of music you are working with (refer to Figure 1.4 to see an example of this information).

NOTE The iTunes window can look different depending on the content with which you are working, your preference settings, and other factors. Many of these options are covered throughout this part of the book in the context where you use them (for example, iTunes Store options are explained in Chapter 2).

As noted earlier, you can use the MiniPlayer to collapse the iTunes window down to the minimum size so that you have the basic controls available without using very much desktop space with the iTunes window (see Figure 1.7 for the MiniPlayer on a Mac or Figure 1.8 to see it on a PC). To move into the MiniPlayer on a Mac, click the **MiniPlayer** button on the toolbar or choose **Window**, **MiniPlayer**. To do the same on a PC, open the **iTunes** menu and choose **Switch to MiniPlayer** or press Ctrl+Shift+M.

FIGURE 1.7

The MiniPlayer enables you to get information about and control music while using a minimum of screen real estate.

FIGURE 1.8

When you hover over the MiniPlayer, playback controls appear.

Information about the music that is playing appears in the window along with some of the buttons that also appear in the toolbar when the iTunes window is visible. If you move the pointer over the MiniPlayer, playback controls appear; you can use these to control playback just like when you are using the iTunes window.

To return to the iTunes window, click the **iTunes window** button.

Working with Different Types of Media

iTunes organizes your media by type, such as music, movies, podcasts, and so on. You determine the type of media with which you want to work by opening the **Source** menu located just under the playback controls at the top of the screen;

the name of this menu is the type of content currently being displayed, such as Music (see Figure 1.9).

FIGURE 1.9

Choose the type of media with which you want to work on the Source menu.

When you make a selection on this menu, iTunes displays the content of the selected type in the Content pane, which fills the center part of the window. At the top of the Content pane, you see buttons that you can use to change how you are seeing the content. For example, when Music is selected, you can choose to view the music by song, album, artist, composer, genre, video, and so on.

When you change how you are viewing content, the Content pane is reorganized. In Figure 1.9, the **Albums** button is selected, and the music is organized by album. When you click **Genres**, the Content pane updates so that the list of genres is on the left side of the window; when you select a genre by clicking it, the music in that genre is displayed on the right side of the window (see Figure 1.10).

FIGURE 1.10

When you view music by genre, select a genre on the left; the music in that genre is displayed on the right. (In this figure, music in the Rock genre is being displayed).

 NOTE If you are just getting started with iTunes, you may not have much (or any) content in the application. The Source menu includes only those options for which there is content in your iTunes Library (for example, if you don't have any movies, you won't see Movies on the menu).

Working with the other types of content and options you see is similar. For example, if you choose Podcasts, you see a list of your podcasts on the left. Select the podcast with which you want to work, and you see its episodes on the right (see Figure 1.11). You can use the buttons at the top of the Content pane to change the view to display only unplayed episodes or to show all episodes in a list.

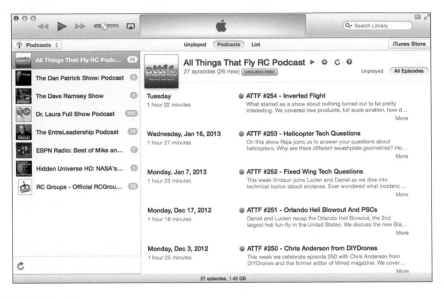

FIGURE 1.11

When you view podcasts, you can select a podcast on the left to see its episodes on the right.

With some options, you can use the Column Browser to move through your content quickly. For example, in the Music source, you can use the Column Browser when you choose **Songs** or **Playlists**.

You can show or hide the Column Browser by pressing ⌘-B (Mac) or Ctrl+Shift+B (Windows). The Column Browser opens and appears at the top of the Content pane (see Figure 1.12).

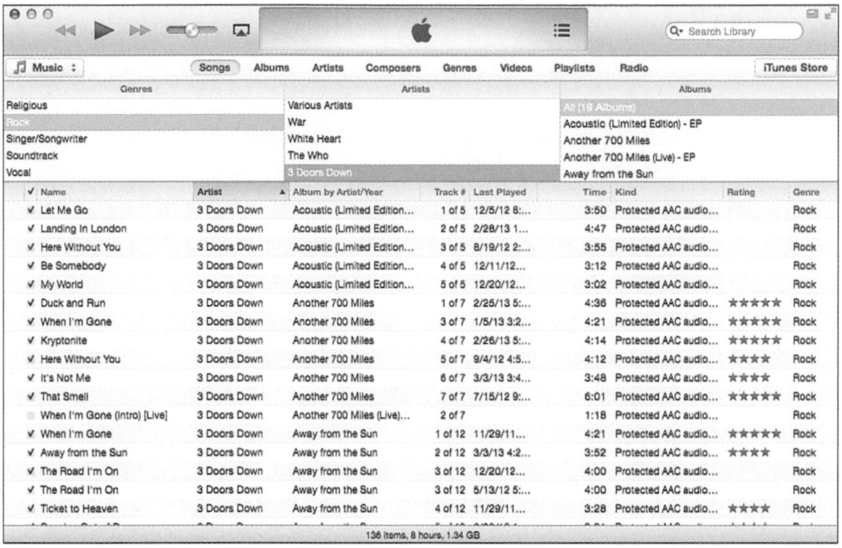

FIGURE 1.12

You can use the Column Browser to rapidly navigate through your content.

The Column Browser presents the contents of the selected source at a summary level and displays various columns of information, such as genre, artist, and album. You can view the contents of the selected source by clicking what you want to browse in the appropriate columns.

As you make a selection in one column, the contents of the next column reflect the selection you made. The "path" you are browsing is indicated by the highlighted text. For example, in Figure 1.12, I have selected the Rock genre. The Artists column then shows all the artists in my library that have music in the Rock genre. On the Artists list, I've selected the band 3 Doors Down, so all the Rock albums by this group that I have in my library are shown in the Albums column. Because All is selected in the Albums column, the Content pane shows all the Rock music I have by 3 Doors Down. I could select an album; if I did, only the songs on that album would be displayed in the Content pane.

You can configure the columns shown in the Column Browser by opening the **View** menu and choosing **Column Browser**. Then choose the columns you want to see in the Column Browser, such as **Genres**, **Artists**, **Albums**, and so on; some options apply only to specific types of content (for example, Seasons applies to TV shows). When you select a column so that it is marked with a check mark, it appears in the Column Browser. If you uncheck a column, it doesn't appear in the Column Browser.

The Column Browser is one of the best ways to find content that you want to listen to or watch because you can quickly and easily navigate through your library.

In the following chapters, you learn how to work with the various types of content you can enjoy with iTunes, but hopefully you already see the general iTunes pattern: Select the type of content you want, choose the way you want that content organized, and then use that view's tools to find and play what you want to hear or watch.

THE ITUNES SIDEBAR

In iTunes version prior to 11, the primary method of selecting content was using the iTunes Sidebar, which appeared in a pane along the left side of the window. The iTunes Sidebar serves a similar purpose to the Source menu, meaning you can use it to choose the type of content with which you want to work. The Sidebar remains in iTunes version 11, but it is hidden by default. To show the sidebar, choose **View**, **Show Sidebar** (on a Windows PC, you need to show the iTunes menu bar to access the View menu). The Sidebar opens and the Source menu disappears. You can work with a type of content by clicking its icon on the Sidebar, such as Movies. Because a hidden Sidebar is the default, the rest of this book assumes it is hidden. However, if you prefer to use the Sidebar, you can leave it open and use it instead of the Source menu.

Moving Ahead with iTunes

Before you can use iTunes, you need to stock your library with music, movies, audiobooks, and so on. You can download content directly from the iTunes Store (see Chapter 2) or add content you already have, such as music on CD or movies on DVD (refer to Chapter 3).

After your library contains content, you use a similar pattern to work with it, which is the following:

1. Find the content that you want to listen to or watch. You can do this by browsing for it, searching for it using the Search tool, or by selecting a playlist or other source that contains the specific content in which you are interested.

2. Select the content you want to hear or see. You can click an item to select it. For example, you can click a song that you want to listen to.

3. Use iTunes' playback and other tools to control the content. For example, you can play or pause it, use AirPlay to stream it to another device, and so on.

This pattern holds no matter what type of content you are working with. Listening to a song is similar to watching an episode of a TV series, although the details are a bit different.

As you move forward in this book, you'll get much more information about each of these steps. For example, in Chapter 4, you'll learn all the ins and outs of listening to music, and in Chapter 7, "Creating and Using Playlists," you learn how to create playlists so you can get to the specific content you want even easier and faster.

THE ABSOLUTE MINIMUM

In this chapter, you gained an overview of iTunes, which covered the following topics:

- If you use a Windows PC, you may need to download and install iTunes. Then you can configure the application so that it automatically checks for new versions to ensure you are always using the current version.

- On a Mac, iTunes is installed by default. You should configure OS X to automatically update your Mac App Store software, notably iTunes, so that you use the current version of the application to take advantage of the improvements Apple makes.

- The iTunes window provides lots of tools you can use to find and play your content. The iTunes toolbar provides controls to play your content, stream it to other devices, and so on. You can work with different types of content by choosing the type you want on the Source menu; then by using the options that appear, you can configure how you view that content.

2

WORKING WITH THE ITUNES STORE

The iTunes Store is a great way to add content to your iTunes Library. By content, I mean music, movies, TV shows, books, podcasts, audiobooks, apps for iOS devices, and so on. The iTunes Store has a huge selection of content that you can browse or search. When you find something you want, you can add it to your iTunes Library with just a couple of mouse clicks. Because the iTunes Store is fully integrated into iTunes, it is this easy: you can move between your iTunes Library and the Store with just a mouse click. If you use iCloud (which you learn about in Part II, "iCloud"), when you download content on one device, such as a Mac, your music, book, and app downloads are automatically downloaded to all your devices (such as an iPad, iPhone, Windows PC, and so on).

Getting Started in the iTunes Store

To use the iTunes Store, you need to have an account that you can use to purchase or rent content to download to your iTunes Library. The good news is that you may have one already. If any of the following is true, you already have an iTunes Store account:

- You have an Apple ID.

- You have an iCloud account.

- You've previously shopped in the Apple Store online.

- You have an AOL account.

The other good news is that even if you don't already have an Apple ID, you can have one in just a few minutes.

Your Apple ID enables you to download content from the iTunes Store, and you can use the same Apple ID to work with iCloud (which is covered in Part II of this book). You can sign into your account directly in iTunes, which enables you to shop for and download content. You can also use iTunes to create a new account, and manage your account, such as when you want to change your information.

If you already have an iTunes account or Apple ID, skip ahead to the section "Signing In to Your iTunes Store Account." If you don't yet have an Apple ID, continue to the next section.

TIP   If you don't already have an email address that you want to use as your Apple ID, instead of performing the steps in the next section, obtain an Apple ID by creating an iCloud account (see Chapter 10, "Obtaining and Configuring an iCloud Account"). When you create an iCloud account, you also get an iCloud email account, which will become your Apple ID. When you have created an Apple ID by signing up for iCloud, come back to this chapter and move to the section "Signing In to Your iTunes Store Account."

Creating an Apple ID

If you don't already have an Apple ID, create one by perform the following steps:

1. Open **iTunes**.

2. Click the **iTunes Store** button located in the upper-right corner of the iTunes window. iTunes connects to the Internet and moves into the iTunes Store. The iTunes Store appears in the iTunes window.

3. Click the **Sign In** button located in the upper-left corner of the iTunes Store window. The Sign In dialog appears (see Figure 2.1).

 NOTE If you see an Apple ID instead of the Sign In link, iTunes is already logged in to an account. If the account is yours, skip to the section, "Viewing and Updating Your iTunes Store Account." If the account shown isn't yours, click the account shown in the button and then click Sign Out so that you can create your account by performing step 3.

FIGURE 2.1

Use the Sign In dialog to start creating your Apple ID.

4. Click **Create Apple ID**. You move to the Welcome to the iTunes Store screen.

5. Click **Continue**.

6. Read the license agreement (yeah, right!), check the **I have read and agree to these terms and conditions** check box, and click **Agree**.

7. Read the information and follow the onscreen instructions to provide the rest of the information required. This includes entering your primary and rescue email addresses (optional), creating a password, choosing security questions and answers, and providing credit card information.

8. After you've provided the required information, click **Create Apple ID**. An email is sent to the email address you provided for your account.

9. Switch into your email application and open the email you received on your primary address.

10. Click the **Verify Now** link in the verification email message you receive (see Figure 2.2). You move to the My Apple ID website.

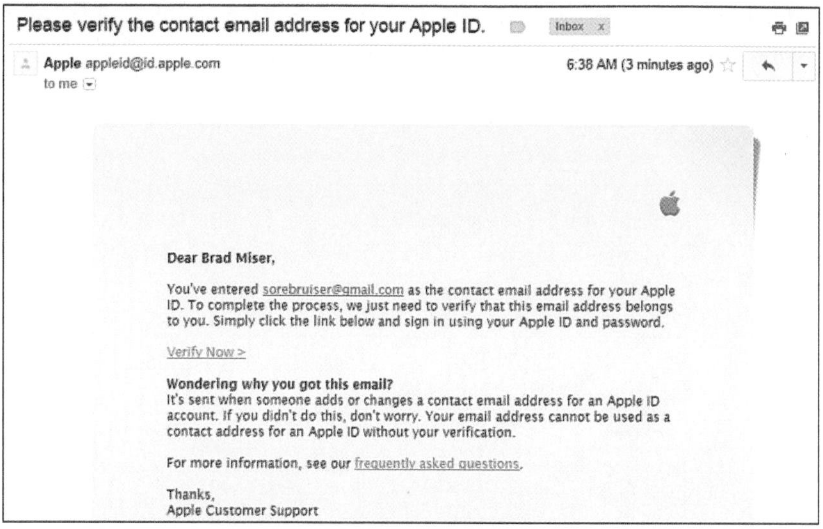

Please verify the contact email address for your Apple ID.   Inbox x

Apple appleid@id.apple.com   6:38 AM (3 minutes ago)
to me

Dear Brad Miser,

You've entered sorebruiser@gmail.com as the contact email address for your Apple ID. To complete the process, we just need to verify that this email address belongs to you. Simply click the link below and sign in using your Apple ID and password.

Verify Now >

Wondering why you got this email?
It's sent when someone adds or changes a contact email address for an Apple ID account. If you didn't do this, don't worry. Your email address cannot be used as a contact address for an Apple ID without your verification.

For more information, see our frequently asked questions.

Thanks,
Apple Customer Support

FIGURE 2.2

Apple sends this email to the address associated with your Apple ID to confirm that you did create an account.

11. Enter your email address in the Apple ID field.

12. Enter your password in the Password field.

13. Click **Verify Address**. If you are able to sign in, your Apple ID is ready to go and you can log in to the iTunes Store.

14. If you elected to provide a rescue email address, repeat steps 9 through 13, except this time open the verification email that is sent to your rescue address.

 NOTE A rescue address is used to communicate with you if you lose access to your primary email address.

Signing In to Your iTunes Store Account

To access the iTunes Store, you need to sign in to your account. You need to do this only once because iTunes remembers your account information and signs you into the store automatically thereafter.

1. Open iTunes.

2. Click the **iTunes Store** button.

3. Click the **Sign In** button located in the upper-left corner of the iTunes Store window. The iTunes Sign In dialog appears.

4. Enter your Apple ID.

5. Enter your password.

6. Click **Sign In** (see Figure 2.3). You are logged in to your iTunes Store account. Your Apple ID replaces the Sign In button to indicate that you are signed into the account shown.

FIGURE 2.3

After you successfully sign in to the iTunes Store, iTunes keeps you signed in.

 TIP If you are using a computer that you don't control, one that you share with others, or if you want to change the account being used, you can sign out of your account to protect your information. To do so, click the account that is signed in, which replaces the Sign In button in the iTunes window. In the resulting dialog, click **Sign Out**.

Viewing and Updating Your iTunes Store Account

In some situations, you might need to change information about your account, such as your email address or the alert settings. You probably won't need to do this when you first start using the iTunes Store, but your information can change over time, and so it is a good idea to know how to manage your account's information. You can access your account's information through the iTunes Store.

1. If the iTunes Store isn't already displayed, click the **iTunes Store** button.

2. Sign in to the iTunes Store using the account you want to manage (if this account is currently signed in, skip this step).

3. Click the account that is currently signed in; this is shown in the location where the Sign In button appears.

4. Click **Account**. The Account Information screen appears (see Figure 2.4).

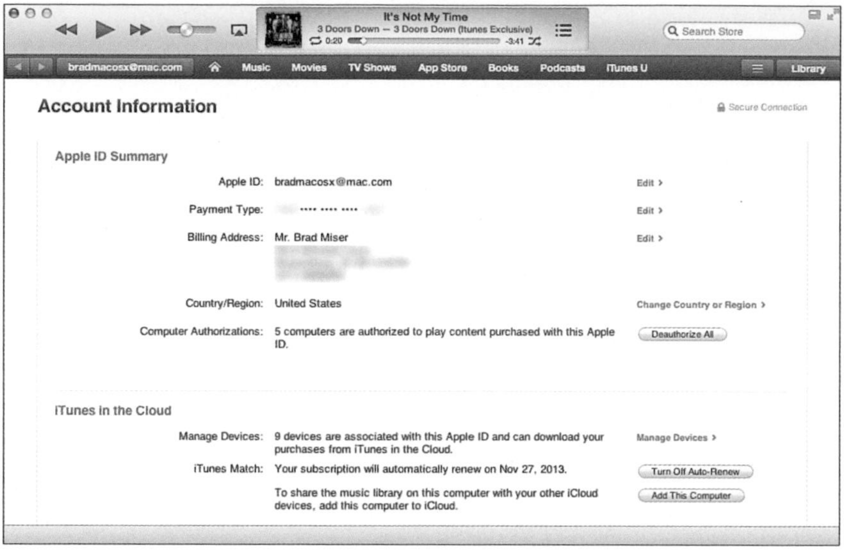

FIGURE 2.4

You can use this screen to manage your iTunes Store account.

TIP You can also access your account information by clicking the downward-facing arrow next to the account that is shown in the upper-right corner of the screen and clicking **Account** on the resulting drop-down list.

5. On this screen, you can perform the following actions:

- **Change your personal information**—Click the **Edit** links next to Apple ID, Payment Type, Billing Address, or Country/Region to change any of that information. You move to the edit screen for the type of information you select; there, you can make changes to it.

- **Deauthorize all computers associated with your account**—Some iTunes Store content has Digital Rights Management (DRM) applied so that the device with which you use that content must be authorized with your account to play it. (See the section, "Understanding Digital Rights Management," later in this chapter for a more detailed explanation.)

  If you ever need to reset the devices that are authorized to play content you've downloaded (such as if you lose or sell some of your devices), click **Deauthorize All** to remove your account authorization from all the devices that currently have it. Each device has to be authorized the next time you use that device to play content you downloaded from the iTunes Store.

- **Manage devices automatically downloading content**—In Part II, you learn how to configure iCloud so that anytime you download content from the iTunes Store onto one device, it is downloaded to your other devices automatically. To stop a device from downloading content, click the **Manage Devices** link. On the resulting screen, click the **Remove** button next to any device on which you want to stop automatic downloads.

- **Manage iTunes Match**—You can use iTunes Match to upload all the music in your iTunes Library into iCloud. From there, you can stream your music to any device with access to your account. This eliminates the need to sync music across your devices, which is especially useful if a device doesn't have enough storage space for all of your music (such as an iPad mini). You'll learn about iTunes Match in Chapter 12, "Streaming Your Music with iTunes Match." For now, know that you can specify whether your iTunes Match account automatically renews or add a computer to your iTunes Match account using the two iTunes Match buttons.

 NOTE If you haven't set up iTunes Match, you don't see the iTunes Match controls on the Account screen as described here. Instead, you see a link that enables you to learn more about iTunes.

- **Review your purchases**—If you click the **See All** link in the Purchase History section, you see all the purchases you have made under your account.

- **Nickname**—If you want to use a nickname to post reviews, click **Create Nickname**, enter your nickname, and then click **Submit**. When you post reviews of content, your review appears under your nickname.

- **Change settings**—Use the **Manage** links in the Settings section to change the various settings you see. For example, you can click **Manage** next to Reviews and Ratings to see all the ratings and reviews you have posted. You can remove a rating or review by clicking its **Remove** button. The other settings work similarly.

6. When you are done working with your account, click **Done**.

ACCOUNT/PASSWORD PROBLEMS?

We all have more user accounts and passwords than we can typically remember. If you have problems with your Apple ID account, such as forgetting your password, you can use the My Apple ID website to reset your password and manage other aspects of your account. To get started, open your web browser and move to iforgot.apple.com. Enter your **Apple ID** and click **Next**. The website will lead you through the process of resetting your password so that you can regain access to your account. You can even look up your Apple ID if you can't remember what it is.

Setting iTunes Store Preferences

iTunes has a few Store preferences you should set to tweak the way it works:

1. Open the iTunes Preferences dialog (on a Mac, choose **iTunes**, **Preferences;** on a Windows PC, display the iTunes menu bar if it isn't shown by pressing Ctrl+B and on the menu bar, choose **Edit**, **Preferences**).

2. Click the **Store** tab.

3. Check the **Always check for available downloads** box so that iTunes automatically looks for items that are available for you to download; when this is the case, you're prompted to download the content. For example, if a download was interrupted at some point, when you open iTunes again, you're prompted to complete the download.

4. Check the **Download pre-orders when available** box if you want items you preorder to be downloaded as soon as they are available in the store. For example, you can preorder music when it is announced. With this setting enabled, that music is downloaded to your computer as soon as it becomes available in the store.

5. On the drop-down list, choose the High Definition option you want to use when you download video. The options are **720p** or **1080p**. If your computer is capable of playing 1080p content, you should choose that option to experience the highest quality playback.

6. To have content you purchase under your iTunes Store account on other devices downloaded to your computer automatically, check the **Music**, **Apps**, and **Books** check boxes. These settings are useful because they ensure that new content is added to your iTunes Library automatically. For example, if you

buy a song using the iTunes app on an iPhone, that song is added to your iTunes Library automatically.

7. Click **OK** (see Figure 2.5).

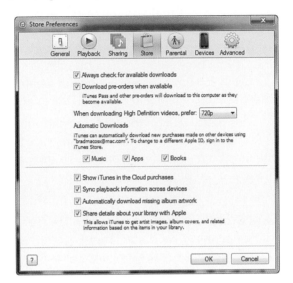

FIGURE 2.5

Use this dialog to configure how you want the iTunes Store to work for you.

8. If you are prompted to, enter your account's password and click **OK**; if you aren't prompted, you don't need to do anything else. You're ready to go shopping.

Adding Content from the iTunes Store to Your iTunes Library

Now that your iTunes account is ready and you've set your Store preferences, you can use the iTunes Store to find, preview, and download content. You'll find a large amount and variety of content available in the store, and the general steps you use to find and download content are similar.

There are two main parts of the shopping process. Begin by finding content in which you are interested and previewing it (if you want to); you can find content by browsing or searching. After you've found content you want, download it to your iTunes Library.

Browsing the iTunes Store

Browsing the iTunes Store is useful when you aren't sure what you want and just want to poke around to see what is available. Browsing can lead you to discover music or other content that you might not have been thinking about. The downside to browsing is that it can take a long time to find something you are really interested in. If you have some idea of what you are looking for, you can limit the scope of your browsing so it is a bit more efficient in getting you to where you want to go. If you have a specific idea of what you want, search for it instead (see the next section, "Searching in the iTunes Store").

Browsing for content is pretty straightforward; mostly, you click on objects you see in the iTunes Store. These can be text links, graphics (such as album covers), and so on. In fact, just about everything you see on the pages of the iTunes Store takes you to content you can browse.

The following steps show how to browse for Rock music:

1. Click the **iTunes Store** button. You move into the iTunes Store and see its Home page in the center pane of the iTunes window. Along the top of the iTunes Store window, you see tabs for various kinds of content, such as Music, Movies, and so on; the Home button takes you back to the iTunes Store's Home page. You can click a tab to take you to the Home page for that type of content and then browse from there. Or you can hover over a tab and click the downward-facing arrow that appears to select a subset of the content to browse. For example, in Figure 2.6, you see the Music tab's menu with the Rock genre being selected.

FIGURE 2.6

By selecting Rock, I'll be browsing music in the Rock genre.

2. Select the subcategory of the content that you want to browse. You move to the Home page for that subcategory and see content only in that subcategory, such as a music genre.

3. Click any graphic or text link that looks interesting. There are many options, such as various lists, specific catalogs, and so on. When you click something, you move into whatever that "something" is. It could be a specific artist's albums, a list of songs organized in some way, or just about anything else.

4. Eventually, you get to specific content that you can preview and download (see Figure 2.7). See "Previewing and Downloading Content in the iTunes Store" to perform these tasks.

FIGURE 2.7

Here I'm browsing the contents of a specific album.

POWER BROWSING

Just clicking around to browse is okay, but it can sometimes take a long time to get to what you want if you are even able to find it (you can't get to all the Store's content by browsing Home pages). You can browse more effectively by using the Column Browser. To do this, choose **View**, **Column Browser**, **Show Column Browser**. The iTunes Store window is reorganized to use a browser that is similar to the one the iTunes window uses. You can quickly get to specific content to browse by choosing the type from the iTunes Store column, such as Music. The rest of the browser is configured for that type and contains columns you can choose from to browse more selectively. When you narrow your search by clicking an entry in a column, you see the list of items you are browsing at the bottom of the window. From there, you can preview and download content the same as you can from other locations.

Searching in the iTunes Store

Browsing can be fun when you are in the mood to explore the Store for content. However, in those cases in which you have some specificity in what you are looking for, searching is a much faster and more effective way to find content:

1. Click the **iTunes Store** button. You move into the iTunes Store and see its Home page in the center pane of the iTunes window.

2. Click in the Search Store bar located in the upper-right corner of the iTunes window.

3. Enter the information for which you want to search, such as Artist, Song, Genre, Album, and such. As you type, iTunes presents a list of possible matches (see Figure 2.8).

FIGURE 2.8

Searching gets you to specific content quickly and easily.

4. If something on the results list is what you want to search for, click it; if not, keep typing until you've typed all of the search term and then press the Enter key. Items that meet your search display in the Content pane (see Figure 2.9). The results are organized into logical groups based on the type of content you found. For example, when you search for music, you see albums, songs, and music videos. You see other kinds of groupings for different types of content.

FIGURE 2.9

Here I've found songs by a particular artist in just a few seconds, which is impressive given the huge number of songs in the iTunes Store!

5. Preview what you've found and download any content that you want to add to your iTunes Library. (See the next section to perform these tasks.)

TIP   To leave the iTunes Store and return to your iTunes Library at any time, click the **Library** button located in the upper-right corner of the iTunes window.

Previewing and Downloading Content in the iTunes Store

When you've located content in which you are interested, you can preview it. If the content is audio, you hear a portion of the content. For example, when you preview most songs, you hear 1.5 minutes. For video content, you see a preview of the actual content or something related to it, such as a movie's trailer.

1. Browse or search to get to specific content.

2. To preview music, move the pointer over the song you want to hear and click the **Play** button that replaces the track number (see Figure 2.10). After you click the button, a preview plays; the length of the preview depends on the specific content you are previewing.

FIGURE 2.10

Previewing content gives you the opportunity to "try before you buy."

3. To preview video, hover over its thumbnail and click the **Play** button that appears. The video preview plays in a pop-up window (see Figure 2.11).

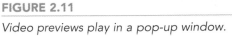

FIGURE 2.11

Video previews play in a pop-up window.

4. When you want to purchase and download content, click its BUY button. This button can include different information depending on the content you are viewing. It always shows the price of the content. It can also describe what you are buying. For example, when you browse a TV show, one BUY button enables you to purchase the entire season, or you can use the BUY buttons next to each episode to purchase individual episodes.

 TIP If you click the **Remember password for purchasing** check box in the Sign In dialog, or the **Don't ask me about buying again** or other similar check boxes in the various confirmation dialogs, when you click BUY or RENT buttons in the future, content is purchased or rented immediately. This is convenient, but it also doesn't give you a chance to reconsider.

5. If prompted, enter your account's information and click **BUY,** or just click the **BUY** button depending on the prompt you see. The content you purchase is downloaded to your computer and added to your iTunes Library. During the download process, you see information about it in the Info window at the top of the iTunes window. You also see the Download button in the upper-right corner of the iTunes window.

6. Click the **Download** button to see the specific content being downloaded. The Downloads window appears (see Figure 2.12). You can see the progress of the download process in this window.

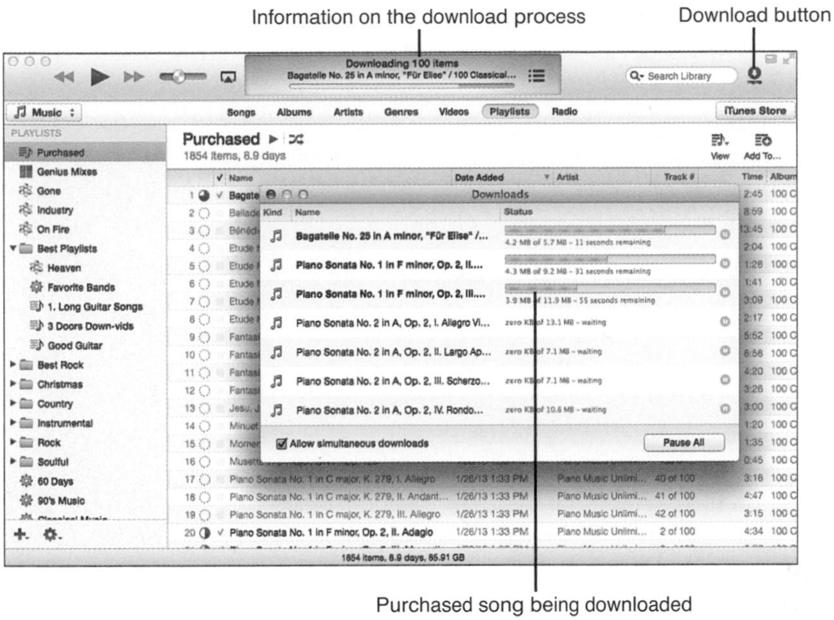

Information on the download process   Download button

Purchased song being downloaded

FIGURE 2.12

You can use the Downloads window to monitor the progress of content being downloaded to your computer.

7. To see all the content you have downloaded, click the **Library** button to return to your iTunes Library, choose **Music** on the Source menu, click the **Playlists** button, and click the **Purchased** source (you can see this in the background in Figure 2.12).

After content has been downloaded to your iTunes Library, it is ready for you to listen to, watch, add to your devices, and so on.

MORE THAN BUY

If you click the downward-facing arrow to the right of BUY buttons, you see a menu with various commands, such as Gift This (Album, Song, and the like), which enables you to give the content to someone else or Share on Facebook, which enables you to provide information about the object on your Facebook page, and so on. One useful option is Add to Wish List, which enables you to add content to your wish list, which is much like a shopping cart where you can store content you might be interested in purchasing at a later time. After you add content to your wish list, you can move back to it by clicking the My Wish List link in the QUICK LINKS section of the iTunes Store Home page. From your wish list, you can preview or purchase content.

Understanding Digital Rights Management (DRM)

Some digital content is protected with Digital Rights Management (DRM) technology. What this means is that the content has been encoded to prevent you from doing certain things with it. For example, you may be limited to storing the content on one device at a time, or there may be a limit to the number of devices the content can be played on.

Much of the content in the iTunes Store—all of the music, in fact—doesn't have any DRM attached to it. You can do pretty much whatever you want with this content.

Most of the video content, such as movies and TV Shows, and some books do have DRM attached. DRM content has some limitations on how you can use it. The primary limitation is that the device on which you play the content must be authorized to play that content. To be authorized, the device must be associated with the iTunes Store account used to purchase that content. You can have up to five devices authorized under a single iTunes Store account. If you try to authorize more than the allowed number, you won't be able to authorize the additional device and so won't be able to play content from the account on it.

In most cases, iTunes prompts you if you try to do something that requires authorization. When you see the authorization prompt, enter the appropriate account information (Apple ID and password) and click **Authorize**; if the authorization process is successful, you are able to do whatever you were trying to do. If not, you have to deauthorize other devices to do it.

 NOTE   After you authorize a device once, you don't need to authorize it again (unless it becomes deauthorized).

You can also authorize a device by choosing **Store**, **Authorize This Computer** (on a Windows PC, you need to show the iTunes menu bar to access this command). In the resulting dialog, enter the Apple ID and password for the account you want to authorize on the device; then click **Authorize**. If the process is successful, you're able to use the protected content. If not, you either entered the incorrect account information or there are already five authorized devices for the account, in which case, you need to deauthorize at least one device to be able to authorize another one.

Although you can play DRM content on only up to five devices at a time, you can store it on as many devices as you'd like.

Content you rent from the iTunes has the most restrictive limitations on it. These include the following:

- **Store rented movies on one device at a time**—Unlike all other content, rented movies can be stored in only one place at a time. So if you sync a rented movie from your computer to an iOS device, it disappears from your computer and moves onto the iOS device. Because of this, you can watch rented content on only one device at a time.

- **Limits on storing rented movies**—You can store rented content for up to 30 days from the time you download it to a device. When 30 days passes, the content is deleted automatically, whether you have watched it or not. You see various warnings as the 30-day countdown proceeds.

- **Limits on watching rented content**—Rented content has a limited watching window. In the United States, this is a 24-hour period; outside the United States, this limit is 48 hours. The playback period starts as soon as you play rented content. After the playback period expires, the content is deleted automatically. So, make sure you finish watching rented content within the playback period. You can watch rented content as much as you want to during the playback period.

If you want to deauthorize a computer, choose **Store**, **Deauthorize This Computer**. Enter the account information and click **Deauthorize**. The device is no longer able to play protected content nor does it count against the five-device limit.

TIP To deauthorize all the devices for your account, open the Account Information window (as described earlier in the chapter) and click **Deauthorize All**. To use any content downloaded under the account, you have to authorize each device on which you want to play it. (You deauthorize a device that you are going to sell so your content can't be used on that device.)

THE ABSOLUTE MINIMUM

In this chapter, you learned about the iTunes Store. Specifically, you learned that the following:

- To start using the iTunes Store, create an Apple ID (if necessary) and then sign in to the store.

- You should configure iTunes' Store preferences to automate some of the tasks for which you use the iTunes Store, such as to automatically download content you preorder.

- There are two ways to find iTunes Store content. Browsing is useful when you aren't sure what you want or when you want to explore what is available in the iTunes Store. Searching is better when you want to get to specific content quickly. After you've located content, you can preview it. You can download content to your iTunes Library with just a few mouse clicks.

- Some iTunes Store content is protected by DRM. Fortunately, all music is not. Even when you have content that is protected by DRM, using it isn't a big deal; you just need to authorize devices to play it.

3

BUILDING YOUR ITUNES LIBRARY

Your iTunes Library is where you store and organize the content (music, videos, books, and so on) that you can then enjoy on your computer and on iOS devices (iPads, iPhones, and iPod touches). You can add many types of content to your library from a number of sources. Before you start building up your library, it's a good idea to understand where iTunes stores your content and how you can configure the application to keep your content organized. Then you can stock your digital library's shelves with music, movies, books, podcasts, and more from CD, DVD, the iTunes Store, Amazon.com, and so on. In later chapters, you learn how to work with the content you've added to your iTunes Library.

Determining Where Content Is Stored

All the items (songs, movies, and so on) you see within the iTunes Library are really pointers to files stored on your computer (or on external drives connected to your computer). Those files contain the actual content, which iTunes accesses using the pointers stored in the iTunes Library.

It is important to realize that the location where iTunes stores content is different than the location of the iTunes application itself. The implication of this is that you can reinstall the iTunes application without impacting the content stored in your library.

The default location of the iTunes content folder depends on the operating system your computer uses. If you want to, you can change this location to change where your iTunes content is stored.

Keeping Your iTunes File Organized

You should set a couple of preferences to keep your iTunes Library as organized as possible.

1. In iTunes on a Windows PC, open the **iTunes** menu and choose **Preferences**; on a Mac choose **iTunes**, **Preferences**.

2. Click the **Advanced** tab (see Figure 3.1). In the iTunes Media folder location field, you see the current location of the folder in which your iTunes content is stored.

FIGURE 3.1

The location shown in the iTunes Media folder location box is where the content of your iTunes Library is stored.

3.   If it isn't checked already, check the **Keep iTunes Media folder organized** check box. This places your media files into logical groups, such as artist, album, and so on.

4.   If it isn't checked already, check the **Copy files to iTunes Media folder when adding to library** check box. When you add content to your iTunes Library, the associated files are stored within your iTunes Media folder. If you leave this unchecked, the files are left in their current location after you add them. If you are limited on hard drive space, you can leave this box unchecked so files you add remain where they are and a copy is not made; just realize your content files aren't organized within the single iTunes Media folder.

5.   Click **OK**. iTunes is now configured to keep your content organized.

Changing the Location of Your iTunes Files

If you want to store your iTunes content in a different location, such as on an external hard drive, use the following steps to reset its location (most iTunes users should leave the folder in its default location):

1.   Open the Advanced pane of the iTunes Preferences dialog as described in the previous steps.

2.   Click **Change**.

3.   Use the resulting dialog to move to and select the location in which you want your iTunes content to be stored. This can be a folder on your computer or on an external drive.

4.   Click **Select Folder** (Windows) or **Open** (OS X). You return to the Advanced tab and the new location is shown in the iTunes Media folder location box.

5.   Click **OK**. After you respond to the resulting dialog, the new location is used for your iTunes content.

Exploring the iTunes Media Folder

To view your iTunes content on a Windows 7 computer, open Windows Explorer and then open the following folders: **Libraries**, **Music**, **iTunes**. On a Mac, open a new Finder window and click the **Music** icon on the Sidebar. Within the iTunes folder, you see several subfolders and files. One of the files is the iTunes Library file, which is where iTunes stores all the pointers, playlists, and other data the application uses. In the iTunes Media folder, you see the types of content you have stored in iTunes, such as Music, Books, Movies, Podcasts, and so on (see Figure 3.2). You can open these folders to see the specific content of that type.

For example, open the Music folder, and then open an artist's folder to see the albums from that artist that you have added to your iTunes Library.

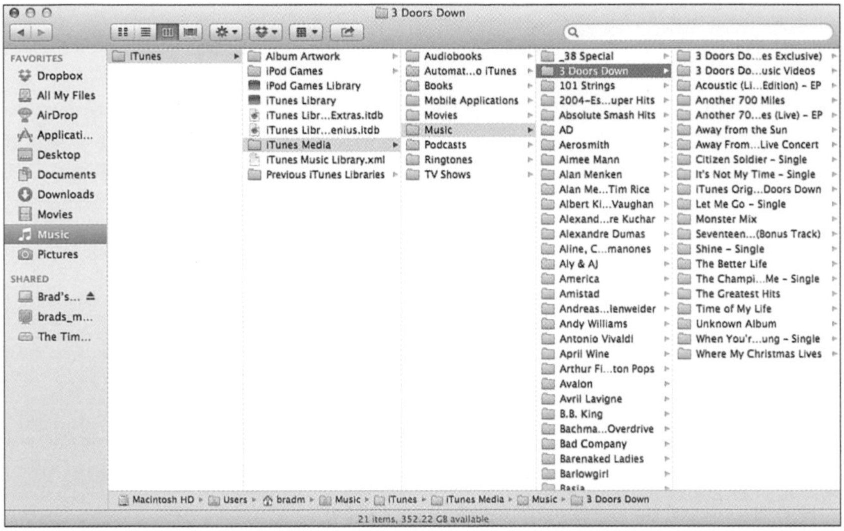

FIGURE 3.2

Here you see the contents of my Music folder with the group 3 Doors Down selected; the albums in my library from this group are shown on the right.

BACKING UP

Over time, you're likely to add a lot of content to your iTunes Library. Like other files on your computer, at some point it's almost a certainty that something will happen to at least some of these files so that they either get lost or become unusable. You should implement some kind of backup system to protect your iTunes content and other important files stored on your computer. Many backup options are available, such as online backup services (two examples are carbonite.com and mozy.com), automated local backup systems (such as OS X's Time Machine feature), or even manual backups.

The specific option you choose matters less than choosing one and using it to protect your iTunes content. Should something happen to your iTunes Media folder, a good backup system saves you an enormous amount of time in recovering your files versus rebuilding your library from scratch. It can also save you money if you have content that can't be recovered without paying for it again.

Adding Music from Audio CDs to Your Library

Importing audio CDs is one of the most useful ways to get music and other audio content into your iTunes Library because you probably already have a lot of music on CD already, and moving that music into iTunes is easy and free!

First, set up iTunes for importing content from a CD, as explained in the next section; you have to do those steps only once. Second, import your CDs into your iTunes Library.

Configuring iTunes to Import Music from CDs

Set iTunes up for quick and easy CD importing by performing the following steps:

1. Open the iTunes Preferences dialog as described earlier.

2. Click the **General** tab (see Figure 3.3).

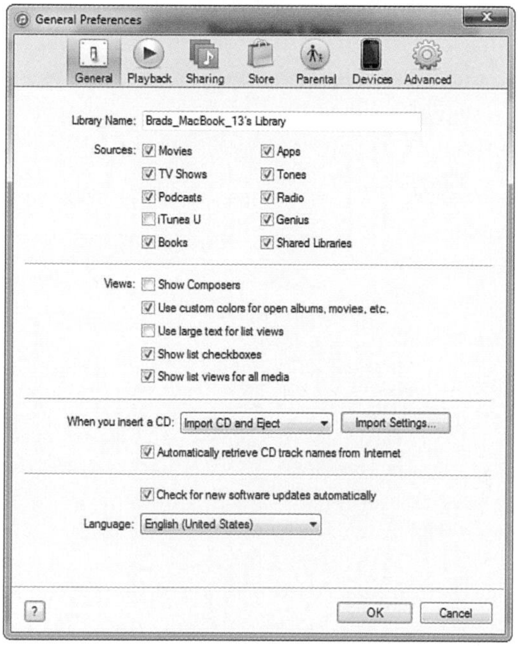

FIGURE 3.3

Set up iTunes to import CDs quickly and easily by using the General tab of the Preferences dialog.

3. On the When you insert a CD menu, choose **Import CD and Eject**.

4. Click **Import Settings**.

5. On the Import Using drop-down menu, choose **AAC Encoder** if it isn't selected already.

6. On the Setting drop-down menu, choose **iTunes Plus** if it isn't selected already.

7. Click **OK**. You return to the General tab.

8. If it isn't checked already, check the **Automatically retrieve CD track names from Internet** box.

9. Click **OK**. You're ready to import CDs.

Adding Audio CDs to Your Library in a Hurry

If you set up iTunes as described in the previous section, importing audio CDs is a snap: Insert a CD into the computer. iTunes connects to the Internet and identifies the CD. When that's done, the import process starts. You don't have to do anything else because iTunes manages the import process for you (see Figure 3.4). As the contents are added to your library, information about what is happening is shown in the Info window. After tracks have been imported, they are marked with the green check mark icon. The track currently being imported is marked with the rotating circle icon. When the process finishes, iTunes plays an alert sound and ejects the disc.

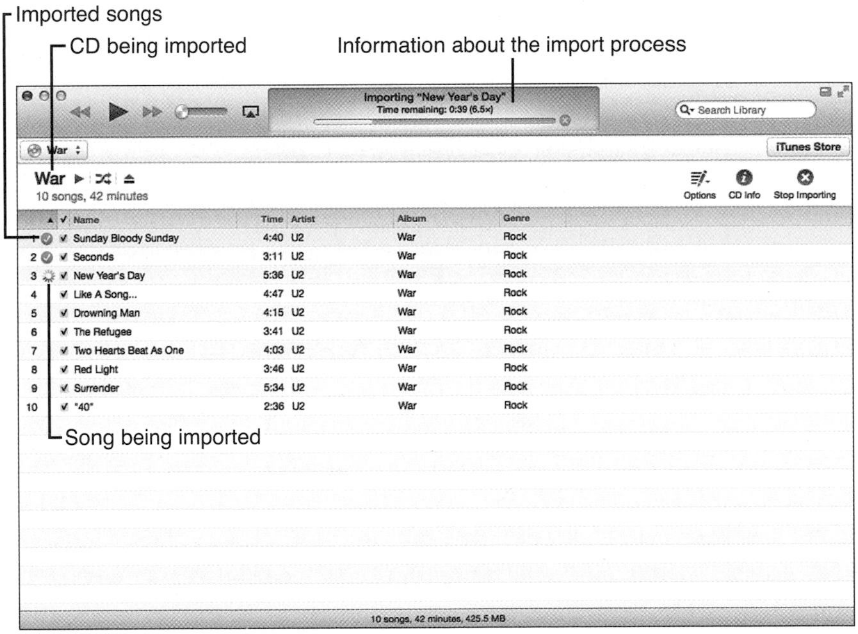

FIGURE 3.4

To add its contents to your iTunes Library, you insert an audio CD into your computer and iTunes does the rest for you.

Insert the next CD you want to import. After it has been ejected, insert the next CD and so on, until you've added all the music from your CDs that you want to have in your iTunes Library.

LIVING CD FREE

After you import a CD into your iTunes Library, you won't likely ever need to use it again on your computer. So after you are finished importing CDs, change the iTunes On CD Insert setting to **Ask To Import CD** so that you don't accidentally import multiple copies of the same CD in the rare case you do insert a CD into your computer again. (Don't worry, though; if you leave the setting as is, iTunes prompts you the next time you insert the CD to see if you want to replace the current version.)

Adding Content from the iTunes Store to Your Library

In Chapter 2, "Working with the iTunes Store," you learn how to set up an account and use the iTunes Store to find (by browsing or searching) content you want to add to your iTunes Library. As you now know, this is an easy process; it is also seamless because the iTunes Store is integrated into the iTunes interface.

The iTunes Store is a great source of content for you because it has a huge selection of many types of content that you can add to your iTunes Library with just a few clicks.

In Chapter 2, you saw some examples of downloading music or video content. In this chapter, a couple of examples of other types of content may help you add even more content to your own iTunes Library.

Renting Movies from the iTunes Store

As you learned in the previous chapter, you can rent movies from the iTunes Store. When you rent a movie, you can watch it as many times as you'd like within a 24-hour period (48 hours outside of the United States), which starts when you play the rented content within a 30-day window (starting when the movie is downloaded into iTunes). After either the 24- or 48-hour viewing or 30-day rental period expires (whichever comes first), the rented movie is removed from iTunes automatically. To rent a movie, follow these steps:

1. Move into the iTunes Store and click the **Movies** tab.

2. Browse or search for movies in which you might be interested; for example, click a thumbnail to view movies related to it.

3. Click a movie's thumbnail or links to see detailed information about it, including the cost to rent it (see Figure 3.5).

FIGURE 3.5

A movie's page in the iTunes Store provides lots of information about it and enables you to watch a trailer and add it to your library.

4. To watch the movie's trailer, click the thumbnail of the trailer you want to watch.

5. To rent a movie, click its **Rent Movie** button; you can often choose to rent a high-definition (HD) version or the standard definition (SD) version. (HD versions are more expensive and have larger file sizes, but they are also higher quality.) If you've allowed iTunes to remember your Apple ID information for purchasing, the movie downloads immediately.

6. If iTunes doesn't remember your Apple ID, provide your information and click the **Rent** button.

7. To access movies you've rented, move back to your iTunes Library by clicking the **Library** button, opening the Source menu, choosing **Movies**, and clicking **Rented**. (Be sure not to play rented content until you're sure you can watch all of it within the viewing period, because that period starts as soon as you play it.)

NOTE   Movie files are very large. If your Internet connection has a limit to the amount of data you can download, you must be aware of that limit while you are downloading movies and other video files from the iTunes Store or other sources. If you exceed this limit, you might be charged overage fees, which can be quite expensive. Check the details for your Internet account to make sure you won't be using all your data allowance by downloading movies from the iTunes Store.

Subscribing to Podcasts in the iTunes Store

Podcasts are radio-like audio or video episodes that you can subscribe to and listen to or watch. Even better, most podcasts are free.

1. Move into the iTunes Store.

2. Click the **Podcasts** tab.

3. Open the Categories menu (labeled All Categories initially) and choose the category you are interested in, such as **Business**.

4. Browse the results.

5. Click a podcast to get more information about it (see Figure 3.6).

FIGURE 3.6

You can read about and listen to a podcast before you subscribe to it.

TIP   You can search for podcasts by typing the podcast's name into the Search Store bar in the upper-right corner of the screen. When you do this, you search across all content, so you might also find music, movies, and so on, in addition to podcasts.

6.   Read about the podcast.

7.   Hover over an episode and click the **Play** button to preview it; if it is a free podcast, you can listen to the entire episode without subscribing to it.

8.   To subscribe to the podcast so it is automatically downloaded, click **Subscribe**; like other action buttons, the Subscribe button shows the cost of the podcast. When you can subscribe to a podcast for free, the button is **Subscribe**.

 NOTE   You can download and listen to an individual episode of a podcast by clicking its **Free** button. However, if you are not limited to the amount of data you can download by your Internet provider, it's just as easy to subscribe to a podcast to download episodes to your computer. If you end up not wanting to keep it, select the podcast and press the **Delete** key.

9.   Click **Subscribe** at the prompt. The most recent episodes are downloaded to your iTunes Library; future episodes will be downloaded automatically.

10. To see the podcasts to which you are subscribed, click the **Library** button to return to your iTunes Library and, on the Source menu, choose **Podcasts**. On the left side of the window, you see the podcasts to which you are subscribed. Select a podcast to see the available episodes on the right side of the window. You learn about listening to and managing your podcasts in Chapter 8, "Subscribing and Listening to Podcasts."

Downloading Apps from the iTunes Store

The iTunes Store has many thousands of apps for iOS devices that you can download and install. Many of these are free, whereas others have a license fee; most license fees are less than $5, and many others are less than $10.

You can use the iTunes Store to browse for and download apps as follows:

1.   Move into the iTunes Store.

2.   Click **App Store**. You move to the App Store Home page.

3.   Click the tab for the device for which you want to download apps, such as the **iPhone** tab.

4. Click the various links you see to browse for apps, or you can search for specific apps using the Search Store tool. You can browse or search for apps just like other content, such as music, movies, and so on.

5. When you find an app in which you are interested, click its icon. You move to the app's description screen, where you can read about it (including user reviews) and look at screenshots (see Figure 3.7).

FIGURE 3.7

An app's Home page provides detailed information about it, including screenshots.

6. Check the requirements to make sure the app is compatible with your device. For example, you need to make sure your device is running the required or later version of the iOS.

> **NOTE** Some apps have a plus (+) sign next to their download menus. This indicates that the app is a universal app, meaning that it runs on iPhones/iPods touches and iPads.

7. Review the description, view screenshots, and read the user reviews on the app's page.

8. When you're ready to download the app, click the **Download** or **Free App** button, or the **Buy App** button, which also shows the price, if it has a fee.

9. If you aren't signed into your iTunes Store account, do so at the prompt by entering your Apple ID and password and then clicking **Buy** or **Get** (depending on whether the app is free); if you are already signed in, you may see a Buy prompt. Click **Buy**. The app is downloaded to your iTunes Library; you can move it onto a device through the sync process, which is explained in Chapter 14, "Synchronizing iTunes Content with iOS Devices."

Adding MP3 Music from Amazon.com to Your Library

Amazon.com has a large catalog of MP3 music that you can download and use in iTunes. Because it isn't integrated into iTunes, this is a bit more complicated than downloading music from the iTunes Store, but fortunately, once you get things set up, the process is just about as simple.

TIP If you're very particular about the quality of the music to which you listen, look for the music from the iTunes Store first. The encoding format of the music in the iTunes Store is of higher quality than the MP3 format used for music in Amazon.com. If you aren't concerned about these kinds of differences, you can choose the source based on price or other factors.

Setting Up Amazon.com Music Downloads

When you download music from Amazon, the MP3 Downloader application automatically makes that music available in iTunes so the process is almost as seamless as downloading music from the iTunes Store.

NOTE To use the Amazon MP3 Downloader application, you must have an Amazon.com account. If you don't already have an account, use a web browser to move to Amazon.com and create an account before performing the following steps.

To download and install the MP3 Downloader application, perform the following steps:

1. Open a web browser and move to amazon.com.

2. Click the **Help** menu command.

3. In the Search Help bar, enter **MP3 Downloader** and click **Search Help**.

4. Click the **Amazon MP3 Downloader** link.

5. Scroll down the page and click the **Amazon MP3 Downloader Installation** link. If you aren't already logged in to your Amazon.com account, you're

prompted to sign in; move to step 6 now. If you are already signed in to your account, your web browser takes you to the Installer page for the type of computer you are using, and you can skip to step 7.

6. Enter your Amazon account information and click **Sign In**. You're taken to the installer page for the type of computer you are using.

7. Click **Install**. The install process for the type of computer you are using starts.

8. Follow the onscreen instructions to download and install the MP3 Download application. See the following paragraph that applies to the type of computer you are using.

   On a Windows computer, the prompts lead you through running the installer application; when prompted, you must allow any changes for the installer to be able to work. When the process is complete, you see a dialog saying so. Clear the dialog by clicking **OK**. You're ready to open and use the Downloader application. Open the Windows menu, choose **All Programs**, click the **Amazon** folder, and then click **Amazon MP3 Downloader**. When the application opens, move to step 9.

   On a Mac, the disk image file is downloaded to your Downloads folder. Open this folder and click the **AmazonMP3DownloaderInstall.dmg** file. In the resulting window, double-click the **Amazon MP3 Installer** icon. Follow the onscreen prompts to complete the installation. When the Installation Complete dialog appears, click **OK**. The Amazon MP3 Downloader application opens automatically, and you are ready for the next step.

9. Choose **File**, **Preferences** (Windows) or **Amazon MP3 Downloader**, **Preferences** (OS X).

10. On a Windows computer, ensure that **Add it to iTunes** is selected on the When an item finishes downloading drop-down list; on a Mac, make sure that the **Add downloaded tracks to iTunes** check box is checked.

11. On a Windows computer, click **OK**; on a Mac, close the Preferences dialog.

 NOTE   By default, the Amazon MP3 Downloader application stores downloaded content in the Amazon MP3 folder. This folder is located in the Music folder on Macs and on Windows 7 computers. You can open this folder to see content that the MP3 Downloader application has downloaded from Amazon.com.

BUT WAIT, THERE'S MORE

Amazon.com offers video content (movies and TV shows) and eBooks, too. The video content is not used in iTunes, but instead uses Amazon's own tools. Likewise, books you download from Amazon.com aren't managed in iTunes because they are in the Kindle format. You use the Kindle app to read these books on your computer or on an iOS device.

Downloading MP3 Music from Amazon.com

With the Amazon MP3 Downloader installed and configured, adding music from Amazon.com to your iTunes Library is also quite simple:

1. Move to www.amazon.com.

2. Open the **Shop by Department** menu and choose **MP3s & Cloud Player**; then choose **MP3 Music Store**.

3. Browse or search in the music store until you find music that interests you (see Figure 3.8).

Play button

FIGURE 3.8

You can preview Amazon.com's MP3 music and read other people's opinions about it to help you decide if you want it.

4. Click the **Play** buttons to preview music.

5. Read user reviews and other information.

6. When you're ready to download music, click the **Buy** button for what you want to download, such as a song or an album.

7. Follow the onscreen instructions to complete the purchase.

8. When the purchase process is complete, click **Download your purchase**. The music is downloaded to your computer.

9. Respond to any prompts that appear, such as allowing the Amazon MP3 Downloader application to open (you see some of these only the first time you download music). The Amazon MP3 Downloader application launches and downloads the music (see Figure 3.9). When the download process is complete, the music is added to your iTunes Library.

 NOTE If you download one song at a time, the Amazon MP3 Downloader doesn't open automatically. You might need to perform a secondary click on the downloaded song and then choose to open the downloaded.amz file using the Amazon MP3 Downloader application to add it to iTunes.

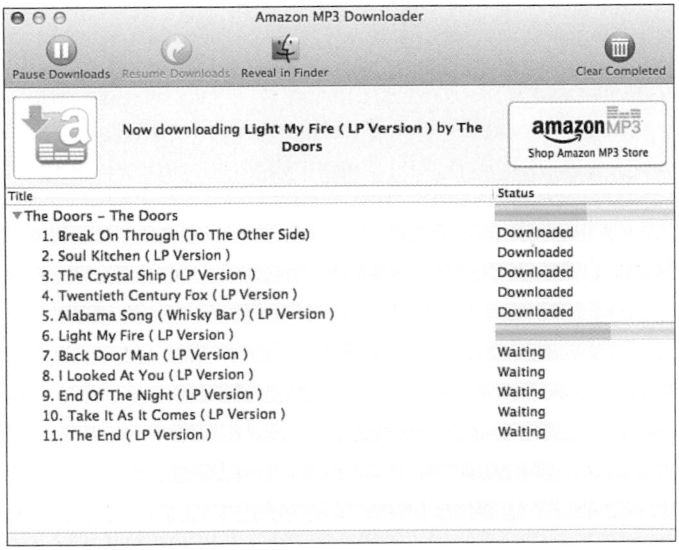

Title	Status
▼ The Doors – The Doors	
1. Break On Through (To The Other Side)	Downloaded
2. Soul Kitchen (LP Version)	Downloaded
3. The Crystal Ship (LP Version)	Downloaded
4. Twentieth Century Fox (LP Version)	Downloaded
5. Alabama Song (Whisky Bar) (LP Version)	Downloaded
6. Light My Fire (LP Version)	
7. Back Door Man (LP Version)	Waiting
8. I Looked At You (LP Version)	Waiting
9. End Of The Night (LP Version)	Waiting
10. Take It As It Comes (LP Version)	Waiting
11. The End (LP Version)	Waiting

Now downloading Light My Fire (LP Version) by The Doors

amazon MP3
Shop Amazon MP3 Store

Pause Downloads   Resume Downloads   Reveal in Finder   Clear Completed

Amazon MP3 Downloader

FIGURE 3.9

The Amazon MP3 Downloader application automatically launches and downloads music.

NOTE The first time the downloader finishes downloading, you see a prompt that enables you to view the music in iTunes or on your desktop. Click the **Don't show this message again** check box and click **OK** if you don't want to be prompted each time.

NO TUNES IN ITUNES ON A MAC?

If music you downloaded doesn't appear in iTunes, open a Finder window and find the music on the desktop (by default, it is located in the Amazon MP3 folder in your Music folder). Perform a secondary click on the song's file and choose **Open With**. On the resulting menu, choose **QuickTime Player.app**. Choose **File**, **Export To**, **iTunes**. The file is added to your iTunes Library. This trick works for other types of content too, such as video. So, if you're unable to add content to iTunes directly, send it into iTunes through the QuickTime Player application.

Adding Video from DVDs to Your Library

You probably have some movies, TV shows, and other video content on DVD that you'd like to have in your iTunes Library. Unfortunately, iTunes can't import this content for you as it can with audio CDs.

To add DVD video to your iTunes Library, you have to perform two steps. First, use an application to convert the DVD content into a digital format that can be used in iTunes. Second, add the content to your iTunes Library.

 NOTE If you use content you import from a DVD for purposes other than your own enjoyment on your devices, you are likely violating copyright laws. In other words, if you keep it to yourself, you're probably in good shape from the legal perspective. If you distribute the content, you likely aren't.

Preparing DVD Content for iTunes

To convert DVD content into a format that iTunes can work with, you need to use an application that can perform this function. There are many available for both Windows PCs and Macs. You can use a web browser to search for and download an application for the type of the computer and operating system that you use.

The following example shows the steps to use the HandBrake application on a Mac to convert an episode of a TV show into an iTunes-compatible format. HandBrake is also available for Windows PCs. Other applications will have different details, but the overall process should be similar.

 NOTE   To download HandBrake, go to http://handbrake.fr.

1. Insert the DVD into your computer.

2. Open HandBrake.

3. Click the **Source** button on the toolbar.

4. Move to the DVD you inserted in step 1, select it, and click **Open**. HandBrake scans the DVD to identify its contents. This process can take a few minutes. When it is complete, the drop-down lists and other interface elements become active.

5. Choose **Window**, **Presets Drawer**. The drawer slides open on the right side of the application window. This enables you to select preset configurations for specific devices.

6. Select the preset you want to use; for example, if you want to be able to put the content on an iPad, click **iPad** on the list of presets under the Devices section. HandBrake configures its settings based on the preset you selected.

7. On the Title menu, choose the content you want to convert. You see only the track number and time for each element on the DVD, so it is sometimes a guessing game. But you can usually tell what the actual content is based on its running time. Menu elements have a runtime of only a few seconds, whereas episodes of TV shows will be more than 20 minutes, and movies typically run more than 90 minutes.

8. In the File bar, name the file and choose a location; leave the file extension as it was created by HandBrake (see Figure 3.10).

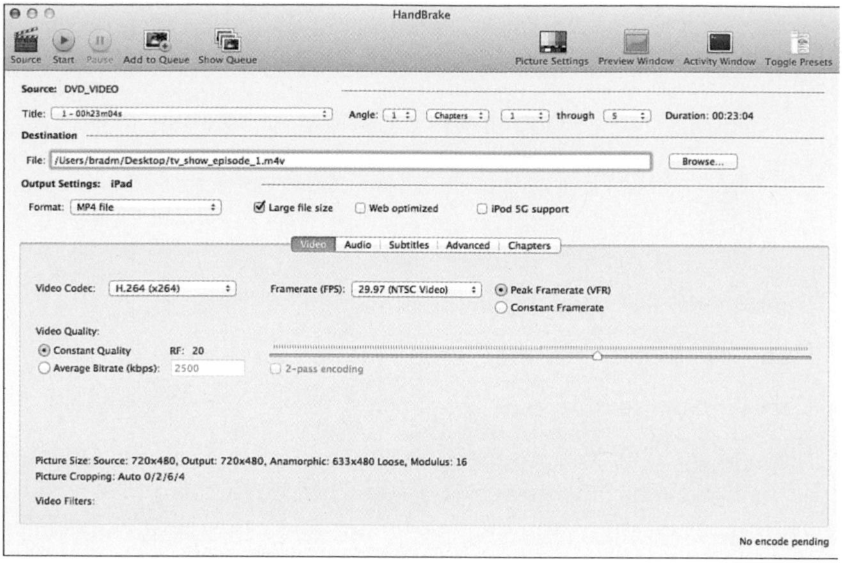

FIGURE 3.10

Here I've selected an episode of a TV show to convert into an iPad-compatible format.

9. Click the **Start** button on the HandBrake toolbar. HandBrake starts the encoding process. A progress bar appears at the bottom of the window to show you how it is going. Converting DVD content can take quite a while, especially for a long movie. You can continue to use your computer for other tasks while HandBrake works.

10. If you want to convert multiple items on the same disc, repeat steps 7 and 8 to select and name it.

11. Click **Add to Queue**. The content is added to HandBrake's queue. When the first content has been converted, HandBrake automatically starts on the next content.

12. Repeat steps 10 and 11 until you've selected all the content on the disc that you want to convert. When HandBrake is done encoding the content (if you've selected lots of content, this may take a couple of hours), the Process Complete message is displayed. You are ready to add the converted content to your iTunes Library.

 TIP To see the progress of the items in the queue, click **Show Queue**. In the resulting window, you see the status of each item you've added to the queue.

Importing Converted DVD Content into iTunes

After you've encoded DVD content, adding it your iTunes Library is a snap:

1. In iTunes on a Windows PC, open the iTunes menu and choose **File**, **Add File to Library**. If you are using iTunes on a Mac, choose **File**, **Add to Library**.

2. Move to and select the DVD content you encoded using the steps in the previous section.

3. Click **Open** (see Figure 3.11). The content is moved into your iTunes Library and is ready for you to watch or move onto an iOS device.

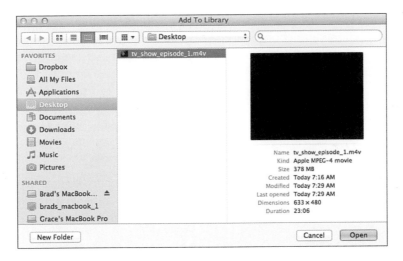

FIGURE 3.11

Adding converted content to iTunes is the easy and fast part of the process.

 TIP   Converted video content likely won't have the information needed to be easy to identify in iTunes. You should add the appropriate information to the content after you move it into your iTunes Library. For help with this, see Chapter 6, "Working with Information in Your iTunes Library."

Adding Content from Other Sources to Your Library

So far, we've looked at several very useful sources of content you can use to build up your iTunes Library, which included the iTunes Store, audio CDs, Amazon.com, and DVDs. However, there are many other sources of music, video, ebooks, and other content that you may want to have in your own library. The good news is that it is simple to add any content on your desktop to your iTunes Library (assuming it is in a compatible format). In fact, if you read through the previous section, you already know how.

To add content from your desktop to your iTunes Library on a Windows PC, open the iTunes menu and choose **File, Add File to Library**. If you are using iTunes on a Mac, choose **File, Add to Library**. Move to and select the content you want to add; you can select a folder of content to add multiple items at the same time. Click **Open**. Compatible content you selected is added to your iTunes Library.

 NOTE iTunes supports many types of audio, video, and other content. The easiest way to see if a particular file is compatible with iTunes is to try to add it to your iTunes Library.

In most cases, you'll want to add information to the content to make it easier to keep organized so that you can also find it more easily when you want to do something to it. That topic is explained in Chapter 6.

 TIP If you made sure that the **Copy files to iTunes Media folder when adding to library** check box is checked as described earlier, you should delete the original files from your computer after you are sure they have been added to your iTunes Library successfully. If you don't, you'll have two copies of the files on your computer: the original one and the copy iTunes added to the iTunes Media folder when you added the content to your iTunes Library.

THE ABSOLUTE MINIMUM

In this chapter, you learned how to add various kinds of content to your iTunes Library. As you create your own content collection, keep the following points in mind:

- Use the iTunes Advanced Preferences tab to determine the location of the iTunes Media folder, which is where your iTunes content is stored on your computer.

- You can import music and other audio content on CDs into your iTunes Library. After you've set up the process to be automatic, all you have to do is insert a CD into your computer.

- The iTunes Store is a great source of all types of content that you can add to your iTunes Library with just a few mouse clicks.

- When you have the Amazon MP3 Downloader application installed and configured on your computer, adding music from the Amazon.com MP3 store is almost as easy as using the iTunes Store.

- You can add video content from DVDs to your iTunes Library by first encoding (also known as ripping) that content using a separate program (such as HandBrake) and then adding it to your iTunes Library.

- You can add many types of content to your iTunes Library by using the Add File to Library (Windows) or Add to Library (Mac) command.

4

LISTENING TO MUSIC WITH ITUNES

In the previous chapters, you learned some very important iTunes tasks, such as setting up the application and, more importantly, filling your iTunes Library with content that you want to listen to or watch. Now it's time for some fun. iTunes offers lots of features that enable you to listen to music with much more flexibility (you might even say style) than a typical stereo system or boom box. Before you jump into listening, though, take a few moments to set some preferences related to music and other audio.

Setting Audio Playback Preferences

You should set a couple of tabs on the iTunes Preferences dialog box now because they impact how your music looks and, to a lesser extent, how it plays.

Open the General pane of the iTunes Preferences dialog box (on a Windows PC, open the iTunes menu and choose **Edit**, **Preferences**, and then click the **General** tab. On a Mac, choose **iTunes**, **Preferences**, and then click the **General** tab) to see several settings you might want to configure (see Figure 4.1):

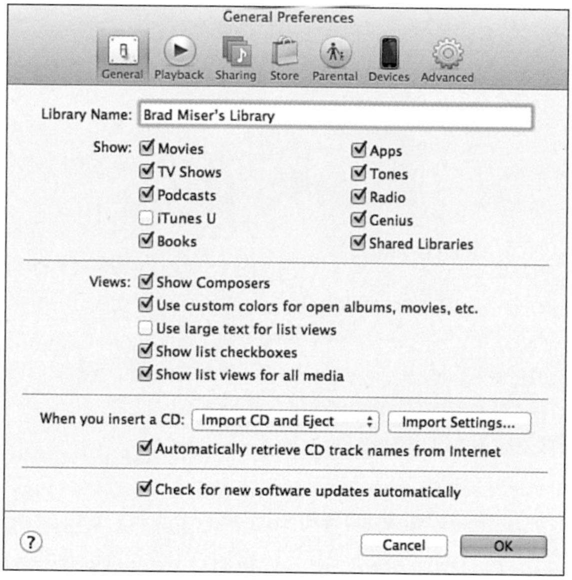

![General Preferences dialog box showing the General pane with Library Name field set to "Brad Miser's Library", Show checkboxes for Movies, TV Shows, Podcasts, Books, Apps, Tones, Radio, Genius, Shared Libraries; Views options; CD import settings; and software update options.]

FIGURE 4.1

The General pane of the iTunes Preferences dialog box provides preferences that impact a number of iTunes areas.

NOTE   For consistency with this book, it's a good idea to set your iTunes to use the same preferences as those shown in these figures. When you are comfortable using iTunes, you can change them to match your own preferences.

- **Library name**—This name identifies your iTunes Library to other iTunes users on your network (iTunes enables you to share your library with other people who are on the same network so they can listen to or watch your content). You can use the default name or edit it to be what you want it to be.

- **Show check boxes**—As you learned earlier, the Source menu contains many different sources of content, such as music, movies, podcasts, and so on. If you uncheck a source's check box, it will be hidden and so won't be available within iTunes. Nothing happens to the content in that source, it is simply hidden from view. You can check a source's check box to display it again.

- **Show Composers**—When checked, the Composers button appears when you are working with music. This enables you to view music based on its composer.

- **Custom colors**—When you view albums and other content, iTunes uses background color to provide more visual appeal. Ensure the **Use custom colors for open albums, movies, etc.** check box is checked to have a more colorful view of your content.

- **List Text**—When checked, the **Use large text for list views** check box changes the size of the text used in the lists you see in the Content pane.

- **Show list check boxes**—When this is checked, a check box appears next to songs, episodes of a TV series, and so on when you are using the List view. You can check that check box to have iTunes take action (such as to play an item), or you can uncheck a song's, movie's, or other item's check box to have iTunes ignore that item.

- **List view**—The List view is very useful because you can see all of a source's content in a convenient list that is easy to navigate, especially when you use the Column Browser. To have the List view available as much as possible, ensure that the **Show list views for all media** box is checked.

 NOTE You learned about the other preferences on the General tab in previous chapters, such as the CD settings you can use to import music from audio CDs.

You can use iTunes Playback preferences to control some aspects of how your music plays. You can take advantage of these features by clicking the Playback pane of the iTunes Preferences dialog box. On this pane, you can configure the following preferences for your music (see Figure 4.2):

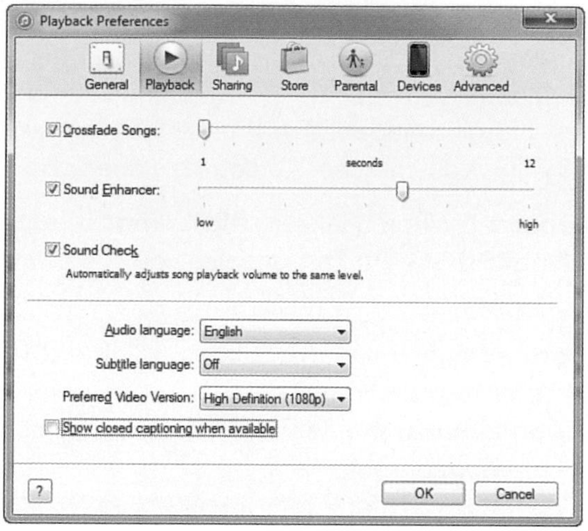

FIGURE 4.2

Control how your music sounds with the Playback preferences.

- **Crossfade Songs**—This effect causes one song to fade out and the next one to fade in smoothly, eliminating the gaps of silence between songs. To activate it, check the **Crossfade Songs** check box and use the slider to see the amount of fade time. If you move the slider to the left, songs fade out more quickly. If you set it to 1, there is almost no fading and as soon as one song ends, the next one starts. If you move the slider to the right, the fades last longer.

- **Sound Enhancer**—This effect is iTunes' attempt to "add depth and enliven" the quality of your music. The actual result of this effect is a bit difficult to describe, so the best thing to do is try it for yourself. Check the **Sound Enhance** check box and use the slider to set the relative amount of enhancement. Listen to some music. If it sounds better to you, increase the amount of the effect; if not, decrease it. Keep playing with the level of enhancer until you get it "just right." If you decide you don't want your music "enhanced," uncheck the box to turn it off.

- **Sound Check**—This effect sets the relative volume level of all songs to be the same. It is useful if you have music in your library that is recorded at different levels (such as classical versus acid rock). When this check box is checked, iTunes attempts to adjust the volume of music as it plays so that there aren't jarring differences in volume when you move from one song to the next.

When you've set the General and Playback preferences, click **OK** to save your changes and close the dialog.

Listening to Audio the iTunes Way

No matter which type of audio you listen to, iTunes follows a consistent pattern in how you listen and the tools that are available to you. Here's the general iTunes way of listening to your content:

1. On the Source menu, choose the source containing the type of content to which you want to listen. Because the focus of this chapter is music, you should select **Music** to access all the music in your library. As you learn in later chapters, you can listen to or watch the content in other sources, such as Podcasts or Movies, using similar steps.

2. Choose how you want to browse the source you are working with. For the Music source, there are quite a few options, which include Songs, Albums, Artists, Composers, Genres, and so on. Each of these offers different features and options; you'll probably use most or all of these options at different times.

3. Browse or search for the specific audio you want to hear.

4. Play the audio and control it from within the iTunes window as well as from the desktop.

You learn much more about each of these general steps throughout the rest of this chapter.

Selecting a Source

Your iTunes Library has a number of sources containing content you can watch or listen to; you choose the source you want to work with by selecting it on the Source menu, whose name is the source you are currently showing. When you open the menu, as shown in Figure 4.3, you see the list of all the types of content in your iTunes Library. After you make a selection, the Content pane shows you the content of that type that you have in your library.

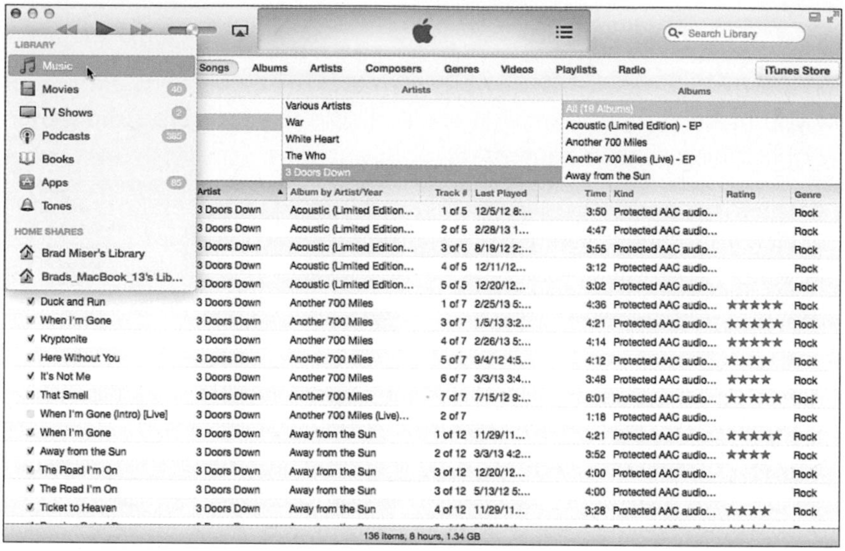

FIGURE 4.3

Choosing an option on the Source menu takes you to the content of that type.

 NOTE The Source menu works similarly for all types of sources as you see in later chapters. The remainder of this chapter is dedicated to the Music source, which offers the most browsing and viewing options.

Browsing for Music

When you choose Music on the Source menu, the Content pane reflects the browsing options available, including Songs, Albums, and so on. In the following sections, you learn about the most useful of these (and after you've learned to use them, you can pick up the others easily).

The Songs option enables you to use the List view and Column Browser, so that is a good place to start.

Browsing for Music by Songs

When you click the **Songs** button, you see all the songs in your library in the List view (see Figure 4.4). This view is all about efficiency. It presents the most information in the least amount of space, making it very useful to navigate through large amounts of content quickly. The downside to the List view is that it doesn't display any graphics, so it is not the most attractive way to see your content.

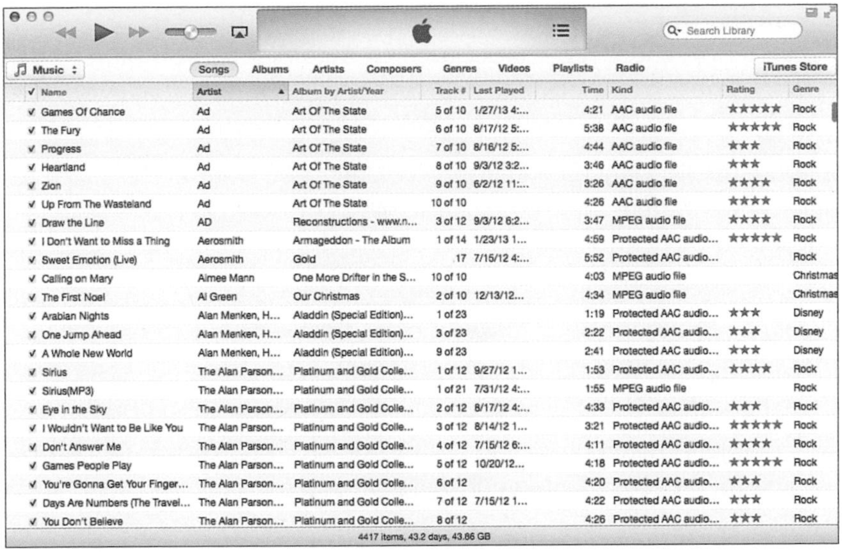

FIGURE 4.4

Here I am browsing all of my music by song title.

The List view offers some handy tools you can use to get to content you want efficiently:

- **Sort Order**—You can click a column heading to sort the list by the column; for example, if you click the Artist column, the tracks are sorted by artist. The column heading by which the column is currently sorted is highlighted in dark gray. The direction of the triangle in that column indicates the sort order; click the triangle to reverse the sort order. The sort order determines the order in which the songs play, starting at the top and moving toward the bottom of the screen.

- **Column width**—Drag the right edge of a column heading to the left to make it narrower or to the right to widen it.

- **Column order**—Drag column headings to the left or right to change their order. You can move any column except the first one, which displays the track number when you are viewing a playlist or album; it is empty when the track number doesn't apply.

- **Scrolling**—If there are more columns than can be displayed in the pane, scroll to the left or right to view all of them. Scroll up or down to browse the entire list.

- **Columns Displayed**—You can change the columns that are displayed by choosing **View**, **View Options** (on a Windows computer, press **Ctrl+B** to show the iTunes menu bar if you don't see the View menu). In the resulting dialog box, check the check boxes for the columns you want to be displayed and uncheck the check box next to any column to hide it. Click **OK,** and the list updates to show only those columns whose check box is checked.

Configure the list until it contains the columns you want at the width and in the order you want them. Then you can scroll up or down and left or right in the window to browse your songs until you find the songs of interest to you.

You can make the Songs list even better to browse because it allows you to use the Column Browser, which makes it even more efficient to browse for specific content. If the Column Browser is not shown, press **Ctrl+Shift+B** (Windows) or **⌘-B** (Mac). The Column Browser opens at the top of the window.

Now, configure the columns you want to see in the browser. Do this by choosing **View** and then choose **Column Browser** (if you are on Windows, you need to show the iTunes menu bar to see the View menu). On the resulting menu, you see all the columns that are available. Columns marked with a check mark are displayed in the Column Browser; if a column doesn't have a check mark, it is not displayed. Select a column that is currently displayed that you want hidden or that is currently hidden that you want to be displayed. Repeat this process until only the columns you want to be in the Column Browser are shown.

Use the following steps to use the Column Browser (these assume the Genres, Artists, and Albums columns are shown):

1. Click the genre shown in the Genres column in which you are interested. When you do, the categories in the other two columns are scoped down to include only the artists and albums that are part of that genre.

2. To narrow the music down further, click an artist in which you are interested in the Artists column. The Albums column is reduced down to show only those albums associated with the artist selected in the Artist column, and All is selected (by default) in the Albums column. The Content pane then shows all the songs on all the albums listed in the Albums column.

3. To see the contents of a specific album, click it in the Albums column. The Content pane shows only the tracks on the selected album (see Figure 4.5). The path to the content you are seeing in the Content pane is highlighted in the Column Browser (in Figure 4.5, this is Rock, 3 Doors Down, Time of My Life).

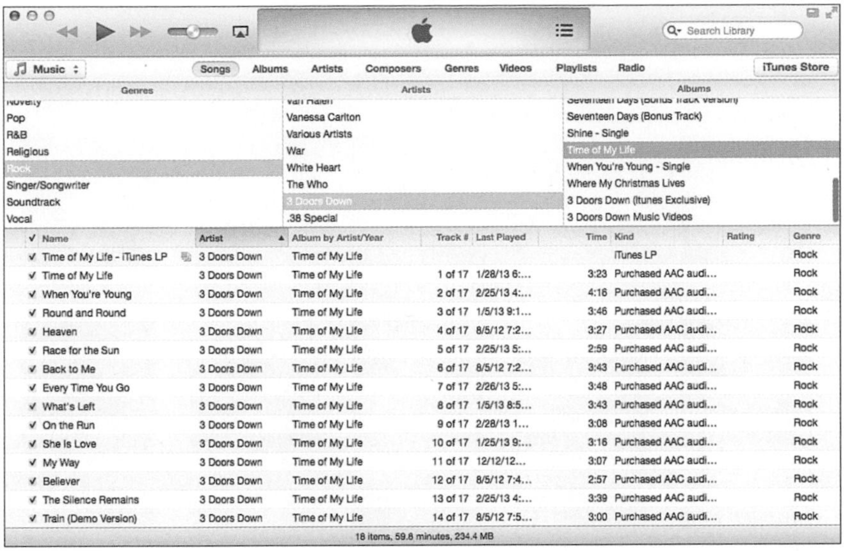

FIGURE 4.5

Here I've browsed to a specific album; its songs are shown in the Content pane in the lower part of the window.

4. You can browse the content you've selected in the Content pane, which fills the lower part of the window. In the Content pane, you see the content as determined by the selections in the Column Browser.

> **TIP** The Column Browser takes space in the iTunes window. After you've used the Column Browser to navigate to content with which you want to work, you can quickly hide the browser by pressing Ctrl+Shift+B (Windows) or ⌘-B (Mac). When hidden, the Content pane expands to fill the window. To show the Browser again, press Ctrl+Shift+B (Windows) or ⌘-B (Mac).

To play a song, double-click it. You can then use iTunes controls to listen to the music (see "Playing Music," later in this chapter).

Browsing for Music by Album

To browse your music collection by album, click the **Albums** button. You see all the albums in your collection, organized from top to bottom alphabetically by artist (see Figure 4.6). Although this can be a visually appealing view, if you have many albums, it can take a while to find a specific one you want to listen to.

FIGURE 4.6

Using the Albums view, you get to see how the music you are browsing is grouped along with its artwork.

Scroll up and down the window to find an album of interest. When you get to it, click its cover. The contents of the album expand out below the cover (see Figure 4.7). You see the songs on the album along with controls you can use to play it. To play the album, click its **Play** button.

To play a song, double-click the song, or select it and click the **Play** button on the toolbar.

You can then use iTunes controls to listen to the music (see "Playing Music," later in this chapter).

Close   Play Album

![iTunes window showing Jon McLaughlin albums in grid view with "Forever If Ever" album expanded showing track listing]

FIGURE 4.7

Click an album's thumbnail to expand its contents.

To collapse the album's contents, click the **Close** button.

NOTE   The Radio category enables you to listen to Internet radio stations. Click **Radio** and you see the types of streams available. Click the triangle next to a type of stream, such as Blues, to see the radio stations available. Double-click a stream to play it.

Browsing for Music by Artist

To browse your music collection by artist, click the **Artists** button. Along the left side of the window, you see the list of artists with music in your library. You can scroll up and down the artist list until you find the artist you want to listen to. When you click an artist, you see the list of albums for that artist in the right part of the window (see Figure 4.8). At the top of the window, you see the number of albums and songs under the artist's name. To play all the songs by the artist, click the **Play** button next to the artist's name.

FIGURE 4.8

You can easily browse all your music by specific artists.

To play a specific album, move the pointer near its name; controls appear. Click the **Play** button next to the album's name.

To play a song, double-click it.

You can then use the iTunes controls to listen to the music (see "Playing Music," later in this chapter).

TIP   You can see content related to what you are currently viewing by clicking the **In the Store** button. You move into the iTunes Store and see music related to what you are browsing. This can be a good way to find music to add to your collection.

Browsing for Music by Genre

To browse your music collection by genre, click the **Genres** button. Along the left side of the window, you see the genres of music in your library. You can scroll up and down the list until you find a genre that interests you. When you click a genre, you see the list of albums in that genre in the right part of the window (see Figure 4.9). At the top of the window, under the genre's name, you see the number of albums and songs. To play all the songs in the genre, click the **Play** button next to its name.

FIGURE 4.9

The Genres option shows you albums grouped by their genre.

The options for Genres are quite similar to those for Artists. For example, when you point to an album, its playback controls appear. And, like the other areas, you can play a song by double-clicking it or by selecting it and clicking the Play button in the toolbar.

You can then use iTunes controls to listen to the music (see "Playing Music," later in this chapter).

 NOTE The Match option, which you see only when iTunes Match is turned on, enables you to add the current iTunes Library to your iTunes Match account, which makes your music available through your iCloud account. This is explained in Chapter 12, "Streaming Your Music with iTunes Match."

 NOTE If it is enabled in preferences, you also see the Composers option. This works just like the Artists option, except music is displayed by who composed it rather than who performs it.

Browsing for Music by Playlist

Playlists are custom collections of music that you create directly or that are created by the iTunes Genius. You learn how to create and manage playlists in Chapter 7, "Creating and Using Playlists." You can listen to the content of playlists similar to the way you listen to other sources.

To browse music through playlists, click the **Playlists** button. Along the left side of the window, you see your playlists. They are organized by type, starting at the top with Purchased, which contains everything you have downloaded from the iTunes Store; Genius Mixes, which are playlists iTunes creates for you; Genius playlists, which are collections of music the iTunes Genius created based on a song you selected; playlist folders, which contain playlists; and of course, the playlists themselves, which contain any music you have placed in them manually or by defining criteria (smart playlists). A playlist's type is indicated by the icon next to its name.

When you select a playlist on the left, you see its contents in the right part of the window.

The Playlists source has view options that you can access by clicking the **View** button, which is located in the upper-right corner of the window. Choose the view you want. You can choose from the following views:

- **List**—When you choose this option, you see the content of the selected playlist in a list. This list works the same as the list you see when viewing the Songs source. Also like the Songs source, you can use the Column Browser with playlists, as shown in Figure 4.10.

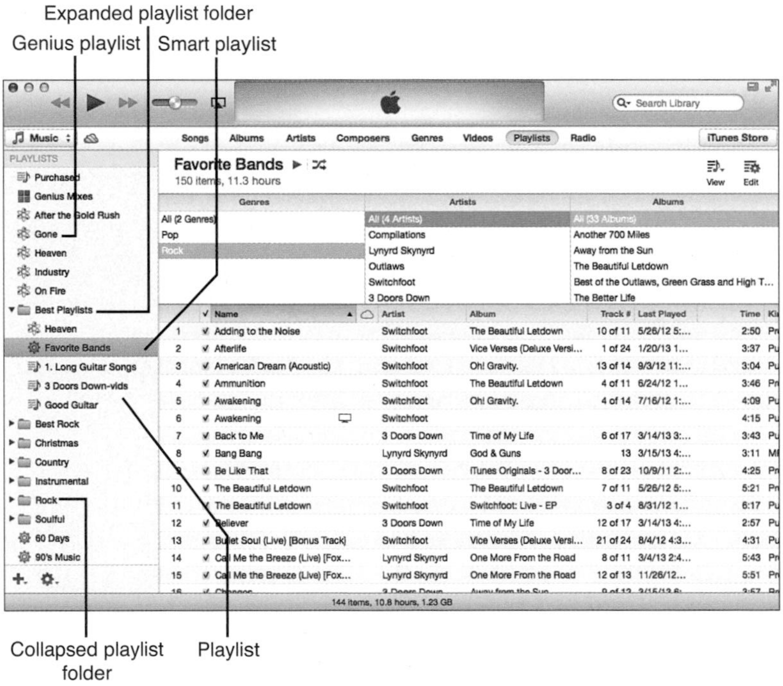

FIGURE 4.10

One of the advantages of the Playlists source is that you can view it in List view and show the Column Browser.

- **Grid**—The Grid view groups the songs in the playlist by the albums from which they come. This view is just like the Albums source. For example, you can click an album's cover to expand it to see the songs it contains. The difference here is that you see only the songs in the playlist from the album, not the full contents of the album that you see when you are using the Albums source.

- **Artist List**—This view organizes the Content pane into two sections. On the left, you see the list of artists whose music is in the playlist. When you select an artist, you see the list of songs from that artist that are in the playlist on the right side of the window. This view is very similar to working with the Artists source.

TIP At the top of many lists, such as artists or albums, you see the All category. When you select this category, you see all the content in the selected source. For example, when you click All in the Albums column in the Column Browser, you see all the albums for the selected artist.

To browse and play music with playlists, use the following steps:

1. Click the **Playlists** button.

2. Browse the list of playlists and select the one you want to work with. You need to expand playlist folders to see the playlists they contain.

TIP To expand the contents of a playlist folder so that you can see the playlists it contains, click the right-facing triangle next to its icon. To collapse a folder, click the downward-facing triangle next to its icon.

3. Configure the view you want to use by using the **View** button, showing the Column Browser (when you use the List view), and so on.

4. Use one of the following options to play content:

   - To play all the playlist's songs, click the **Play** button located by the playlist's name at the top of the window.

   - To play a specific song, double-click it.

   - To play all the songs on an album in the playlist, expand the album and click the **Play** button by its title (Grid view).

   - To play all the songs by an artist (when you use the Artist List view), select the artist and click the **Play** button by the artist's name.

When music is playing, you can control it using iTunes' playback tools, which are explained in the section, "Playing Music."

MUSIC VIDEOS

If your music collection includes music videos, click the **Videos** button to see them. To play a video, move the pointer over its thumbnail and click the **Play** button that appears. Then use iTunes video controls to watch it; these are explained in Chapter 5, "Watching Video with iTunes."

Searching for Music

When you want to hear something very specific, you can use the iTunes Search tool to search for it; this can be an even faster and easier way to get to individual songs, albums, and so on than browsing using the options described in the previous sections. You can search for songs by any of the following criteria:

- Entire Library (searches all your content)
- Artist
- Album
- Composer
- Song

To search for music in your library, perform the following steps:

1. If you want to search a specific source, select it; if you want to search your entire library, skip this step. For example, to search the contents of a playlist, select it so you see its contents in the Content pane.

2. Click the **magnifying glass** icon in the **Search** tool. You see a menu containing the options by which you can search.

3. To search across the entire library, ensure there is a check mark by the Search Entire Library option (if there isn't, click it); to search only the selected source, ensure there isn't a check mark by that option (if there is, click it to remove the check mark).

4. Choose how you want to search by clicking **All**, **Song**, **Album**, **Artist**, or **Composer** (see Figure 4.11). The currently selected search attribute is marked with a check.

FIGURE 4.11

By selecting Song on the menu, you can search for specific songs in the selected source (in this case, the entire library).

 TIP If you want to repeat a search, you don't need to make selections on the search menu because iTunes remembers your previous selections and uses those until you change them.

5. Type the data in the field for which you want to search. As you type, iTunes searches the selected source and presents the songs that meet your criterion in the Content pane. It does this on-the-fly so the search narrows with each keystroke. As you type more text or numbers, the search becomes more specific.

    If you selected the Search Entire Library option, the results appear in a list organized by type of content, such as Albums, Songs, Music Videos, and so on (see Figure 4.12). To move to and select one of the results, click it. For example, if you click an album, that album opens and you see the songs it contains. If you click a song, it is selected.

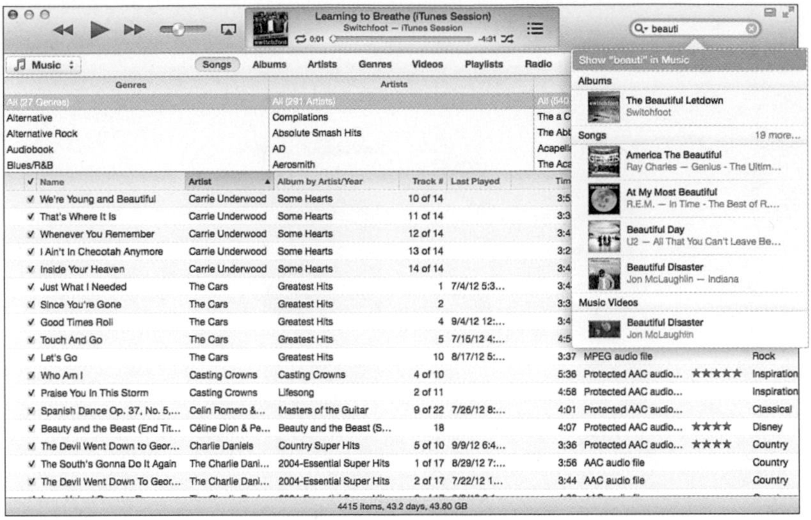

FIGURE 4.12

Here I'm searching for songs related to "beauti"; iTunes has found an album, several songs, and a music video that might be what I'm looking for.

If you disable the Search Entire Library option, the contents of the selected source are narrowed so that you see only items related to your search term (see Figure 4.13). You can work with results the same as other sources.

FIGURE 4.13

In this example, Search Entire Library is disabled, and so iTunes is showing those songs in the selected playlist folder that have "beauti" in their name.

6. Play the content in the search results the same as when you browse for music. Move ahead to the section, "Playing Music," to learn how to control music.

To clear your search and the search results displayed in the Content pane, click the **Clear** button (x) that appears in the Search tool after you have typed in it.

Playing Music

As you learned in the previous sections, iTunes offers many ways to find the music you want to hear. It also offers lots of tools to enable you to play music and other audio content in many ways. You can use the iTunes toolbar to control playback. You can also use the tools that appear within the Content pane. As if that isn't enough, the Up Next list provides yet another way to control your music.

In general, iTunes determines the order in which songs play by the order in which they are listed in the Content pane, starting from the top of the pane and moving toward the bottom. When you are playing an album using the Albums source, songs play by their track number, starting with track 1 and moving to the end of the album.

When you are working with the List view, you can set the order by sorting the list (you click a column heading to sort the list by that heading, and click it again to reverse the order).

In some sources, such as playlists, you can manually drag tracks up or down the screen to set the order in which they play (playlists are covered in detail in Chapter 7).

To start music playing, you can use one of the options listed in the previous sections, such as clicking the relevant Play button or double-clicking a song. The music starts to play and you see information about it in the Information window at the top of the screen (see Figure 4.14). The song currently playing is marked with the speaker icon.

FIGURE 4.14

Even if you can't hear it, you can see that the song "Beautiful Disaster" is playing; the speaker icon displays next to its name and the Information window at the top of the screen shows the song information.

 TIP To skip a song, uncheck its check box (these appear only in certain views, such as Songs and Playlists). When iTunes comes to that song, it skips over it and the song isn't played. Check the song's check box to have iTunes play it.

Controlling Music from the iTunes Toolbar and Controls Menu

When music is playing, there are lots of ways in iTunes to control it using the tools on the toolbar and commands on the menu bar:

- Click the **Pause** button (when music is paused, this is the **Play** button); choose **Controls, Pause**; or press the **spacebar**. The song pauses. To start playing it again, click **Play**; choose **Controls, Play**; or press the **spacebar**.

- Control the volume by dragging the **Volume** slider to the left to turn it down or to the right to turn it up. You can also control the volume by selecting **Controls, Increase Volume** or **Controls, Decrease Volume**. For yet another option, press the **Ctrl+Up arrow** and **Ctrl+Down arrow** keys on Windows PCs or the **⌘-Up arrow** and **⌘-Down arrow** keys on Macs to set the volume from the keyboard.

Using the Volume slider within iTunes changes the volume of iTunes relative to your computer's master volume. If you can't make the music loud or quiet enough using only iTunes Volume slider, adjust your computer's volume level up or down and then set the volume using iTunes Volume slider. Think of the computer's volume setting as the baseline; the iTunes volume level changes the music volume relative to that baseline.

- When a song is playing and you click and hold the **Rewind** or **Fast Forward** button, the song rewinds or fast-forwards until you release the button.

- If a song is playing and you single-click (but don't hold the button down) the **Rewind** or **Fast Forward** button, the previous or next song, respectively, plays. You can also select **Controls**, **Next** or **Controls**, **Previous** to move to the next or the previous song. And for yet another method to do the same thing, you can press the **Ctrl+Right arrow** and **Ctrl+Left arrow** keys on a Windows PC or the ⌘**-Right arrow** and ⌘**-Left arrow** keys on a Mac to move to the next or previous song.

- To see the song currently playing, choose **Controls**, **Go to Current Song**. The song that is playing is located and highlighted in the Content pane.

TIP   iTunes "remembers" the song currently playing so you can navigate around even if you pause the song and move off the Content pane screen that shows it. When you click the Play button, it resumes playing again. To "clear" the song, choose **Controls**, **Stop**. This stops the playback and clears the iTunes "memory" of what you were listening to.

Using the Information Window

While music is playing, you can view information about it in the Information window. At the top of the window, you see the name of the current song. Just under that you see its artist and album (see Figure 4.15).

FIGURE 4.15

The Information window provides information about what iTunes is doing and the controls you can use.

At the top of the window, you see information about the music playing, including song title, artist, and album.

On the left side of the window, you see the album art associated with the current song. If you click the art, a separate window appears. This window shows the album art at a large size and includes controls you can use to play the music (see Figure 4.16). If you move the pointer off this window, after a few moments, the window controls and toolbar disappear. Move back over the window to display them again. When you are done with the window, close it using the standard **Close** button.

FIGURE 4.16

If you like to view album art while you listen, click the artwork thumbnail in the Information window, and you see the art in all its glory.

You can set iTunes to repeat an entire source once or to repeat only a single song. To have iTunes repeat an entire source, click the **Repeat** button located just to the right of the album art thumbnail. The Repeat button is highlighted to show you that it is active. iTunes plays all the songs in the current source, such as a playlist, and repeats them until you stop the music.

To repeat only the selected song, click the **Repeat** button a second time. A "1" appears on the Repeat button to indicate that only the current song will be repeated.

To turn off the repeat function, click the **Repeat** button until it is no longer highlighted in blue.

 NOTE The neat thing about the Information window is that it changes based on the context of what you are doing. You have seen how it works when you listen to music. When you add music to your library, the information and tools in the window become those you use for the import process. When you sync an iOS device, the window displays information about the sync process.

Underneath the album and artist information is the Timeline bar. This displays the elapsed time (the amount of time a song has been playing) and remaining time (the amount of time a song has left) or total time (the song's total length). To change the display from remaining time to total time, click the time at the right end of the timeline bar.

 TIP You can find Shuffle, Repeat, and a number of other commands on the Controls menu. This menu also has the Play Recent command that you can use to play songs, albums, playlists, and so on that you have played recently.

For a little variety, you can have iTunes play songs in a random order using the Shuffle feature. To use this feature, click the **Shuffle** button located at the right end of the Timeline bar (two "crisscrossing" arrows). The Shuffle button is highlighted in blue to indicate that it is active.

 TIP When iTunes is doing more than one thing, such as playing music and syncing an iOS device, up and down arrows appear at the right end of the Information window. Click these to change the information being displayed, such as to move from information about the sync process to see information about the music currently playing.

You can choose how content is shuffled by choosing **Controls**, **Shuffle** and then choosing **By Songs**, **By Albums**, or **By Groupings**. When By Songs is selected, iTunes randomly selects among songs in the selected source. If you choose one of the other options, iTunes plays the songs in order in the current album or grouping and then randomly selects another album or grouping and plays all the songs in that album or grouping in the order in which they are listed.

To return the source so that it plays in order again, click the **Shuffle** button again.

At the right side of the Information window, you see the **Up Next** button. When you click this button, a list of songs that will play appears (see Figure 4.17). At the top of the list, you see the source of the music, such as playlist or genre. To the right of that is the Clock button; click this to change the list from what is going to be played to what has been played recently. Click the Clear button to clear the list.

FIGURE 4.17

The Up Next list shows the songs that will play, in the order in which they will play.

To see all on the songs on the list, scroll up or down it.

You can play any song on the list by double-clicking it.

To remove a song from the list so that it won't play, hover over it and click the **Remove** (x) button.

Controlling Music from the Contextual Menu

When you see the right-facing arrow, which happens when you expand an album or hover over a song's title in the Content pane or in the Information window, you can click it to open a contextual menu (see Figure 4.18).

FIGURE 4.18

Clicking the right-facing arrow reveals a menu that contains a number of useful commands.

The commands you see on this menu can include the following:

- **Play Next**—This causes the song to play after the current one finishes.

- **Add to Up Next**—This adds the song at the top of the Up Next list but places it after a song on which you've used the Play Next command so that the song you applied the Play Next command to will play next.

- **Genius controls**—The Genius controls enable you to activate the iTunes Genius (these features appear only when the Genius is enabled). This is covered in Chapter 7.

- **Add To**—When you choose this, you see a list of your playlists and playlist folders. Click a playlist to add the song to that playlist.

- **Go to**—These commands take you to related music in your iTunes Library, such as to all of the artist's music or the album the song comes from.

- **Show in Tunes Store**—This command takes you to related music in the iTunes Store, such as to an album containing the song.

 TIP The Shuffle button appears next to playlist titles, album titles, artists, and other objects in the various views. You can click it in those locations to shuffle whatever the button is associated with.

THE ABSOLUTE MINIMUM

In this chapter, you learned how to listen to music and other audio content. As you enjoy the music, keep the following points in mind:

- You can set iTunes Playback preferences to have music play at a similar volume level, have little or no gap between songs, and to "enhance" the sound.

- iTunes follows a similar pattern for any type of content. First, choose the source containing the content you want to listen to or watch. Second, choose how you want to view the source, such as by Albums or Playlists when you are working with music. Third, browse or search for the specific content you want. Fourth, use the iTunes controls to play that content.

- The Source menu provides access to the various types of media in your library, such as Music, Movies, TV Shows, Podcasts, and so on.

- There are lots of ways to browse your music. After you select Music on the Source menu, you can click the buttons along the top of the Content pane to choose how you want to browse. For example, click **Songs** to see your music in a song list, or click **Albums** to see graphic thumbnails of the albums in your collection.

- You can use the Search tool to find music by song, album, artist, and so on. Searching can be a faster way to get to specific music than browsing for it.

- iTunes provides lots of controls you can use while listening to music. These are located on the toolbar, in the Information window, and on the contextual menu that you can access by clicking the right-facing arrow that appears when you point to a song's title.

5

WATCHING VIDEO WITH ITUNES

As you might suspect from this chapter's title, you can use iTunes to watch various types of video. You may have also noticed that this is a short chapter; that's because using iTunes to watch video is similar to using it to listen to audio. You use the same basic steps, which include selecting the source of video you want to watch, choosing how you want to browse that video, browsing or searching for the specific video content you want to watch, and playing the video. Only the last step has significant differences from working with audio, which is where this chapter comes in.

Selecting Video Content to Play

As you learned in Chapter 2, "Working with the iTunes Store," and Chapter 3, "Building Your iTunes Library," you can stock your iTunes Library with video. The sources of video that you can manage in iTunes include the following:

- **Music**—The Music source contains music videos you have downloaded from the iTunes Store or added to your library from your computer's desktop. To see the music videos in your music collection, choose **Music** on the Source menu and click the **Videos** button (see Figure 5.1).

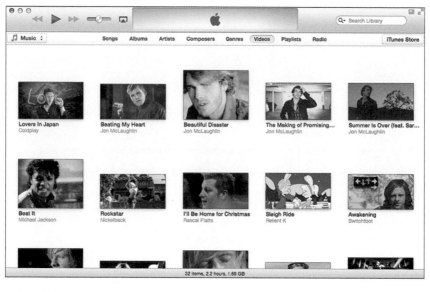

FIGURE 5.1

To view the music videos in your collection, open the Music source and click the Videos button.

- **Movies**—This source contains movies you have downloaded from the iTunes Store along with those you have added in other ways, such as movies you have converted from DVD. To access your movies, choose **Movies** on the Source menu. You can browse your movies in a number of categories, which include Rented, which shows movies you have rented from the iTunes Store; Unwatched, which shows you only movies you haven't watched; Movies, which contains all your movies; Genres, which organizes your movie by genre; Home Videos, which contains video you've uploaded into iTunes from other sources; and List, which presents all your movies in a list.

- **TV Shows**—You can also download TV shows from the iTunes Store or use an application to convert them into digital format from a DVD and then add them to your iTunes Library. To view your TV shows, choose **TV Shows** on the Source menu. You can choose from the following options by clicking the respective button: Unwatched, which shows you only those shows you haven't watched yet; Shows, which presents your TV shows by season; Genres, which shows the series organized by their genre; and List, which presents all the content in a list.

- **Podcasts**—Most podcasts are audio only, but there are quite a few that are video. To view video podcasts, choose **Podcasts** on the Source menu and look for episodes marked with the video screen icon.

To watch video content, perform the following general steps (if you read Chapter 4, "Listening to Music with iTunes," these steps should be familiar to you):

 NOTE   Movies and TV shows that you haven't watched yet are marked with a blue circle. As you watch video content, its blue circle empties. When you have watched all of it, the circle disappears.

1. Select the source containing video that you want to watch by choosing it on the Source menu. For example, choose **TV Shows** to see shows in your library.

2. Choose the option for the selected source. For example, click **List** to see the content organized in a list with which you can use the Column Browser, as shown in Figure 5.2.

√ Name	Time	Show	▲ Season	Description	Plays
√ Mini-series	3:02:26	Battlestar Galactica	Season 1		1
√ 33	45:00	Battlestar Galactica	Season 1		1
√ Water	43:58	Battlestar Galactica	Season 1		1
√ Bastille Day	43:44	Battlestar Galactica	Season 1		1
√ Act of Contrition	43:59	Battlestar Galactica	Season 1		1
√ You Can't Go Home Again	43:57	Battlestar Galactica	Season 1		1
√ Litmus	43:55	Battlestar Galactica	Season 1		1
√ Six Degrees of Separation	44:00	Battlestar Galactica	Season 1		1
√ Flesh and Bone	44:01	Battlestar Galactica	Season 1		1
√ Tigh Me Up, Tigh Me Down	44:01	Battlestar Galactica	Season 1		1
√ The Hand of God	44:00	Battlestar Galactica	Season 1		1
√ Colonial Day	43:59	Battlestar Galactica	Season 1		1
√ Kobol's Last Gleaming, Part 1	44:00	Battlestar Galactica	Season 1		1
√ Kobol's Last Gleaming, Part 2	44:01	Battlestar Galactica	Season 1		1
√ Scattered	43:39	Battlestar Galactica	Season 2	With Commander Adama near death after...	1
√ Valley of Darkness	43:33	Battlestar Galactica	Season 2	A Cylon virus has penetrated the Galactica...	1

77 TV shows, 2.5 days, 59.48 GB

FIGURE 5.2

Here I'm viewing the TV Shows source as a List with the Column Browser shown.

3. Browse or search for the specific video you want to watch. This works just like browsing or searching for music.

4. Select and play the video (playing video is explained in detail in the following section).

Watching Video in iTunes

Using iTunes to watch video is fairly straightforward. The application offers different ways to watch. Although those ways look different, the basic controls are similar.

iTunes enables you to watch video in the following locations:

- **iTunes Window**—This option fills the area below the toolbar with the video.

- **A Separate Window**—When you select this mode, the video plays in a window that is independent of the iTunes window.

- **Full Screen**—Using the Full Screen mode, the video content fills your entire screen; the iTunes controls are automatically hidden so nothing clutters your view of the content.

You should experiment with each of these views to see which works best for you.

To play video and choose how you want to watch it, perform the following steps:

1. Use the Source menu to choose the type of video you want to watch, such as **TV Shows**.

2. Use the category options to organize the video. For example, click **List** to see the content in a list.

TIP   You can use the Column Browser to work with any content in the List mode. If the Column Browser isn't shown, press ⌘-B on a Mac or Ctrl+Shift+B on a Windows PC. The Column Browser appears on top of the list. Choose **View, Column Browser,** and then choose a column you want to see so that it is marked with a check mark. Repeat this process until all the columns you want to be displayed are shown. Then you can browse the content on the list by clicking the items in each column.

3. Double-click the video you want to watch. It plays in the mode you most recently used.

4. Perform a secondary click on the video. A contextual menu appears (see Figure 5.3).

FIGURE 5.3

Use this contextual menu to choose the video viewing option you want to use.

5. Choose the view mode you want to use. The video window changes accordingly.

6. Use the playback tools available in the mode you are using. Details for each mode are provided in the following sections.

  NOTE iTunes remembers the last mode in which you watched video and uses that mode automatically until you select a different view.

Watching Video in the iTunes Window

When you choose to watch video in the iTunes window, the video fills the iTunes window under the toolbar, and you see something like Figure 5.4.

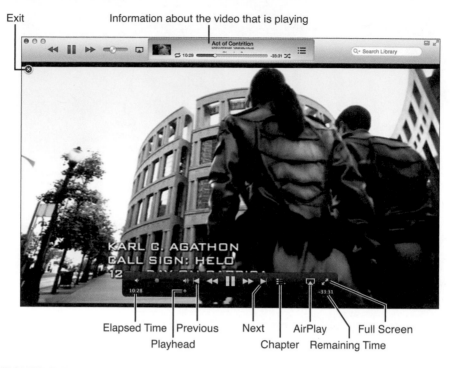

Exit   Information about the video that is playing

Elapsed Time | Previous   Next | AirPlay | Full Screen
Playhead   Chapter   Remaining Time

FIGURE 5.4

Here I'm watching an episode of the TV show Battlestar Galactica *in the iTunes window.*

When you watch video in the iTunes window, you can control it in the following ways:

- **Play/Pause**—When video is playing, click to pause. When paused, click to play. You can also press the spacebar to do the same things.

- **Fast Forward/Rewind**—Click and hold these buttons to fast forward or rewind.

- **Volume slider**—Drag to the left to reduce volume or to the right to increase it.

- **Chapter**—Click this to see a list of the chapters in the video (see Figure 5.5). To jump to a chapter, select it on the menu.

FIGURE 5.5

You can use the Chapter menu to move to a specific chapter in the video.

TIP You can also change chapters using the Chapter menu.

- **AirPlay**—Use this to send the video to an AirPlay-enabled device (this topic is covered in detail in Chapter 9, "Streaming Music and Video Through an AirPlay Network."

- **Full Screen**—Click to switch into Full Screen mode.

- **Playhead**—Drag to the left to move back in the video or to the right to move ahead in it. The current position of the Playhead is indicated by the Elapsed time while the remaining time is shown at the right end of the Timeline bar.

As the video plays, you see information about it in the Information window at the top of the iTunes window. You can also use the controls on the iTunes toolbar to play/pause, fast forward, and so on.

After video plays for a few moments, the onscreen controls are hidden. To show them again, move the pointer over the video.

When the video reaches the end, it stops playing, and you return to the Content pane. You can stop the video and return to the Content pane at any time by clicking the **Exit** button or by pressing the Esc key.

NOTE iTunes also remembers where you were in a video when you stop playing it. The next time you play that video, playback starts at the position where you left off.

Watching Video in a Separate Window

When you choose this option, a new, separate window opens (see Figure 5.6). This window is independent of the iTunes window, so you can move it around on your desktop, move it to a different display, and so on. The controls you see at the bottom of the window are the same as those that appear when you play video in the iTunes window (see the previous section for details).

Window controls   Video that is playing

Video controls   Resize handle

FIGURE 5.6

Here the video is playing in a separate window.

The title of the video you are watching appears in the window's title bar along with the standard window controls for Windows or OS X. In the lower-right corner of the window is the Resize handle that you can use to change the size of the video window.

Also, just as when you watch in the iTunes window, the controls and title bar disappear after a few moments. Move the pointer over the window to cause them to reappear.

When you are done watching, close the video window.

TIP Because you want to see the video playing in iTunes, it is helpful if the movie window remains in the front. To ensure this, open the Advanced tab of the iTunes Preferences dialog box and check the **Keep movie window on top of all other windows** check box. Then click **OK**.

Watching Video in Full Screen

Full Screen mode causes the video to fill the entire screen so that it is as large as possible (see Figure 5.7). Depending on the proportion of the video and your display, you may see black bars on the tops or the sides of the video.

Back

FIGURE 5.7

Full Screen mode is the one you will likely use most often because it provides the best viewing experience.

In Full Screen mode, you have almost the same set of controls as when you watch video in the iTunes window. The exception is the **Back** button. When you click this button, the video continues to play, but the mode returns to the one you used previously, such as playing in the iTunes window or in a separate window.

Also like the other modes, after video plays for a few moments, the controls are hidden. Move the pointer over the video to show them again.

When the video finishes playing, you return to the iTunes window. You can stop the video at any time and return to the iTunes window by clicking the **Exit** button.

TIP   If your computer supports High Definition (HD) video (most current computers do), open the **Playback** tab of the iTunes Preferences dialog box. On the **Preferred Video Version** menu, choose the highest resolution video that your computer supports, such as **High Definition (1080p)**. Click **OK** to save your preference.

THE ABSOLUTE MINIMUM

In this chapter, you learned how to use iTunes to watch video:

- Most of the playback process for video is the same as for audio. You choose a source of video, browse or search for the video you want to watch, and then play it.

- Unlike audio, you can watch video in several modes: in the iTunes window, in a separate window, or in full screen.

- Controlling video playback is straightforward. If you've used a DVD player, you'll get the hang of iTunes video playback very quickly. However, iTunes provides more control than does a standard DVD player. For example, you can drag the Playhead to get to any position in the video you are watching.

IN THIS CHAPTER

- Understanding information in your iTunes Library
- Viewing and changing information
- Configuring a track's options
- Working with art
- Changing the information you see

6

WORKING WITH INFORMATION IN YOUR ITUNES LIBRARY

As you've seen in the previous chapters, iTunes presents a lot of information about the content in your iTunes Library, such as song and movie names, artists, genres, and so on. This information is important because you use it to identify content, and it determines how you are able to browse or search for content to play. This information also impacts how you can use other iTunes tools, such as smart playlists (which you learn about in Chapter 7, "Creating and Using Playlists"). Much of the information about the content in your iTunes Library is automatically created by iTunes when you add content to iTunes, such as by downloading it from the iTunes Store. However, you can also configure information for your content to improve your ability to keep your iTunes Library organized, making it much easier to work with

Understanding Information in Your iTunes Library

In previous chapters, you saw how you can browse or search your iTunes content by various categories, such as artist, genre, season (TV shows), and so on. This is possible because of the information associated with the content in your library.

Two basic types of information are attached to the content in your library: information that iTunes assigns for you and that you can't change or information that you or iTunes assigns and that you can change.

An example of the type of information that iTunes applies and you can't change is the account used to download content from the iTunes Store and the date on which it was downloaded. When you download content from the iTunes Store, iTunes automatically applies this information to the content when it is added to your library. This information stays the same over time.

An example of information that iTunes assigns to content and you can change is the genre by which music is categorized. For example, when you import music from an audio CD into your library, iTunes applies a genre to it based on the information it gathers from the CD and Internet. However, you can change this information as needed.

There are also lots of types of information about content that may initially be blank. You can add information to these empty information fields and change it whenever you want to.

As you have learned, you can include different types of media in your iTunes Library, including music, movies, TV shows, and so on. Each type of media can have different categories of information associated with it. For example, video content includes information about the type of media it is (movie, TV show, and the like), whereas music does not have this information because it doesn't apply. When you view the information for a specific type of content, you see only the information applicable to the type you are viewing.

iTunes includes a number of ways to view information about your iTunes content. It also enables to you to change the information that is editable and to add information where there isn't any.

 NOTE You don't have to add information where none exists; in fact, you probably won't add very much of it. Lots of the information that is possible for specific content can be blank if you have no need to use that information. However, in certain situations it is good to know how to add information to content when you need to.

Viewing and Changing Information

In previous chapters, you learned how to browse, search for, and view music, movies, podcasts, and other types of media. When you do these tasks, you are using the information associated with that content.

Viewing Information in the Content Pane

Whenever you view music, movies, podcasts, or other types of media in the Content pane, you are viewing it based on the information associated with that content. This is true of detailed views, such as when you view music by Artist, as well as when you use a more general view, such as Genre. When you use the Column Browser, it presents content based on the high-level categories associated with that content. For example, in Figure 6.1, you see the Songs view with the Column Browser displayed. You are able to use the Column Browser to find specific music because of the information associated with that music. For example, because each song is categorized by its genre, you can use the Genres column to select and browse music in a specific genre.

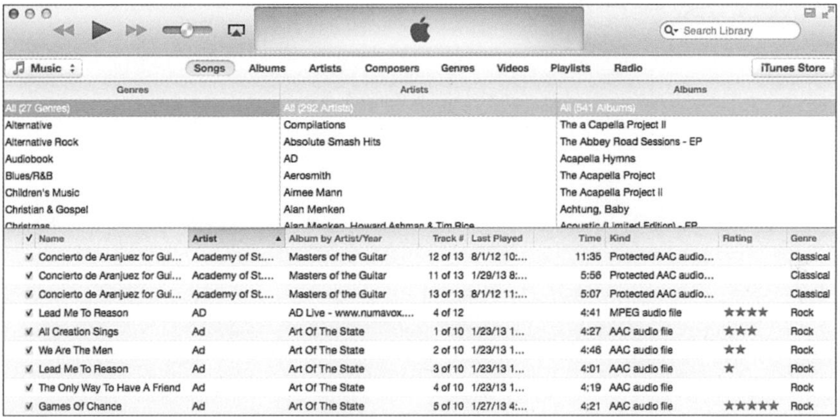

FIGURE 6.1

When you view songs, you see lots of information that you can use to work with those songs.

NOTE You can change how information is displayed in the iTunes window, so the information you see in iTunes on your computer may not be the same as that shown in the figures in this chapter. You learn how to configure the information that you see in the section, "Changing the Information You See," later in this chapter.

Viewing Information in the Info Window

You can use the Info window to view all the information associated with your media and to change some of it. To view the Info window, select a song, a movie, an episode of a TV series, a podcast, or other item in your library and choose **File**, **Get Info** or press **Ctrl+I** (Windows) or **⌘-I** (Mac). The Info window appears; at the top of the window, you see the name of the item whose information you are viewing (see Figure 6.2). This window has a number of tabs that you learn about throughout the rest of this chapter.

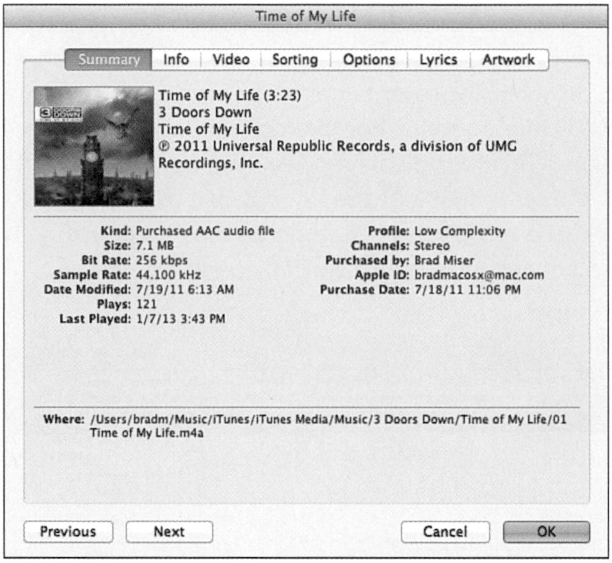

FIGURE 6.2

The Info window enables you to view the information associated with tracks, and you can change many of them.

To change to a different set of information, click the tab for the type of information that you want to view, such as Info, Video, or Artwork.

You can change the item about which you are getting information without closing the Info window. Click **Next** to move to the next item in the current source you are viewing (such as a playlist) or **Previous** to move to the previous item. When you do so, the next or previous item's information is displayed in the Info window.

To close the Info window, click **OK**.

Viewing Information on the Summary Tab

The first tab in the Info window is the Summary tab that provides an overview of the item's information; you can't directly change any of the information on this tab because iTunes manages this information for you. Some of the information on this tab never changes, such as information about the download process when the content came from the iTunes Store, whereas other information changes as you use the content, such as the number of times a song has been played.

Explaining the Summary information you see for music will help you understand the information you see for other types of media, although as noted earlier, the specific information you see depends on what kind of media you are getting information about.

When you are viewing information about a song, at the top of the tab you see art associated with the song, along with its name, length, artist, album, and publisher.

In the center part of the pane, you see more technical information that includes the following:

- **Kind**—The item's media type, such as Purchased AAC audio file, AAC audio file, MP3, and so on.

- **Size**—The amount of disk space required to store the file.

- **Bit Rate**—The quality level at which the sound was encoded. Larger numbers, such as 128Kbps, mean the track was encoded at a higher quality level (and also has a relatively larger file size).

- **Sample Rate**—The rate at which the music was sampled when it was captured. When music is converted from analog to digital, the music is "sampled," at which point the music is recorded digitally. The faster the rate of this sampling, the higher the quality the resulting digital music plays with and the larger its file size.

- **Date Modified**—The date on which the media's file was last changed.

- **Plays**—The number of times the media has been played.

- **Last Played**—The last time the media was played.

- **Profile**—A categorization of the media's complexity.

- **Channels**—Whether the track is stereo or mono.

NOTE   Not even all media of the same type, such as music, has the same categories of information. You see only information that is applicable to a specific song based on the type of song it is and where it came from. For example, only music downloaded from the iTunes Store has information about the purchaser. And information for a Purchased AAC audio file, which is what is described in this list, is different from music in the MP3 format.

- **Purchased by**—The name of the person associated with the Apple ID used to download the content from the iTunes Store.

- **Apple ID**—The account under which media was downloaded from the iTunes Store.

- **Purchase Date**—This is the date when the track was downloaded from the iTunes Store.

At the bottom of the tab, you see the Where information. This shows a path to the track's file on your computer along with its filename.

Viewing Information on the Info Tab

Click the **Info** tab to view different categories of information about the current item; in Figure 6.3, you see the Info tab for a song. You can use the fields on this tab to view or change the item's information. (The steps to change it are in the section, "Changing an Item's Information.")

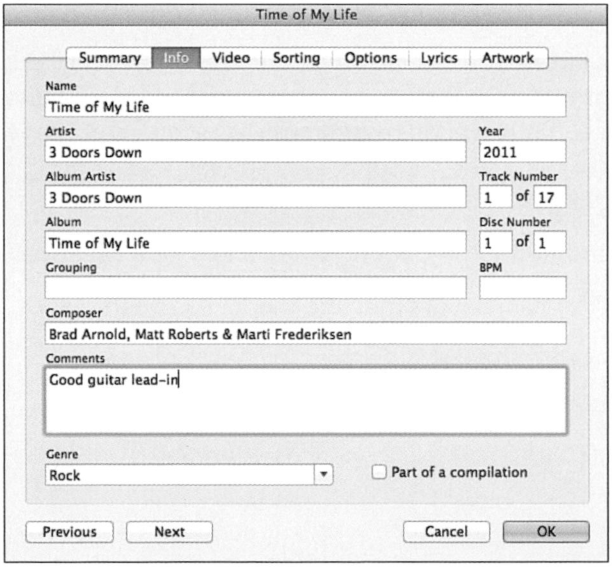

Time of My Life

| Summary | Info | Video | Sorting | Options | Lyrics | Artwork |

Name
Time of My Life

Artist | Year
3 Doors Down | 2011

Album Artist | Track Number
3 Doors Down | 1 of 17

Album | Disc Number
Time of My Life | 1 of 1

Grouping | BPM

Composer
Brad Arnold, Matt Roberts & Marti Frederiksen

Comments
Good guitar lead-in

Genre
Rock | ☐ Part of a compilation

| Previous | Next | | Cancel | OK |

FIGURE 6.3

You can use the Info tab to change an item's (in this case, a song's) information.

Information for songs on the Info tab include the following:

- **Name**—The name of the song.

- **Artist**—The person or group who performs the song.

- **Album Artist**—This is typically the same as the artist. However, when songs on the same album come from different artists, they can be split up when you browse music by artist. To keep them together, you can input an album artist and choose to have music grouped by this field instead of by artist.

- **Album**—The name of the album or compilation from which the song comes.

- **Grouping**—This is a label you can assign to group songs together. You can then organize songs by their group, collect them in playlists, and so on.

- **Composer**—The people who are credited with composing the song.

- **Comments**—This is a free-form text field in which you can make comments about a song.

- **Genre**—This associates a song with a genre, such as Jazz or Classical.

- **Year**—The year the song was created.

- **Track Number**—The song's position on the CD from which it came, such as "2 of 12."

- **Disc Number**—The number of the CD or DVD. This is meaningful for multiple-disc sets.

- **BPM**—The song's beats per minute.

- **Part of a Compilation**—When checked, this check box indicates that the song is part of a compilation, meaning a CD or other grouping that contains songs from a variety of artists, such as "Best of 1970s Southern Rock."

Understanding Other Tabs in the Info Window

You might find several other tabs in the Info window useful:

- **Video**—The Video tab is active when you are getting information about movies, TV shows, or other types of video. This tab provides information you might want to include for TV shows, such as episode ID, season number, and so on.

- **Sorting**—The Sorting tab enables you to add information that you can then use to sort content in the Content pane. For example, you can add an album artist to music and then sort music by album artist instead of the artist associated with songs.

- **Options**—This tab provides tools you can use to configure certain aspects of how audio and video plays in iTunes. This is covered in the section, "Configuring an Item's Options in the Info Window."

- **Lyrics**—The Lyrics tab enables you to store lyrics or other text associated with an item. Type or paste the lyrics or other text in the box on the Lyrics tab and click **OK**. Unfortunately, there isn't really a good way to view lyrics while music plays in iTunes. You see them only on the Lyrics tab. However, on some iOS devices, such as an iPhone, you can display lyrics on the Now Playing screen, which makes them much more convenient than they are in iTunes.

- **Artwork**—This tab shows the artwork associated with an item. It is covered in the section, "Working with Art."

Changing an Item's Information

You can use the Info window to change an item's information, as you can see in the following steps:

1. Open the Info window for the song or other item that has information you want to add or change.

2. Click the **Info** tab, and the Info pane appears (refer to Figure 6.3).

3. Enter or change the information shown in the various fields. For example, you can add grouping information or comments.

4. To change a item's genre, select the new genre from the **Genre** menu.

5. When you are done entering or changing information, click **OK**. The Info window closes, and any changes you made are saved.

 TIP If a genre by which you want to classify media isn't listed on the Genre menu, select the genre selection so it becomes highlighted and type in the genre you want to add. That genre is added to the menu and associated with the current item. You can use the genres you create in this way the same as you can use the default genres.

Changing Information for Multiple Items at the Same Time

You can change some information, such as Genre, for a group of tracks at the same time. This can be a faster way to enter information because you can change multiple items with one action. Here are the steps to follow:

1. Select the items whose information you want to change.

2. Choose **File**, **Get Info**. You're prompted to confirm that you want to change the information for a group of items.

3. Click **Yes** to clear the prompt. The Multiple Item Information window appears (see Figure 6.4). The information and tools in this window work in the same way as they do for individual items, except that the information and settings apply to multiple items at the same time.

Multiple Item Information	
Info Video Sorting Options	
Artist	Year
☐ 3 Doors Down	☐ 2008
Album Artist	Track Number
☐ 3 Doors Down	☐ of ☐ 13
Album	Disc Number
☐ 3 Doors Down (Itunes Exclusive)	☐ 1 of ☐ 1
Grouping	BPM
☐	☐
Composer	Artwork
☐ Brad Arnold, Matt Roberts, Todd Harrell & Chris Hendersc	
Comments	
☐	☐
Genre	Rating
☐ Rock ▾	☐ · · · · ·
	Cancel OK

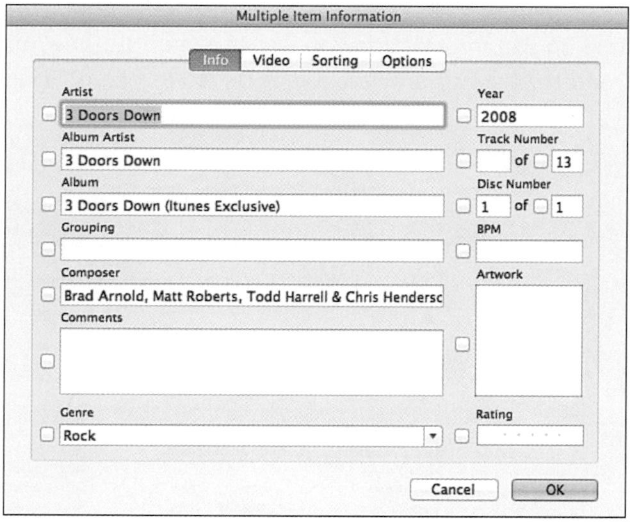

FIGURE 6.4

You can use this window to change the information for multiple items at the same time.

 TIP   Many iTunes dialog boxes have a check box you can check to prevent the dialog from being displayed again. For example, if you don't want to be warned when you use the Multiple Item Information tool, check the **Do not ask me again** check box in the prompt.

4. Enter data in the fields, make changes to existing data, or use the other tools to configure the information associated with items you have selected. When you change something, the check box next to that information becomes checked to show that you are changing that information for all the selected items.

5. When you are finished making changes, click **OK**. The window closes, and the changes you made are saved.

Changing Information in the Content Pane

You can also change information within the Content pane:

1. If you aren't in a view that displays a list, switch to one that does, such as Songs or List. (See Chapter 4, "Listening to Music with iTunes," for information about working with views.)

2. Click once on an item to select it.

3. Click once on the information you want to change. The information becomes highlighted to show that it is ready to be edited (see Figure 6.5).

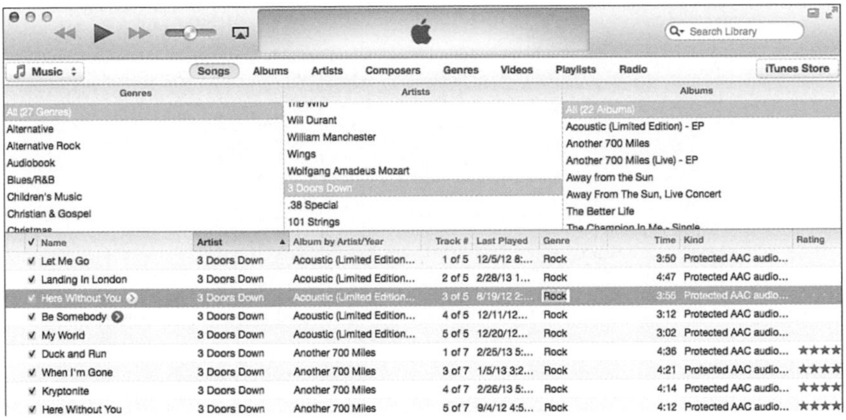

FIGURE 6.5

You can also change information on the Content pane (in this case, the Genre is being edited).

4. Type the new information, choose a value on the information's drop-down list, or click to set a value (for example, to rate a song).

5. Press **Enter**. The changes you made are saved.

Configuring an Item's Options

The Options tab enables you to configure various aspects of how audio and video plays in iTunes. The specific tools available on the Options tab depend on the type of media you have selected. For example, music has different options than movies or podcasts do. The options you may see include the following:

- **Relative Volume**—You can change an item's relative volume so it is either louder or quieter than "normal." This is useful if you like to listen to songs recorded at a variety of volume levels, because the volume remains somewhat similar as you move from song to song.

- **Equalizer Preset**—You can use the iTunes Equalizer to configure the relative volume of sound frequencies. When you set an Equalizer preset for a song, the settings in that preset will be used each time the song plays.

- **Media Kind**—You can use this field to change how some types of media are classified. For example, you can set this to be TV Show for episodes of a TV show that you've imported into your library (by default, they come in as a Movie).

- **Rating**—You can give songs a rating from one to five stars. You can use ratings in various ways, such as to create criteria for playlists (for example, include only my five-star songs) or to sort lists.

- **Start and Stop Time**—You can configure items to start or stop playing at specific times. This can be useful if you don't want to hear all of a song, such as when it has an introduction you don't want to hear each time it plays.

- **Remember Playback Position**—When this option is enabled, iTunes starts playing an item from the point at which you last played it. This is a really useful option for audiobooks, podcasts, movies, or TV shows because you can stop playing that content and do something else, such as listen to or watch other content. When you come back to the item with this option enabled, iTunes picks up where you left off. This prevents you from hearing or seeing the same content again or from searching for the point at which you stopped listening or watching.

- **Skip When Shuffling**—If this option is enabled for an item, it is skipped when you use the Shuffle mode. This is useful for items you don't want to hear when you shuffle (such as those that make sense only in the content of the album from which they come) or for content that doesn't make sense when you shuffle (such as episodes of a podcast or an audiobook).

NOTE iTunes is pretty smart and makes your listening and viewing life as easy as possible. For example, when you add podcasts, video, or audiobooks from the iTunes Store to your library, the Playback Position and Skip options are set appropriately. If you add this kind of content from other sources (such as importing them from your computer's desktop), you should make sure these options are set the way you want them.

Configuring Options in the Info Window

Configuring the options for any type of media is done similarly. The steps showing you how to set options for a song demonstrate them well:

1. Select the song whose options you want to set.

NOTE   You can set some of the options for multiple items at the same time, such as the equalizer, skip when shuffling, and so on. Others, such as start and stop time, can be set only for a single item at a time.

2. Choose **File**, **Get Info**.

3. Click the **Options** tab (see Figure 6.6).

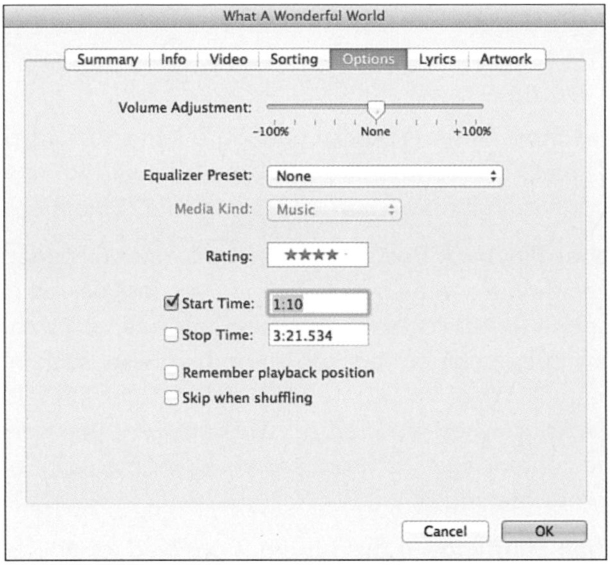

What A Wonderful World

Summary | Info | Video | Sorting | Options | Lyrics | Artwork

Volume Adjustment:
-100%   None   +100%

Equalizer Preset: None

Media Kind: Music

Rating: ★★★★

☑ Start Time: 1:10
☐ Stop Time: 3:21.534

☐ Remember playback position
☐ Skip when shuffling

Cancel   OK

FIGURE 6.6

Using the Options tab, you configure an item's optional settings.

4. To set the song's relative volume, drag the **Volume Adjustment** slider to the left to make it quieter or to the right to make it louder.

5. To apply an equalizer preset to the song, choose the preset you want to be used when it plays on the **Equalizer Preset** menu. On this menu, you see a large number of presets that are available to you. When you choose one, the song's playback is adjusted accordingly. For example, if you choose Bass Booster, the relative volume of the bass frequencies is increased.

6. To rate the song, click the dot representing the number of stars you want to give it in the **Rating** field. For example, to give the song three stars, click the center (third) dot. Stars appear up to the point at which you click. In other words, before you click, you see a dot. After you click a dot, it becomes a star, as do the rest of the stars to its left.

7. To set a song's start time, check the **Start Time** check box and enter a time in the format *minutes:seconds*. When you play the track, it starts playing at the time you enter. The default value is 0:00, which is the initial starting time all songs.

 NOTE   When you set a start or stop time, you don't change the item's file in any way. You can play the whole item again by unchecking the Start Time or Stop Time check box.

8. To set a stop time, check the **Stop Time** check box and enter a time in the format *minutes:seconds*. When you play the song, it stops playing at the time you enter. The default stop time is the total song length. Notice that the default stop time is very precise, even going to two decimal places beyond a second.

 TIP   To determine the start or stop times you want to use, play the song and use the times displayed when the Playhead is at the position where you want the song to start or stop playing. (See Chapter 4, "Listening to Music with iTunes," for information about the Playhead and song times.)

9. If you want iTunes to remember the point at which you stopped playing a song and to start playing the song at that point the next time you play it, check the **Remember playback position** check box. If you always want the song to start playing at the current Start Time, leave the box unchecked.

10. If you want the song to be skipped when you shuffle (when the track is an introduction to the next song, for example), check the **Skip when shuffling** check box.

11. Click **OK**. The window closes and your changes are saved. The next time the song plays, it does so with the options you configured.

Rating Songs in the Content Pane

You can also rate songs in the Content pane, which is more convenient than doing so in the Info window. To rate songs, follow these steps:

1. If you aren't in a view that displays a list of music, switch to one that does, such as **Songs** or **Playlists**. (See Chapter 4 for information about working with views.)

2. Scroll vertically until the song you want to rate appears in the Content pane.

3. Scroll horizontally in the Content pane until you see the **Rating** column (see Figure 6.7).

FIGURE 6.7

You can also rate tracks in the Content pane.

4. If there isn't currently a rating for the song, click the **dot** representing the number of stars you want to give the track. The dots up to and including the one
   on which you clicked become stars. If the song already has a rating, click a star
   to the left of the right-most star to lower the rating, or click a dot to the right
   of the right-most star to raise the rating.

Working with Art

As you've seen in previous chapters, songs, albums, and other content have art
associated with them, such as the "album cover" for songs that you download
from the iTunes Store. You see this art when you browse music and in the Info
area at the top of the iTunes window when that content plays (as you learned in
Chapter 4, you can also view it in a separate window). This makes working with
iTunes much more visually interesting and helps you identify content more quickly
than text alone does. Art also appears on iOS devices when music plays, both on
the Now Playing screen and on the Locked screen.

When you download content from the iTunes Store, its art comes with it. And
even if you didn't get content from the iTunes Store, as long as that content is
available there, iTunes automatically associates artwork with it.

In the rare case that some content in your iTunes Library doesn't have art
associated with it (such as it being content you import from your desktop), you
can add it manually, like so:

> **TIP** Before manually adding art, see if iTunes can retrieve the art for you. Perform a secondary (right) click on one or more tracks. On the resulting menu, choose **Get Album Artwork**. If iTunes is able to locate the appropriate art, it downloads it and attaches it to the selected items.

1. Prepare the artwork you are going to associate with a track. You can use graphics in the usual formats, such as JPG, TIFF, GIF, and so on, that you've created yourself, downloaded from the Internet, and so on.

2. Select the item with which you want to associate the artwork.

3. Open the Info window and click the **Artwork** tab. If the item has artwork with it, you see it in the Artwork pane.

4. Click **Add**. A dialog box that enables you to choose an image appears.

> **TIP** You can also add artwork to an item by dragging the image file from your desktop directly onto the Artwork pane.

5. Move to and select the graphic file that you want to associate with the track.

6. Click **Open** (Windows) or **Choose** (Mac). The image is added to the Artwork pane of the Info window.

7. You can use the slider under the image box to change the size of the previews you see on the Artwork pane. Drag the slider to the right to make the image larger or to the left to make it smaller. This doesn't change the image you see in the iTunes window; instead, it only impacts the size of the image as you currently see it in the Info window. This is especially useful when you associate lots of images with an item because you can see them all at the same time.

8. Repeat steps 4 through 6 to continue adding images to the Artwork pane until you have added all the images for an item.

9. To change the order of the images, drag them around in the image box. If an item has more than one graphic, place the image that you want to be the default on the left side of the image box.

10. Click **OK**. The window closes and the images are saved.

Changing the Information You See

You can customize the columns (information) that appear in the Content pane in a number of ways. What's more, you can customize the Content pane for each source so that information you see changes as you view different sources of content. The customization you have done for a source (such as a CD or playlist) is saved and used each time you view that source.

You can select the information (columns) that are shown for a source by using the following steps (which demonstrate changing the information displayed for a source containing music):

1. Select the source whose Content pane you want to customize and choose the view you want to configure (such as **Songs** or **Playlists**). Its contents appear in the Content pane.

2. Select **View**, **View Options** or press **Ctrl+J** (Windows) or **⌘-J** (Mac). You see the View Options dialog box (see Figure 6.8). Near the top of the dialog box, you see the name of the source for which you are configuring the Content pane. You also see all the available columns that can be displayed. If a column's check box is checked, that column is displayed; if not, it isn't shown.

FIGURE 6.8

The View Options dialog enables you to change the information displayed in the iTunes window.

 NOTE The View Options dialog changes based on the specific content and view you are using when you open it. Most views have just a few options; the List view has the most.

3. Check the check boxes next to the columns you want to see.

4. Uncheck the check boxes next to the columns you don't want to see.

NOTE   In some cases, such as when you configure the options for something in List view, you need to expand an area by clicking its right-facing triangle to see all the options.

5. Close the dialog. When you return to the Content pane, only the columns you selected are shown.

6. Drag the column headings you see to the left or right to set the order in which they are displayed.

THE ABSOLUTE MINIMUM

In this chapter, you learn about the information associated with the content in your library. Although configuring information isn't the most fun thing to do, it does make iTunes work a lot better for you. As you work with the information about your iTunes content, keep the following points in mind:

- Information in iTunes is important because the information applied to content determines how iTunes organizes that content. The more organized your content is, the easier it is for you to find content you want to work with. Information also helps you create smart playlists and perform other tasks.

- You can view the information associated with the content in your iTunes Library in a number of ways. When you browse content, you see it by its information, such as by genre. When you view a list, each column shows a specific piece of information.

- You can configure the information for content using the Info window. There is a tab for each type of information, such as Info, Options, and Artwork. Different categories of information exist for different types of media, such as music or video.

- iTunes automatically associates art with your content. You can view this art in a number of places, such as in the Info window. If content doesn't have art, you can have iTunes check for and add it, or you can manually add your own graphic files to items.

- You can change the information you see for a specific source (such as a playlist) by configuring View Options.

7

CREATING AND USING PLAYLISTS

Playlists enable you to listen to exactly the music you want to hear, when and how you want to hear it. Do you love a CD but hate a song or two on it? Fine, just set up a playlist without the offensive songs. Wish you could hear different songs from a variety of albums in your own greatest hits collection? Make a playlist and be the judge of what is great and what isn't. How about keeping things interesting by creating collections of music whose contents automatically change as your music collection does? No problem. Would you like it if the tunes you hear are selected for you automatically based on a specific song? With iTunes playlists, you can do all this and more.

Understanding Playlists

Simply put, playlists are customized collections of content that you create or that iTunes creates for you based on criteria you define. After a playlist has been created, you can listen to it, put it on a CD, move it to an iOS device, share it over a network, and so on.

 NOTE Playlists are the most useful for music, which is the focus of this chapter. However, playlists are equally applicable to other kinds of content, such as videos and podcasts. And you can mix and match different types of content in the same playlist. For example, you can include both songs and music videos in a "greatest hits" playlist.

There are several kinds of playlists in iTunes:

- **Standard playlists**—A standard playlist—which I'll usually call just a playlist from here on because that is what it is called in iTunes—is a set of songs, music videos, podcasts, TV shows, and so on that you define manually. You put the specific content you want in a playlist, and then organize how you want it to play. You can include the same song multiple times, mix and match songs from many artists, put songs in any order you choose, and basically control every aspect of that music collection. Playlists are useful for putting music on an iOS device, creating a CD, or making a compilation of specific music you might want to listen to at the click of the mouse. With a playlist, you can determine exactly which songs are included and the order in which those songs play. Playlists are also easy to create, and they remain as they are over time—unless you purposefully change them.

- **Smart playlists**—A smart playlist is smart because you don't put songs or other content in it manually. Instead, you tell iTunes which kind of content you want included in it by the attributes of that content. For music, you can use categories such as genre or artist, and iTunes picks songs with those attributes for you. For example, you can create a playlist based on a specific genre, such as Jazz, that you have listened to in the past few days. You can also tell iTunes how many songs to include.

  The really great thing is that smart playlists can be dynamic, meaning the songs they contain are updated over time based on criteria you define. As you add, listen to, or change the music in your iTunes Library, the contents of a smart playlist can change to match those changes as they happen. Imagine you have a smart playlist that tells iTunes to include all the music you have in the Jazz genre that is performed by Kenny G, the Pat Metheny Group, Joe Sample, and Larry Carlton. If you make this a "live" smart playlist, iTunes automatically adds any new music from any of these artists to it as you add that music to your iTunes Library. Live smart playlists make music more interesting to listen to because those playlists can change over time, giving you a different music experience each time they do.

- **Genius playlists**—iTunes creates this kind of playlist for you too, but instead of telling iTunes the type of music you want included, you choose a song and iTunes creates a playlist containing music that "goes with" the song you selected. How the iTunes "genius" selects songs that go with other songs is a bit of a secret, but you may find that it works really well for you.

  Genius playlists can be very interesting because you might not be able to predict which songs are included. And you can refresh Genius playlists, which results in a new playlist that can have different songs in it that may play in a different order. Because you have to pick only one song, genius playlists are the easiest to create.

NOTE   iTunes includes some playlists by default. The Purchased playlist contains content you've downloaded from the iTunes Store. The Genius Mixes playlist contains genius playlists based on the genres and other types of music in your iTunes Library. There are also some default smart playlists, such as those based on music from a specific era (for example, the 90s) or other criteria (such as your top-rated music).

You access your playlists through the **Playlists** tab of the Music window, as shown in Figure 7.1. Each type of playlist has a specific icon to represent it. As you learn later, you can create folders to keep your playlists organized. The Playlists list is sorted by the following general groups (top to bottom): default playlists, genius playlists, playlist folders, smart playlists, and playlists. Within each group, playlists are sorted alphabetically.

NOTE   In Chapter 1, "Getting Started with iTunes," you learned about the iTunes Sidebar. This chapter assumes the Sidebar is hidden. If you have iTunes show the Sidebar, you use it to select the starting point for the tasks described. For example, you view your playlists by clicking **Playlists** on the Sidebar.

FIGURE 7.1

To view your playlists, click the Playlists tab while you are viewing the music in your iTunes Library.

> **NOTE** Earlier, you read that playlists can contain other media in addition to music, such as music videos, TV shows, and so on, which is true. However, playlists are most useful for music, so this use is the focus of the remainder of this chapter. You can use playlists for other types of media in a similar way. For example, you can manually add a music video to a playlist in the same way you can add a song to it.

Creating and Managing Playlists

Playlists are very useful because you can choose the exact songs included in them and the order in which those songs will play. In this section, you learn how to create, manage, and use playlists.

Creating a Playlist

You can create a playlist in two ways. One is to create a playlist that is empty (meaning it doesn't include any songs). The other is to choose songs and then create a playlist that includes those songs.

The place you start depends on what you have in mind. If you want to create a collection of songs but aren't sure which specific songs you want to start with, create an empty playlist. If you know of at least some of the songs you are going to include, select them first and then create the playlist. Either way, creating a playlist is simple, and you'll end up in the same place.

 TIP By default, you don't see the menu bar when you are using iTunes on a Windows PC. To show this so that you can choose its commands, open the **iTunes** menu and choose **Show Menu Bar**. You can also show or hide the menu bar by pressing the **Alt** key.

Creating an Empty Playlist

You can create an empty playlist from within iTunes by using any of the following techniques:

- Selecting **File, New, Playlist**.
- Pressing **Ctrl+N** (Windows) or ⌘-**N** (Mac).
- Clicking the **Add** button (the + located in the bottom-left corner of the iTunes window) and choose **New Playlist**.

Whichever method you use results in the Playlists pane opening; you see an empty playlist whose name is highlighted to show you that it is ready for you to edit. Type a name for the playlist and press **Enter**. The playlist is named and ready for your content to be added (see Figure 7.2). The song list is empty because you haven't added any songs to the playlist yet. You learn how to do that a bit later in this chapter in the section, "Adding Songs to a Playlist." If you are ready to add songs now, skip to that section; if not, click **Done** to close the playlist.

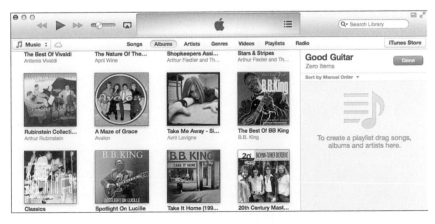

FIGURE 7.2

This brand new playlist is ready for songs to be added to it.

Creating a Playlist with Songs in It

If you know some of the songs you want to place in a new playlist, you can create the playlist so it includes those songs immediately. Here are the steps to follow:

1. Browse or search your music to find the songs you want to include in the new playlist. For example, you can browse for all the songs in a specific genre or search for music by a specific artist.

2. Select the songs you want to place in the playlist.

 TIP Remember that you can select a group of songs that are next to one another by holding down the **Shift** key while you click them. You can select multiple songs that aren't next to one another by holding down the **Ctrl** key (Windows) or the ⌘ key (Mac) while you click them.

3. Choose **File, New, Playlist from Selection**. The Playlist pane appears and the new playlist opens. Its name is highlighted to indicate that you can edit it, and you see the songs you selected in the Content pane (see Figure 7.3).

FIGURE 7.3

This new playlist already has three songs in it.

 TIP When you add a new album to your library, use this technique to quickly create a playlist to make it easy to listen to. Select all the songs in the album and then use the **New Playlist from Selection** command. You can use the resulting playlist to easily select and play the new album.

iTunes attempts to name the playlist by looking for a common denominator in the group of songs you selected. For example, if all the songs are from the same artist, that artist's name becomes the playlist's name. Similarly, if the songs are all from the same album, the playlist's name is the artist's and album's names. Sometimes iTunes picks an appropriate name, and sometimes it doesn't.

4. While the playlist name is highlighted, edit the name as needed and then press **Enter**. The playlist is ready to listen to and for you to add more songs.

5. You can leave the playlist open to add more songs to it (see the next section) or click **Done** to close it.

 NOTE   Playlists have the musical note icon.

Adding Songs to a Playlist

Whether you created an empty playlist or one that already has some songs in it, the steps to add songs to a playlist are the same:

1. Select **Music** on the **Media** menu.

2. Click the **Playlists** tab.

3. Click the playlist to which you want to add songs. You see its current content in the Content pane.

4. Click **Add To**. The Playlist pane opens in the right side of the window and the current content is shown there. You see the playlist name at the top of the pane. The left pane contains the Music source, which you can use to find the songs you want to add to the playlist.

 NOTE   If you haven't closed the playlist and it is still open, you can skip steps 1 through 4.

5. Choose how you want to see your music by clicking one of the tabs, such as **Songs** or **Artists**.

6. Browse or search the music so that songs you want to add to the playlist are shown in the Content pane.

7. Select the tracks you want to add to the playlist by clicking them (remember the techniques to select multiple tracks at the same time).

8. Drag the selected songs from the Content pane onto the playlist to which you want to add them. As you drag, you'll see the songs you have selected in a "ghost" image attached to the pointer. When you are over the playlist, you see a blue line, which indicates where the songs will be placed when you drop them (see Figure 7.4). Move the songs up or down the playlist until this line is at the location where you want to place the songs.

⏮ ▶ ⏭ 🔊━			🍎	☰	Q- Search Library	

| ♫ Music ⌄ ☁ | | Songs | Albums | Artists | Genres | Videos | Playlists | Radio | | | iTunes Store |

✓	Name	☁	Artist	▲	Album by Artist/Year		Track #	Last Played	
✓	Crossfire		Henry Paul Band		Grey Ghost		2 of 10	5/20/12 1...	
✓	Foolin'		Henry Paul Band		Grey Ghost		3 of 10	7/6/12 8:4...	
✓	Wood Wind		Henry Paul Band		Grey Ghost		4 of 10	6/8/12 10:...	
✓	Grey Ghost ⊙		Henry Paul Band		Grey Ghost		5 of 10	8/16/12 6:...	
✓	I Don't Need You No More		Henry Paul Band		Grey Ghost		6 of 10	9/3/12 3:3...	
✓	Lonely Dreamer		Henry Paul Band		Grey Ghost		7 of 10	6/18/12 3:...	
✓	One-Night Stands		Henry Paul Band		Grey Ghost		8 of 10	9/4/12 9:2...	
✓	You Really Know (What I Mean)		Henry Paul Band		Grey Ghost		9 of 10		
✓	All I Need		Henry Paul Band		Grey Ghost		10 of 10		
✓	The Lonely Bull		Herb Alpert and...		Herb Alpert - Classics Vo...		1 of 25		
✓	Acapulco 1922		Herb Alpert and...		Herb Alpert - Classics Vo...		2 of 25		
✓	A Taste of Honey		Herb Alpert and...		Herb Alpert - Classics Vo...		3 of 25		
✓	Green Peppers		Herb Alpert and...		Herb Alpert - Classics Vo...		4 of 25		
✓	The Work Song		Herb Alpert and...		Herb Alpert - Classics Vo...		5 of 25		
✓	I'm Getting Sentimental Over...		Herb Alpert and...		Herb Alpert - Classics Vo...		6 of 25		
✓	Whipped Cream		Herb Alpert and...		Herb Alpert - Classics Vo...		7 of 25		

Good Guitar [Done]
10 songs, 1 hour

Sort by Manual Order ⌄

1. Free Bird (Live) [Undubbed] {Fo...
   Lynyrd Skynyrd
2. Sweet Home Alabama (Live) [Alt...
   Lynyrd Skynyrd
3. Free Bird (Live) [Fox Theatre 20...
   Lynyrd Skynyrd
4. Kryptonite
   3 Doors Down
5. Ain't Talkin' 'Bout Love
   Van Halen
6. The Silence Remains
   3 Doors Down

FIGURE 7.4

To add songs to a playlist, drag them from the Content pane on the left onto the Playlist pane on the right.

 NOTE As you add songs to a playlist, the song count and play time located under the playlist's name is updated.

9. Repeat steps 5 through 8 until you have added all the songs you want to include in the playlist.

 TIP You can add all the songs on an album to a playlist by viewing your music by album and dragging the album's icon onto the playlist.

10. Click **Done**. The Playlist pane closes and you see the playlist's contents in the Content pane (see Figure 7.5). You can use the playlist in the ways you learn about later in this chapter; for example, click the **Play** button to hear the results of your work.

FIGURE 7.5

This playlist contains 11 songs that I think have excellent guitar work.

Removing Songs from a Playlist

If you decide you don't want one or more songs included in a playlist, click the **Playlists** tab and select the playlist from which you want to remove songs. You see the playlist's contents in the Content pane. Select the songs you want to remove in the playlist's Content pane and press the **Delete** key. A warning prompt appears. Click **Remove** and the songs are deleted from the playlist. (If this dialog box annoys you, as it does me, check the **Do not ask me again** check box and you won't ever have to see it again.)

NOTE When you delete a song from a playlist, it *isn't* deleted from the library. It remains there so you can add it to a different playlist or listen to it from the library. If it is included in other playlists, it isn't removed from those, either.

Setting the Order in Which a Playlist's Songs Play

The order in which a playlist's songs play is determined by the order in which they appear in the Content pane. The first song will be the one at the top of the window, the second will be the next one down, and so on. (This assumes you aren't using Shuffle.)

You can drag songs up on the list to make them play earlier or drag them down in the list to make them play later. Open the playlist and drag songs up or down the list to set the order in which they play. (If songs "bounce back" when you try to move them, click the first column heading in the pane so that the track numbers determine the sort order. This must be the case to be able to manually sort the order of the songs, which determines the order in which they play.)

You can also change the order in which songs will play by sorting the playlist by its columns. You do this by clicking the column title in the column by which you want the Content pane sorted.

 TIP Like other music sources, you can change the way you view a playlist's songs by changing the view you are using. Click the **View** button and choose **List**, **Grid**, or **Artist List**.

Creating and Managing Smart Playlists

The basic purpose of a smart playlist is the same as a playlist—that is, to contain a collection of tracks you can listen to, put on a CD, and so on. However, the path smart playlists take to this end is different from that of playlists. Rather than choose specific songs as you do in a playlist, you tell iTunes the kind of tracks you want in your smart playlist, and it picks out the tracks for you and places them in the playlist. For example, suppose you want to create a playlist that contains all your classical music. Rather than picking out all the songs in your library that have the Classical genre (as you would do to create a playlist), you can use a smart playlist to tell iTunes to select all the Classical music for you. The application then gathers all the music with the Classical genre and places that music in a smart playlist.

You create a smart playlist by defining a set of conditions. After you have created these conditions, iTunes chooses songs that match those conditions and places them in the playlist. Another example should help clarify this. Suppose you are a big-time Elvis Presley fan and regularly add Elvis music to your library. You could create a playlist and manually drag your new Elvis tunes to that playlist. But by using a smart playlist instead, you can define the playlist to include all your Elvis music. Anytime you add more Elvis music to your library, that music is added to the playlist automatically—so it always contains all the Elvis music in your iTunes Library.

You can also base a smart playlist on more than one condition at the same time. Going back to the Elvis example, you could add the condition that you want the playlist to include only those songs you have rated four stars or higher—so the smart playlist contains your favorite Elvis songs.

As the previous example shows, smart playlists can be dynamic; iTunes calls this live updating. When a smart playlist is set to be live, iTunes changes its contents over time to match changes to the music in your iTunes Library. If this feature isn't enabled for a smart playlist, that playlist contains only those songs that met the criteria at the time the playlist was created.

Finally, you can also link a smart playlist's conditions by the logical expression **All** or **Any**. If you use an All logical expression, all the conditions must be true for a song to be included in the smart playlist. If you use the Any option, only one of the conditions has to be met for a song to be included in the smart playlist.

Creating Smart Playlists

To create a smart playlist, perform the following steps:

1. Select **File**, **New**, **Smart Playlist**.

   TIP   iTunes includes keyboard shortcuts for many of its commands. If you like to use the keyboard, open the various iTunes menus to see which keyboard shortcuts are available for your favorite commands. For example, you can create a new smart playlist by pressing Ctrl+Alt+N (Windows) or Option-⌘-N (Mac).

2. On the first pop-up menu (which displays Artist by default), select the first category on which you want the smart playlist to be based. For example, if you want to use something different than Artist, you can select Genre, My Rating, or Year tag, among many others.

3. On the second pop-up menu, select the operator you want to use. For example, if you want to match data exactly, select **is**. If you want the condition to be looser, select **contains**.

4. Type the criterion you want to match in the box. The more you type, the more specific the condition is.

   NOTE   As you type the criterion in the boxes, iTunes automatically fills in data that it pulls from your iTunes Library. Using the Elvis Presley example, if you start typing the word "Elvis," iTunes completes the criterion for you with "Presley." If you also have music by Elvis Costello, however, his name comes up first because it comes first in the alphabet. As you continue typing Elvis Presley's name, when you type a P, the last name will change from Costello to Presley.

5. To add another condition to the smart playlist, click the **Add** button (+). A new, empty condition appears (see Figure 7.6). At the top of the dialog box, the All or Any menu appears.

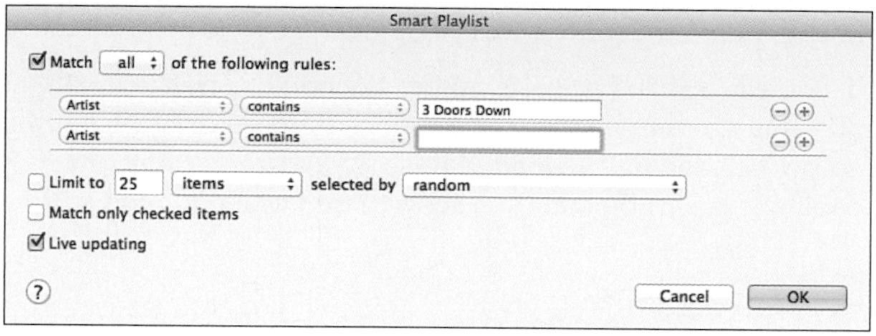

Smart Playlist

☑ Match [all ⇅] of the following rules:

| (Artist ⇅) | (contains ⇅) | 3 Doors Down | ⊖ ⊕ |
| (Artist ⇅) | (contains ⇅) | | ⊖ ⊕ |

☐ Limit to [25] [items ⇅] selected by [random ⇅]
☐ Match only checked items
☑ Live updating

(?)   [Cancel] [OK]

FIGURE 7.6

This smart playlist contains one completed condition and one in progress.

6. Repeat steps 2 through 4 for the new condition.

 NOTE Some of the conditions you choose may be based on dates or numbers instead of text. If you choose one of those, just make selections on the pop-up menus that appear and enter the appropriate type of search term, such as a date (which you either type in or use the up and down arrows to configure).

7. Repeat steps 5 through 6 to add more conditions to the playlist until you have all the conditions you want to include.

8. Choose **all** on the menu at the top of the dialog if all the conditions must be met for a track to be included in the smart playlist, or choose **any** if only one of them must be met.

 NOTE If you include more than one condition based on the same attribute, such as Artist, you usually don't want to use the **all** option because the conditions will likely be mutually exclusive; using the **all** option results in no songs being included in the playlist because no song will be able to meet all the conditions at the same time.

9. If you want to limit the playlist, check the **Limit to** check box.

10. Select the parameter by which you want to limit the playlist in the first menu; this menu defaults to **items**. Your choices include items (the number of items in the playlist), the time the playlist will play (in minutes or hours), or the size of the files the playlist contains (in MB or GB).

11. Type the data appropriate for the limit you selected in the Limit to box. For example, if you selected minutes in the menu, type the maximum length of the playlist in minutes in the box.

12. Select how you want iTunes to choose the songs it includes based on the limit you selected by using the **selected by** menu. For example, to have iTunes include tracks you've rated highly, select **highest rating**.

13. If you want the playlist to include only songs whose check boxes in the Content pane are checked, check the **Match only checked items** box.

14. If you want the playlist to be dynamic, meaning that iTunes updates its contents as the content of your Music library changes, leave the check in the **Live updating** box. If you uncheck this box, the playlist includes only those songs that meet the playlist's conditions when you create it.

15. Click **OK** (see Figure 7.7). You move to the Source list; the smart playlist is added and selected, and its name is ready for you to edit. The songs in your library that match the criteria in the playlist are added to it, and the current contents of the playlist are shown.

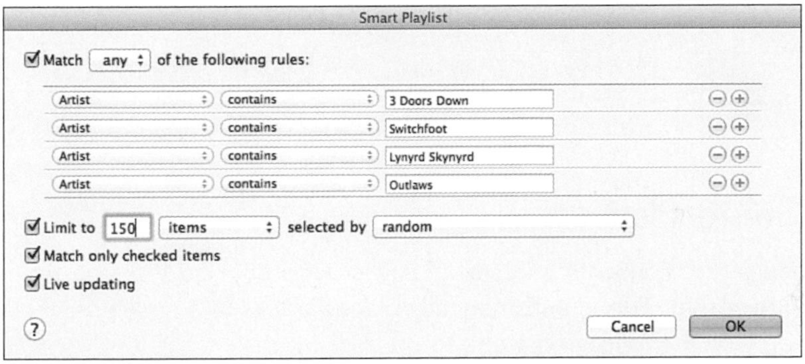

FIGURE 7.7

This smart playlist contains up to 150 songs from the selected artists; its content changes over time.

16. Type the playlist's name and press **Enter**. The playlist is ready for you to listen to and use for other purposes (such as to move onto an iOS device). You see the current content of the playlist in the Content pane (see Figure 7.8). You can work with the smart playlist like other types of content lists, such as sorting it to change the order in which songs play.

FIGURE 7.8

This playlist is ready for my listening pleasure.

NOTE Smart playlists have the gear icon.

Changing Smart Playlists

To change the contents of a smart playlist, you change the smart playlist's criteria (remember that iTunes automatically places tracks in a smart playlist based on its criteria). Use the following steps to do this:

1. Select the smart playlist you want to change.

2. Click the **Edit** button. The Smart Playlist dialog appears, and the playlist's current criteria will be shown.

3. Use the tools in the dialog (most of which you learned about in the previous section) to change its criteria. For example, you can remove a condition by clicking its **Remove** button (-). You can also add more conditions or change any of the other settings for the playlist.

4. Click **OK**. Your changes are saved and the contents of the playlist are updated to match the current criteria.

Creating and Managing Genius Playlists

The iTunes Genius feature creates a playlist of songs that "go together" based on a specific song that you select. It is difficult to predict which songs the genius will group, which is a big part of the fun of using it. The collections of songs you get are a surprise to you and the genius is a good way to make your music fresh because of the unpredictable ways iTunes selects music. Don't let the unpredictability lead you to think that the genius isn't good at what it does though; it seems to do a remarkable job of creating collections of songs that sound really good together.

 NOTE You must have enough of a "type" of music for the Genius to be able to work. If you don't have enough, you see a message from iTunes telling you that the Genius is not able to complete what you are trying to do. You'll have to wait until your iTunes Library has more content that is similar to what you are trying to use the Genius on. If Genius commands are disabled for a song, it also relates to there not being enough content of that type in your iTunes Library.

Starting the Genius

If you see the Genius Mixes playlist at the top of the Playlists list, the Genius is turned on and you are ready to start creating genius playlists.

If you don't see the Genius Mixes playlist, start the Genius by choosing **Store**, **Turn On Genius**. The Genius becomes available on the Playlists screen. Click the **Turn on Genius** button. Sign in using your Apple ID and agree to the terms and conditions. The Genius starts analyzing your music collection. You can continue to use iTunes during this process.

 NOTE If the Genius is turned on and you don't see the Genius Mixes on the list of playlists, there isn't enough content in your library for Genius Mixes to be created.

Creating a Genius Playlist

To create a genius playlist, complete these steps:

1. Play the song on which you want the genus playlist to be based.

 TIP There are other ways to create a genius playlist. One is to hover over a song's name, click the right-facing arrow that appears, and choose **Create Genius Playlist**.

2. Click the right-facing arrow next to the song's name in the Info area at the top of the iTunes window (see Figure 7.9).

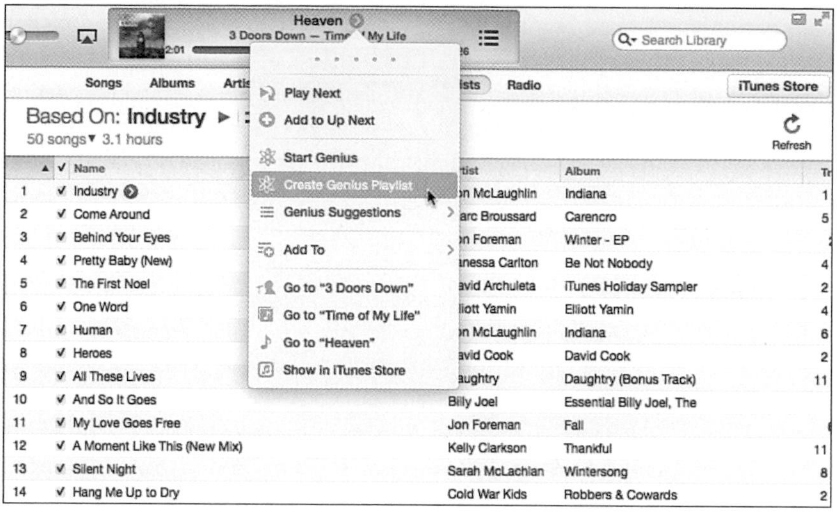

FIGURE 7.9

This genius playlist will be based on the song "Heaven."

3. Choose **Create Genius Playlist**. The playlist is created and appears on the Playlists list. It is selected, and you see its contents on the screen. Just under its name, you see how many songs it contains (25 by default) and its run time (see Figure 7.10). You can play the playlist just like playlists you have created manually.

FIGURE 7.10

This playlist contains songs that "go with" the song "Heaven."

Changing a Genius Playlist

You can change a genius playlist in several ways:

- To refresh its contents, select it on the Playlists list and click **Refresh**. The Genius updates the contents of the playlist. It may add or remove songs or change the order in which they play.

- Like other playlists, you can change the order in which songs play by dragging them up or down the list. (If you refresh a genius playlist, the order you set may be overridden.)

- To change the number of songs in the playlist, click the downward-facing arrow to the right of the number of songs and choose the number you want to be included in the playlist. The options are 25, 50, 75, or 100. If you change the current number, the Genius adds or removes songs to get to the number you selected.

 TIP   If you use the Genius regularly, keep its information current by periodically choose **Store**, **Update Genius**.

Working with Playlists

There are a number of things you can do with your playlists, such as listening to them, keeping them organized in folders, changing their contents on-the-fly, and so on.

Listening to Playlists

After you have created a playlist, you can listen to it by selecting it on the list of playlists and using the same controls you use to listen other music in your iTunes Library. For example, you can browse playlists using the three views (except for genius playlists, for which you are limited to the List view), shuffle them, set them to repeat, use the Up Next list, and so on.

 TIP   You can add one playlist's contents to another by dragging its icon and dropping it on the playlist to which you want to add its contents.

Organizing Playlists in Folders

As you use iTunes, you are likely to create lots of playlists. Over time, your list of playlists can get huge, making it long and unwieldy. Fortunately, you can create folders to organize your playlists and then drag your playlists into the folders you create to organize them. By doing this, you can keep your playlist list neat and tidy and make your playlists easier to use.

To create a folder, choose **File**, **New**, **Playlist Folder**. A new folder opens; its name is highlighted, indicating it's ready for you to give it a name. Type the folder's name and press Enter to save it. It remains open and appears on the playlist list.

 TIP If you have a folder selected when you create a new folder, the new folder is created inside the selected folder. You also can drag a folder inside another one to create "nested" folders.

To place a playlist within a folder, drag its icon onto the folder until that folder's icon becomes highlighted; then drop the playlist on the folder. The playlist is moved into the folder. As soon as you add at least one playlist to a folder, a triangle is added to the folder's icon. You can click this to expand or collapse the folder so that you see or don't see the playlists it contains (see Figure 7.11).

FIGURE 7.11

The folder Best Playlists contains five playlists (one is a genius playlist and one is a smart playlist).

A folder can contain different kinds of playlists (including genius and smart playlists), and they can even contain playlists containing different types of content. For example, you can create playlists of rock music videos and include them in a folder you've created for your playlists that also include rock music.

When you select a folder's icon on the Source list, the contents of all the playlists it contains are displayed (refer to Figure 7.11). You can play all the content in a folder just as you can a playlist; select the folder and use the playback controls to play it. You can also sort it, choose its view options, and so on.

 TIP   To change a folder's name, double-click it, type the new name, and press Enter.

Within folders or not, playlists are listed based on their type (genius, then smart, then standard). Within each group, the playlists are in alphabetical order based on their names. You can make your playlists and folders be listed in another order by appending numbers before their names, such as adding "1." before the name of the playlist you want to appear at the top of the list. You could add "2." to the one you want to be listed next, and so on.

 TIP   To delete a folder, perform a secondary click on it and choose **Delete**. When you delete a folder, any playlists it contains are also deleted.

Adding Songs to a Playlist On the Fly

As you are listening to music, you may decide you want to add specific songs to a playlist. There are several ways to do this:

- Hover over a song's name and, when the right-facing arrow appears, click it. Choose **Add to** and choose the playlist to which you want to add the song (if the playlist is within a folder, you can expand the folder to see the playlist).

- Perform a secondary click (right-click) on a song, choose **Add to Playlist**, and choose the playlist to which you want to add the song.

- Drag the song from the Content pane toward the right side of the iTunes window. The Playlist pane pops open. Drag the song onto the playlist to which you want to add it.

 TIP   These methods work when you have multiple songs selected or with albums, too.

NOTE If a playlist is available on the cloud through iTunes Match, but hasn't been downloaded to iTunes, it doesn't appear on the list of playlists when you add songs to them on the fly.

Deleting Playlists

If you decide you no longer want a playlist, you can delete it by selecting the playlist and pressing the Delete key. A prompt appears; click **Delete** and the playlist is removed. (Be sure to check the **Do not ask me again** check box if you don't want to be prompted in the future.) Even though you've deleted the playlist, the songs in the playlist remain in the library or in other playlists.

NOTE The only time songs or other content are removed from iTunes is when you delete them from a library (such as the Music Library) that is selected. You should do this only when you are absolutely sure you won't want that content again. If you are working with playlists, deleting tracks removes them from only the current playlist so you can always add them again later if you change your mind.

THE ABSOLUTE MINIMUM

In this chapter, you learned about one of iTunes' best features: playlists.

- Playlists are great because they enable you to customize your content so the specific content plays when you want it to. Standard playlists are lists of music that you create manually by placing specific songs in the playlist. Smart playlists are created by iTunes based on criteria you select. Genius playlists are created based on songs that "go with" a song you designate.

- One of the easiest ways to create a playlist is to select one or more songs and choose **File**, **New**, **Playlist from Selection**. Name the new playlist and press **Enter** to save it. You can add more songs to it by dragging them from the Content pane onto the playlist.

- Use a smart playlist to have iTunes create a collection of music based on your criteria, such as your favorite music from specific artists or all the music that you've added to your Music Library within the past 60 days.

- The iTunes Genius is amazingly adept at creating lists of music based on a song that you select. Using genius playlists is a good way to keep your music experience fresh because you probably won't be able to predict the music that gets played.

- You can listen to playlists similar to other sources of content. You can also keep them organized in folders, add songs to them whenever you want, or delete them if their time has passed.

IN THIS CHAPTER

- Adding podcasts to your iTunes Library
- Listening to podcasts
- Managing podcasts

SUBSCRIBING AND LISTENING TO PODCASTS

Podcasts are episodic audio or video series you can add to your iTunes Library for your listening or viewing pleasure. Podcasts exist for just about any topic you can think of and are created by individuals or organizations; for example, almost all radio shows provide their content in podcasts that you can subscribe and listen to in iTunes or on iOS devices. Some podcasts are informative in nature, such as news podcasts, while others are for entertainment.

Most podcasts are provided in episodes. When you want to be able to listen to or view a podcast, you subscribe to it; subscribing to a podcast causes current and future episodes to be downloaded to your computer and added to your iTunes Library automatically. You can also choose to download previous episodes if you want to.

PODCASTS APP

If you exclusively listen to podcasts on iOS devices, there's no need to work with them in iTunes on a computer because the Podcasts app enables you to subscribe to, listen to, and manage podcasts on those devices. If you do listen to them using both iTunes and the Podcasts app, your podcasts can be synced through your iCloud account so that you if you change devices mid-podcast, you pick up right where you left off. Syncing also maintains the status of individual episodes on all the synced devices. For information about working with the Podcasts app, see Chapter 16, "Listening to Podcasts with the Podcasts App."

Adding Podcasts to Your iTunes Library

Like other iTunes content, the first step in enjoying podcasts is to add the podcasts you want to enjoy to your iTunes Library. You can do this in a couple of ways:

- Subscribing to podcasts via the iTunes Store
- Subscribing to podcasts via a website

As you might suspect, you'll learn how to do both of these tasks in the following sections.

Subscribing to Podcasts in the iTunes Store

You can subscribe to and download almost all the podcasts that are available in the iTunes Store for free. Like other content, downloading podcasts from the iTunes Store is easy, as follows:

1. In the iTunes application, move into the iTunes Store by clicking the **iTunes Store** button.

 NOTE For more information on using the iTunes Store, see Chapter 2, "Working with the iTunes Store."

2. Click the downward-facing arrow on the **Podcasts** tab.

3. Choose the category you are interested in, such as **Business** (see Figure 8.1).

FIGURE 8.1

You can choose a category of podcast to browse by selecting it on the Podcasts menu.

 TIP You can search for podcasts by typing the podcast's name in the Search tool. When you do this, you search across all content, so you might see music, movies, and so on, in addition to podcasts.

4. Browse the results.

5. Click a podcast to get more information about it (see Figure 8.2).

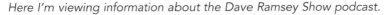

FIGURE 8.2

Here I'm viewing information about the Dave Ramsey Show podcast.

6. If isn't selected already, click the **Details** tab. You see the episodes currently available for the podcast. In some cases, you see many episodes for the podcast, whereas other podcasts don't make past episodes available.

7. Read about the podcast.

> **NOTE** Click the **Ratings and Reviews** tab to see what other people think about the podcast. On the **Related** tab, you see podcasts that are related to the current one, such as being on a similar topic.

8. Hover over an episode and click the **Play** button to preview it; if it is a free podcast, you can listen to the entire episode without subscribing to it.

9. To subscribe to the podcast so that its episodes are automatically downloaded, click **Subscribe**; like other action buttons, the Subscribe button shows the cost of the podcast. In most cases, they are free, so the button is just labeled Subscribe.

10. Click **Subscribe** at the prompt. The currents episodes are downloaded to your iTunes Library; future episodes will be downloaded automatically. In some cases, you can download past episodes from within your iTunes Library, too.

NOTE After you subscribe to at least one podcast, you should configure iTunes Podcast settings for that (and all your other podcasts) to determine how iTunes manages the podcast for you. See "Configuring Podcast Settings," later in this chapter for details.

11. Repeat steps 3 through 10 to subscribe to more podcasts.

12. Click the **Library** button to return to your iTunes Library.

13. Open the **Source** menu and choose **Podcasts**. You see all the podcasts to which you've subscribed. When you select a podcast (see Figure 8.3), you see the episodes available for that podcast. You're ready to listen to and manage your podcasts.

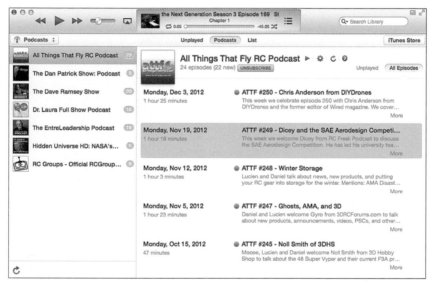

FIGURE 8.3

When you select a podcast, you see the episodes available in your iTunes Library.

Subscribing to Podcasts Outside of the iTunes Store

Although accessing podcasts via the iTunes Store is definitely the easiest way to get to them, not all podcasts are available there (although with the tremendous quantity available there, that's hard to believe). In some cases, you have to subscribe to the podcast outside of the iTunes Store to be able to access it with iTunes.

Typically, you visit the website for the source of the podcast to which you want to subscribe, such as a radio show's website. You use that website to subscribe to its podcast by logging into your account and using the tools provided to access the podcast; if a fee is required, you need to provide payment information.

When you've created an account, add the podcast to your iTunes Library by performing the following steps:

1. Obtain the URL for the podcast. How this works varies by website, but usually it is a matter of clicking a button or link related to the show's podcast. After you've created an account and signed up for the podcast (and paid a fee if required), you can access the URL for that podcast. Select and copy this URL.

 NOTE Some websites provide a button you can click to add the podcast to iTunes. When you click such buttons, the appropriate information is added to your iTunes Library just like when you subscribe to a podcast in the iTunes Store.

2. Move back into iTunes.

3. On the **File** menu, choose **Subscribe to Podcast**. The Subscribe to Podcast dialog appears.

 NOTE If you are using the Windows version of iTunes and don't see the File menu, open the **iTunes** menu and choose **Show Menu Bar.**

4. Paste the URL you obtained in step 1 into the dialog (see Figure 8.4).

FIGURE 8.4

You can subscribe to a podcast by pasting its URL in this dialog.

5. Click **OK**. The podcast is added to your iTunes Library.

6. Choose **Podcasts** on the iTunes **Source** menu to see and work with the podcast to which you subscribed. From this point forward, you can manage the podcast just like those from the iTunes Store.

Listening to Podcasts

After you have subscribed to podcasts, you can use iTunes to listen to or watch them.

Browsing Your Podcasts

As you've seen, when you subscribe to podcasts, they are added to the Podcasts source in your iTunes Library. When you select **Podcasts** on the iTunes Source menu, you see all the podcasts to which you've subscribed shown in the left pane of the window. When you select a podcast, you see its available episodes in the right pane (see Figure 8.5).

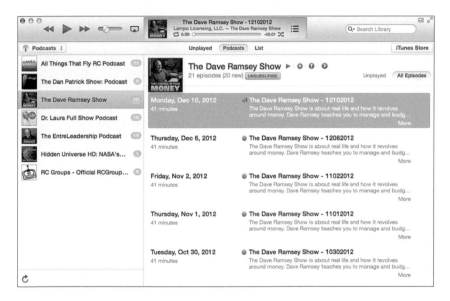

FIGURE 8.5

When you select a podcast to which you've subscribed, you see the episodes available in your iTunes Library.

The following are some tidbits about the information and icons you see when you have a podcast selected (you won't always see all of these):

- **Number of new episodes**—The number to the right of the podcast's name on the podcast list indicates how many episodes you have, but haven't listened to yet.

- **Podcast information**—At the top of the episode list, you see the podcast's name, the total number of episodes, and the number of new (those you haven't listened to) episodes. For each episode, you see the release date, run time, episode title, and a description. Click **More** to read all of an episode's description (if all of the description is shown, click **Less** to collapse it again).

- **Browse played or all episodes**—Click **Unplayed** to see only those episodes to which you haven't listened or **All Episodes** to see all of them.

- **Video**—When an episode contains video content, it is marked with the display icon.

- **Status**—Episodes you haven't listened to are marked with a blue circle. As you listen to an episode, this circle "empties" to indicate how much of the episode you've listened to. When you've listened to all of an episode, the circle disappears.

- **Episodes**—Browse the list of episodes to view all that are available for the selected podcast.

 TIP Click the **List** button to view your podcasts in a single list organized by podcast. You see various columns of information. Within each podcast, you see the episodes sorted by release date. You can collapse or expand podcasts by clicking the triangle next to their names.

Playing Podcasts

Listening to or watching podcasts is similar to other audio and video content in your library. Browse or search for the episode you want to listen to, and double-click it to play it.

 TIP If you click the **Play** button next to the podcast's name at the top of the episode list, the most recent episode plays.

If it is audio podcast, you hear it and see information about it in the Info area at the top of the screen. You can control the audio playback just like music (see Chapter 4, "Listening to Music with iTunes").

If it is a video podcast, it plays according to your current video playback options (see Figure 8.6). Video podcasts play just like other video content, such as movies and TV shows (see Chapter 5, "Watching Video with iTunes").

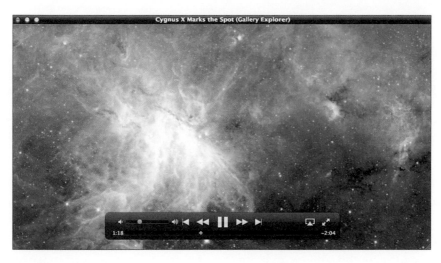

FIGURE 8.6

Here I'm watching a video podcast produced by NASA.

 TIP You can use the Search Library tool to search for podcasts. Type the podcasts or episode information in the search tool. As you type, you see the episodes of the podcast on the results list. Click an episode to jump to it on the episode list.

Managing Podcasts

iTunes features several tools with which you can manage your podcasts. These include the settings iTunes uses to automatically download and keep episodes of your podcasts. You can also manage your podcasts manually.

Configuring Podcast Settings

You can configure iTunes' Podcast settings to determine how it manages your podcasts. You can set the default settings that are used for all podcasts, and you can configure the settings for a specific podcast. Do so by following these steps:

1. Move to the Podcasts source.

2. Select a podcast. It doesn't matter which one, because you want to set your default settings first.

3. Click the **Gear** button at the top of the episode list, just to the right of the podcast's name. The Podcast Settings dialog appears (see Figure 8.7).

Podcast Settings		
Check for new episodes:	Every day ⬍	
	Next check: Today, 6:41 AM	
Settings for:	Podcast Defaults ⬍	
	☑ Use Default Settings	
When new episodes are available:	Download all ⬍	
Episodes to keep:	All unplayed episodes ⬍	
⑦	Cancel	OK

FIGURE 8.7

Use Podcast Settings to determine how iTunes automatically manages your podcasts.

4. On the **Settings for** menu, choose **Podcast Defaults**. This enables you to configure the settings that are used for all podcasts except those for which you individually configure the settings.

5. Choose how often you want iTunes to check for new episodes, using the **Check for new episodes** menu. The options are **Every hour**, **Every day**, **Every week**, or **Manually**. iTunes checks for new episodes according to the time frame you select—unless you select Manually, in which case you must check for new episodes manually.

 NOTE   Underneath the Check for new episodes menu, you'll see when the next check for new episodes will be performed.

6. Use the **When new episodes are available** menu to determine what iTunes does when it finds new episodes of the podcasts to which you are subscribed. Select **Download the most recent one** if you want only the newest episode to be downloaded. Select **Download all** if you want all available episodes downloaded. Select **Do nothing** if you don't any episodes to be downloaded.

7. Use the **Episodes to Keep** menu to determine whether and when iTunes deletes podcast episodes. Select **All episodes** if you don't want iTunes to automatically remove any episodes. Select **All unplayed episodes** if you want iTunes to remove episodes you have listened to, or select **Most recent episode** if you want iTunes to keep only the most recent episode even if you haven't listened to all of them. Select **Last** *X* **episodes**, where *X* is 2, 3, 4, 5, or 10, to have iTunes keep only the selected number of episodes.

8. On the **Settings for** menu, choose a podcast for which you want to configure different settings.

9. If it is checked, uncheck the **Use Default Settings** check box.

10. Use steps 5 through 7 to configure the selected podcast's settings.

11. Repeat steps 8 through 10 to configure the settings for the rest of the podcasts for which you don't want to use the default settings.

12. Click **OK**. iTunes manages your podcasts according to the settings you configured.

Manually Managing Your Podcasts

You can also manage your podcasts manually by doing the following:

- **Download episodes**—If an episode isn't currently downloaded, it is marked with the **Download** button. Click this to download the episode. As the download occurs, you see the download status icon next to the episode's name. When the download process is complete, you see the blue dot indicating that it is a new episode.

 NOTE In iTunes, a new episode is one that you haven't listened to yet. It has nothing to do with the episode's date.

- **Refresh all podcasts**—Click the **Refresh** button located in the bottom-left corner of the iTunes window to refresh the list of episodes available for each podcast to which you are subscribed. The podcast's episodes are downloaded to your computer according to your settings. And episodes are removed based on your settings, too. For example, if you've elected to keep only unplayed episodes, all the episodes to which you've listened are deleted.

- **Refresh a podcast**—Click the **Refresh** button (next to the **Gear** button) to refresh the list of episodes available for the selected podcast.

- **Start downloading a podcast again**—If you haven't listened to or watched episodes of a podcast to which you've subscribed in a while, iTunes stops downloading episodes of that podcast and the Warning button (exclamation point) appears next to the Gear button. When you click this button, you see the message telling you this has happened. Click **Yes** to have episodes downloaded to your computer again.

- **See the podcast in the iTunes Store**—To view the podcast in the iTunes Store, click the right-facing arrow to the right of the podcast's name and choose **Show in iTunes Store**. You move into the iTunes Store and see the podcast's page.

TIP Open a podcast's contextual menu (by right-clicking or performing a secondary click) to see a number of useful commands. You can mark episodes as played or unplayed, update a podcast, show all available episodes, mark an individual episode so that it won't be deleted automatically, and so on.

- **Add the podcast to a playlist**—Click the right-facing arrow to the right of its name and choose Add To. Then click the playlist to which you want to add the podcast. All the episodes (played and unplayed) are added to the playlist.

- **Delete an episode**—To delete an episode from your library (whether it's been downloaded or not), select it and press the **Delete** key. Click **Delete Podcast**. If the file has been downloaded to your library, click the **Move to Recycle Bin** (Windows) or **Move to Trash** (Mac) button to delete the podcasts files from your computer and from the library, or click the **Keep Files** button to remove the podcast from your library but leave its files on your computer.

- **Unsubscribe**—To unsubscribe from a podcast, click the **UNSUBSCRIBE** button. Episodes of the podcast will no longer be downloaded to your computer, although episodes that you have downloaded will remain in your library and you can listen to or delete them. You can subscribe again by clicking the **SUBSCRIBE** button that appears next to a podcast to which you used to be subscribed. If you don't regularly listen to a podcast, you should unsubscribe from it so you aren't wasting disk space storing episodes that you'll never listen to.

TIP To remove a podcast and all its episodes from your iTunes Library, select the podcast and press **Delete**. When you confirm the action, the podcast no longer appears in your iTunes Library. To get it back, you can subscribe to it again (either from the iTunes Store or its website).

THE ABSOLUTE MINIMUM

In this chapter, you learn that podcasts are a great feature because they enable you to listen to and view a huge amount and variety of content. Here's a reminder of some of the information you learned:

- Podcasts are similar to radio or TV, and you can store episodes in your iTunes Library so you can listen to or view them from your computer at a time of your choosing. You can subscribe to podcasts in the iTunes Store or from websites.

- Use the Podcasts source to access the podcasts to which you've subscribed. You browse your podcasts there, and when you find one you want to listen to or watch, you can do so using the same tools you use to listen to music or watch movies or TV shows.

- iTunes includes tools to manage your podcasts for you automatically, such as by downloading podcasts, removing them from your iTunes Library, and so on. You can also manage your podcasts manually.

9

STREAMING MUSIC AND VIDEO THROUGH AN AIRPLAY NETWORK

You're probably going to want to enjoy your iTunes content in different places. With AirPlay, you can easily stream audio and video content to a variety of devices so that you can listen and watch without having to be in front of a computer.

Understanding AirPlay

AirPlay is Apple's streaming technology that works with iTunes on Macs and Windows PCs and on iOS devices. AirPlay works well and is also pretty easy to set up, which is a good combination. An AirPlay network can look like the one shown in Figure 9.1. The devices that stream content to the network can be Macs or Windows PCs running iTunes or iOS devices. The receiving devices can be AirPort Express Base Stations to which speakers are attached, Apple TVs, or AirPlay-capable speakers.

Streaming devices

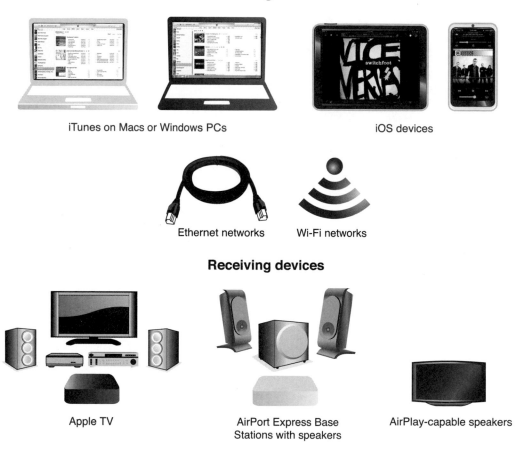

iTunes on Macs or Windows PCs   iOS devices

Ethernet networks   Wi-Fi networks

Receiving devices

Apple TV   AirPort Express Base Stations with speakers   AirPlay-capable speakers

FIGURE 9.1

There are many options for setting up an AirPlay network, and they are all pretty straightforward to set up and use.

You can have any combination of sending and receiving devices on the network, although only one streaming device can be playing on a specific receiving device at the same time.

AirPlay works over a Wi-Fi, wired Ethernet, or a network that includes both types of connections. In any case, the devices that stream and those that receive must be on the same network to be able to communicate with each other.

AirPlay is integrated into iTunes on computers and the iOS. That means you don't have to install any additional software to enable the devices with which you can use AirPlay to communicate with each other. All you need to do is to configure each device to access your AirPlay network.

The streaming device sends its content (audio or video) to the receiving device, which plays it. The content is controlled from the streaming device. For example, if you are streaming from iTunes on a computer, you use iTunes to control playback on the receiving device. If an iOS device is streaming, you control playback with the app you are using on the iOS device, such as the Music app.

To use AirPlay, set up the AirPlay network as described in the next section. Then you can stream your content from any of the streaming devices you have set up, which is the topic of the section "Streaming Content on an AirPlay Network," later in this chapter.

APPLE TV

Apple TV is a small digital media device that you can connect to an HDTV/home theater system. This device enables you to use AirPlay to stream music, movies, podcasts, TV shows, and other content directly from computers and iOS devices onto the HDTV/home theater so you can use that system to watch or listen to your content. Additionally, you can use an Apple TV to access web services such as watching movies, TV shows, and videos on Netflix, Hulu, YouTube, and so on. You also can download content from the iTunes Store; for example, you can rent a movie and start watching it as it downloads to the Apple TV. For more information on Apple TV, use a web browser to visit www.apple.com/appletv.

Creating an AirPlay Network

To set up an AirPlay network, you need to create the local network over which you will stream content. This network can be created over Wi-Fi, Ethernet, or both. Typically, you will have a modem (cable, DSL, and the like) that is connected to the Internet that provides both Wi-Fi and Ethernet connections to which you can connect other routers, AirPort Express Base Stations, computers, and iOS devices. Many configurations are possible, and it is likely you already have a suitable network set up in the location in which you'll be using AirPlay. (The details to set up a local network are beyond the scope of this book, but there are lots of good networking books available if you need help.)

 NOTE Like all technology, AirPlay isn't perfect. If you run into trouble using it, Apple's support website is a good place to search for help: www.apple.com/support. If you have trouble using AirPlay related to a Wi-Fi network, use a web browser to move to http://support.apple.com/kb/HT1595.

Setting Up Streaming Devices

After the network is set up, connect each streaming device (computers and iOS devices) to it.

When a computer running iTunes is connected to a network that includes AirPlay–enabled receiving devices, it automatically recognizes and is able to stream to those devices, so no additional configuration of iTunes (on a Mac or Windows PC) is required.

Likewise, when an iOS device is connected to the network, it recognizes any AirPlay-capable receiving devices on that network automatically and no additional configuration is required.

Setting Up Receiving Devices

Setting up receiving devices isn't much harder than setting up the streaming devices. The options covered here are for an Apple AirPort Express Base Station with speakers, an Apple TV, and AirPlay-capable speakers.

Installing an AirPort Express Base Station with Speakers

An AirPort Express Base Station is a small, wireless networking device produced by Apple that you can use to create or extend Wi-Fi networks. For example, you can connect it to a modem to provide a Wi-Fi network. It also has a jack to which you can connect a set of powered (computer) speakers. This enables you to stream audio from iTunes or an iOS device so that you can listen to the audio on the speakers connected to the base station.

 NOTE For more information about AirPort Express Base Stations, use a web browser to visit www.apple.com/ airportexpress.

To set up an AirPort Express Base Station, perform the following steps:

1. Connect the base station to power.

2. Connect the speaker jack on the base station to the speakers you want to use with it.

 NOTE The AirPort Utility software is installed by default under OS X. To download it for Windows PCs, go to support. apple.com/downloads.

3. On a computer that is in range of the base station, open the AirPort Utility software. To open this software on a Mac, open the **Launchpad**, click the **Other** folder, and click **AirPort Utility**. To open this software on a Windows 7 PC, open the **Windows** menu, choose **All Programs**, and then choose **AirPort Utility**. The application opens and identifies all the base stations within range of your computer.

4. Use the AirPort Utility application to select and configure the base station (see Figure 9.2). To do this on a Mac, click the base station and click **Edit**. On a Windows 7 computer, select the base station on the list on the left side of the window and click **Manual Setup**.

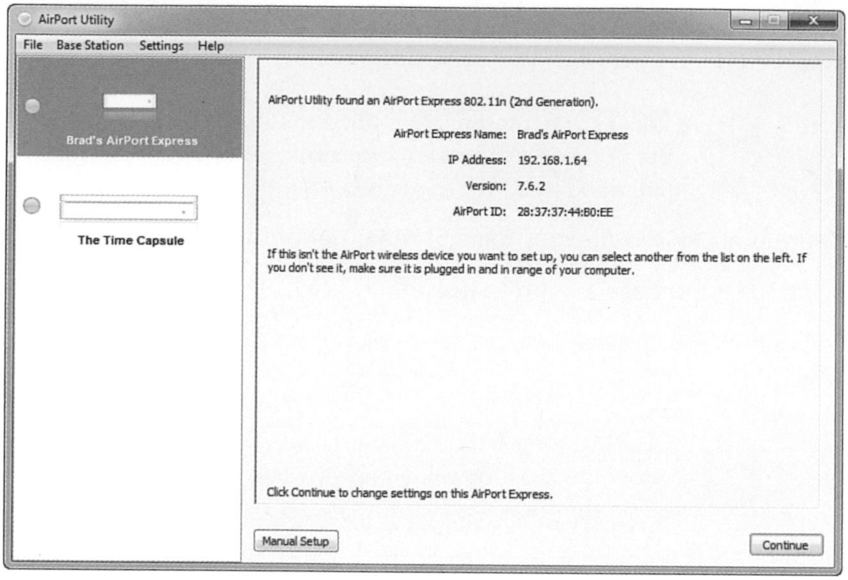

FIGURE 9.2

Use the AirPort Utility application to configure an AirPort Express Base Station so that you can stream content to it.

5. Ensure that AirPlay is enabled on the base station (see Figure 9.3) by clicking the **AirPlay** tab and then ensuring the **Enable AirPlay** check box is checked.

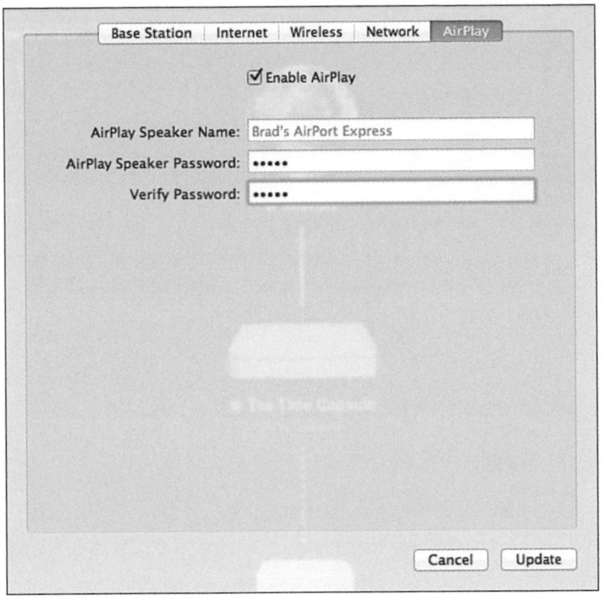

> | Base Station | Internet | Wireless | Network | AirPlay |
>
> ☑ Enable AirPlay
>
> AirPlay Speaker Name: Brad's AirPort Express
> AirPlay Speaker Password: •••••
> Verify Password: •••••
>
> Cancel   Update

FIGURE 9.3

Enable AirPlay on the base station to allow content to be streamed to the speakers connected to it.

6. Name the speakers (you use this name to select them as the playback device in iTunes or on an iOS device).

7. If you want to require a password to be able to stream to the speakers, enter the password and verify it.

8. When you're done configuring the base station, update its settings by clicking the **Update** button. The base station restarts and is ready to receive AirPlay streaming.

 TIP You can also connect the speaker jack on an AirPort Express Base Station to an input on a home theater audio system to be able to stream audio to that system.

Installing an Apple TV

Setting up an Apple TV is also straightforward:

1. Connect the HDMI cable to the Apple TV and to the HDMI input port on a TV or home theater receiver to which a TV is connected.

2. If you want to use the optional optical digital audio cable for sound, connect one end of the cable to the audio input port on your receiver or TV and the other end to the optical digital audio port on the back of the Apple TV.

 NOTE Some devices, such as a home theater receiver, might not be able to get the audio signal via the HDMI connection, in which case you must use the optical audio cable. In many cases, using the optical audio cable provides better sound quality, but using it is optional if all the other components are able to work with the audio through the HDMI connection.

3. If you are using an Ethernet network connection instead of Wi-Fi, plug the Ethernet cable into the port on the Apple TV.

4. Connect the Apple TV to power.

5. Select the Apple TV as the input source on the TV/home theater and follow the onscreen instructions to complete the device's configuration. This will include selecting the Wi-Fi network you want to use (if you aren't using an Ethernet connection); make sure you select the network that the sending devices are on). When the configuration process is complete, you are ready to stream content to the Apple TV.

Installing AirPlay-Capable Speakers

AirPlay-capable speakers have Wi-Fi built in so that they can directly communicate with other AirPlay devices; there is no need to connect these type of speakers to a base station. So, installing AirPlay-capable speakers is very easy. Simply connect the speakers to a power outlet and power them up. Then use the speaker's controls to connect it to the same wireless network that the streaming devices you want to use are on. (See the instructions included with the speakers for the details on how to do this.) After they are connected to that network, you can stream content to them.

Streaming Content on an AirPlay Network

After an AirPlay network is established, streaming content to the devices on it is a snap. You can do this from either iTunes on a computer or from an iOS device.

Streaming Content with iTunes

You can stream audio or video with iTunes. The details for each type of content are a bit different, as described in the following sections.

Streaming Audio Content with iTunes

To stream iTunes audio, perform the following steps:

1. Find and select the content you want to stream (see Part I, "iTunes," for detailed information on this task).

2. Click the **AirPlay** button. The AirPlay menu appears (see Figure 9.4).

FIGURE 9.4

Use the AirPlay menu to select the devices to which you want to stream audio content.

3. If you want to play the audio on more than one device at the same time, skip to step 5; to play it on a single device, click the **Single** tab.

4. Click the device to which you want to stream the content and skip to step 7. The menu closes and the AirPlay button turns blue to indicate you are streaming to an AirPlay device.

5. Click the **Multiple** tab. You see each device that is available for AirPlay streaming (see Figure 9.5).

FIGURE 9.5

You can use AirPlay to stream audio to multiple devices at the same time.

6. Check the radio button next to each device on which you want to play the audio. The button is marked with a check mark and the device's volume slider becomes active.

7. Play the content you selected. It plays on the AirPlay device or devices that you selected in step 4 or 6.

8. If you stream to multiple devices, open the AirPlay menu and use the volume sliders to set the relative volume of each device and the **Master Volume** slider to set the base volume level in iTunes (when streaming to multiple devices).

To play content only on the computer again, open the **AirPlay** menu, click the **Single** tab, and click **Computer**.

CONTROLLING ITUNES REMOTELY

Because you probably won't be in front of your computer when you are streaming iTunes content, it would be a pain to have to go back to the computer to control the audio or video, such as to choose the songs you want to play or change the volume level. You can use Apple's Remote app (available in the App Store) to control iTunes from an iOS device, in which case, the iOS device acts just a like a remote control that works with a TV or other device. Using the Remote app on an iOS device, you can start and pause playback, choose the content you want to watch or hear, and so on. For information about downloading and installing apps, see Chapter 13, "Downloading Content onto iPads, iPhones, or iPod touches."

Streaming Video Content with iTunes

Streaming video content is similar to audio, but you need to use an Apple TV to stream both video and audio, as follows:

1. Find and play the video you want to stream (see Part I for detailed information on this task).

2. Click the **AirPlay** button. The AirPlay menu appears (see Figure 9.6).

FIGURE 9.6

Choose an Apple TV to stream iTunes video to it.

3. Click **Apple TV**. The video streams to the Apple TV, and the Apple TV window replaces the video content in iTunes (see Figure 9.7).

FIGURE 9.7

When you stream video to an Apple TV, you see this window in iTunes.

4. Use the playback controls in the Apple TV window to control the video.

5. Use the volume controls on the HDTV or home theater receiver to control volume.

To return video playback to iTunes, open the **AirPlay** menu on the computer and choose **Computer**.

Streaming Content from an iOS Device

You can stream content from an iOS device to AirPlay devices in a number of apps, such as Music, Videos, and so on.

1. On the iOS device, open the app you want to use to play audio or video and start playing the content you want to watch or listen to. (Using these apps is covered in Part III of this book, "iPads/iPhones/iPod touches.")

2. Tap the **AirPlay** button located at the right end of the toolbar when you are watching video or to the right of the Volume slider in an iOS app. The AirPlay menu opens and you see the devices to which you can stream content (see Figure 9.8).

FIGURE 9.8

You can play content from an iOS device on an AirPlay device by selecting it on this menu.

NOTE   The icon next to the device name on the menu indicates whether it can play audio only (speaker) or both audio and video (display).

3. Tap the device to which you want to stream content. If you are streaming video, the video playback screen appears (see Figure 9.9). If you are streaming audio, you see the app's screen on the iOS device.

FIGURE 9.9

When you stream video from an iOS device, you see this screen on the iOS device.

4. Use the app's tools to control playback, choose different content, and so on (when you stream video, set the volume using the audio controls on the device to which the Apple TV is connected).

To return playback to the iOS device, open the **AirPlay** menu and tap the iOS device.

DISPLAYING THE IOS SCREEN ON AN APPLE TV

You can also use AirPlay to display the iOS itself on Apple TVs. This enables you to show any app or even the iOS desktop on those devices, the same as when the iOS device is connected to an external display (which it is when you use AirPlay). Press the **Home** button twice to open the Multitasking bar. Swipe to the right until you see the AirPlay button. Tap the **AirPlay** button. Tap **Apple TV**. Set the **Mirroring** switch to **ON**. The iOS device's screen appears on the device to which the Apple TV is connected. Anything you do on the iOS device is also shown on the device to which the Apple TV is connected.

THE ABSOLUTE MINIMUM

In this chapter, you learned how easy it is to use AirPlay to stream audio and video.

- AirPlay is Apple's technology that enables iTunes on computers and apps on iOS devices to stream audio and video to AirPlay-compatible devices, such as AirPort Express Base Stations to which speakers are connected, Apple TVs, and AirPort-capable speakers.

- To use AirPlay, you need to connect the streaming devices (computers and iOS devices) to receiving devices (Apple TVs, AirPort Express Base Station, AirPort-capable speakers) using a Wi-Fi or Ethernet network. When connected, iTunes on computers and the iOS automatically recognize the receiving devices.

- Use the AirPlay button in iTunes on a Mac or Windows PC and in iOS apps to stream audio and video to other devices.

10

OBTAINING AND CONFIGURING AN ICLOUD ACCOUNT

Many (dare I say most or even all?) people have multiple devices, such as computers, iPhones, iPads, and so on. Having the same content on all these devices can be a real challenge—if they don't use iCloud, that is. That's because iCloud is a service that connects your iOS devices, Macintosh computers, Windows computers, and Apple TVs to a "cloud," which is a central repository for data storage that is available via the Internet. Each device stores data on the cloud and receives data from the cloud through the various services iCloud offers.

iCloud enables you to share music, photos, books, and other content on each device, no matter where that content came from originally. iCloud can be thought of as the "connection" that enables all your devices to communicate and share content with each other, without being physically connected or even in the same location. Using iCloud enhances your enjoyment of music, books, photos, and much more, because you don't have to think about putting content on specific devices; you can get it all through the cloud, automatically.

Understanding iCloud

iCloud provides storage space on the Internet and manages the flow of data to and from each device through the syncing process, which happens automatically if your devices are configured to allow it.

The result is that you have the ability to access the same content from each device. For example, when you use iTunes Match, any music stored in iTunes on your computer (or more than one computer) is available in your cloud. Each of your devices can connect to the same space in the cloud so that the music can be downloaded from the cloud onto the device to be played there. Similarly, your photos can be stored in iCloud's Photo Stream from where they can be accessed on each device and automatically downloaded onto computers for permanent storage. Likewise, you can set iCloud up so that when you buy a book from the iBookstore on an iPhone, it is automatically downloaded to an iPad or other iOS device; even your current page is synced so that when you read that book on a different device, you see the last page you read on a different device. iCloud maximizes your enjoyment of digital content because that content is available on whatever device you happen to be using at one time (see Figure 10.1).

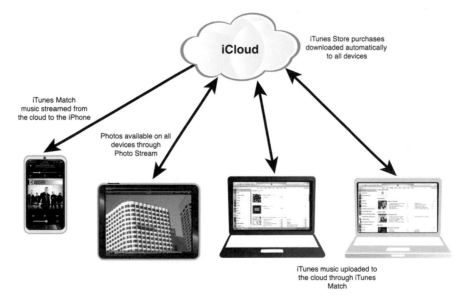

FIGURE 10.1

iCloud provides online storage and a set of services that enable you to link your iOS devices and computers together.

To use iCloud, you first need to accomplish the following two tasks:

1. Obtain an iCloud account. This is explained in the next section.

2. Configure each device to use your iCloud account. This means that you log in to your iCloud account and determine which type of information will be synced on the device. The later sections in this chapter explain how to do this on Macs, Windows PCs, and iOS devices.

After iCloud is set up on each device, you can start working with the various services it provides. You don't have to use all the iCloud services, nor do you have to start using them all at the same time. You can pick and choose which services you want to use and when you want to use them.

The devices that work with iCloud are the following:

- **Macintosh computers**—To use iCloud on a Mac, you must be running OS X Lion, version 10.8.2 or later, along with iTunes 11 or later. If you want to use Photo Stream, you need to have iPhoto 11, version 9.4 or later, or Aperture, version 3.4 or later.

- **Windows computers**—iCloud works with Microsoft Windows 7 or 8. You also need to install version 2.1.1 of the iCloud control panel and have iTunes 11 or later installed.

- **iOS devices**—To use iCloud, iOS devices must be running iOS 6 or later.

NOTE iCloud works with some older versions than those listed in the previous requirements, but not all the features will be available, so you should upgrade your devices to the versions specified.

BUT WAIT, THERE'S MORE

This book is focused on iTunes and related content: music, video, podcasts, books, and photos. iCloud can help you manage a lot more than this. For example, you can use iCloud to keep your contact information in sync, to create and manage online calendars, and so on. To learn about the other areas iCloud supports, see my book *Sams Teach Yourself iCloud in 10 Minutes*.

Obtaining an iCloud Account

To use iCloud, you need an iCloud account. The good news is that you may already have one. The even better news is that an iCloud account is free to obtain and use. A free account includes access to almost all the services described in the previous section, along with 5GB of online storage space. (The exception to iCloud being free is iTunes Match, which requires an annual subscription to use.)

If you have an Apple ID, such as one you create so that you can download content from the iTunes Store, you have an iCloud account as well. That's because an Apple ID account includes access to iCloud. If you haven't created an Apple ID already, see Chapter 2, "Working with the iTunes Store," for the information you need to create an Apple ID.

If you don't have an Apple ID already and don't want to create one as described in Chapter 2, you can also create an Apple ID on an iOS device by performing the following steps:

1. Tap **Settings** on the Home screen. The Settings app opens.

2. Tap **iCloud**.

3. Tap **Get a Free Apple ID**. The New Account dialog appears.

4. Follow the onscreen steps to provide the required information and complete the account creation process. This will include creating your Apple ID, which can be either a new email address or an existing one, along with your password. You'll also provide your identification and other information. When done, you'll have an Apple ID and password, and you'll be ready to use iCloud.

YOUR ICLOUD WEBSITE

With your iCloud account, you get a useful website, too. The website has applications you can use for your email, contacts, calendars, notes, reminders, and documents. The nice thing about this is that you can access these applications and your information from any computer running a supported web browser (current versions of Safari, Firefox, Chrome, or Internet Explorer). You can also use the Find My iPhone feature to locate an iOS device and to secure it if it is out of your control. Using your iCloud website is beyond the scope of this book (see *Sams Teach Yourself iCloud in 10 Minutes* for the details), but you can check it out by going to iCloud.com and logging in with you Apple ID and password.

Configuring iCloud on a Mac

To use iCloud on a Mac, you log in to your iCloud account and enable the iCloud services you want to use. You should also configure iTunes so that any downloads you get from the iTunes, App, or iBookstores are downloaded to your Mac automatically.

Signing In to an iCloud Account on a Mac

The iCloud software is built in to OS X. To start using it, you need to log in to your iCloud account using the following steps:

1. Open the System Preferences application.

2. Click **iCloud**. The iCloud pane opens as shown in Figure 10.2.

FIGURE 10.2

When you log in to your iCloud account on a Mac, you can use the services iCloud provides, which are integrated into OS X.

3. Enter your Apple ID.

4. Enter your Apple ID password.

5. Click **Sign In**. Your Mac logs in to your iCloud account. You're prompted to use iCloud for specific syncing.

6. If you don't want to sync information, uncheck the **Use iCloud for contacts, calendars, reminders, notes, and Safari** check box. You can reconfigure this later, so it doesn't really matter whether you leave this enabled.

7. Uncheck the **Use Find My Mac** check box if you don't want to use this service that can locate your Mac. You can reconfigure this later, so it doesn't really matter whether you leave this enabled.

8. Click **Next**.

9. If you enabled Find My Mac, click **Allow** to allow iCloud to use Location Services to locate your Mac. iCloud services begin working, and the information you enabled is synced with your iCloud account. The iCloud pane reflects the services you have enabled (see Figure 10.3).

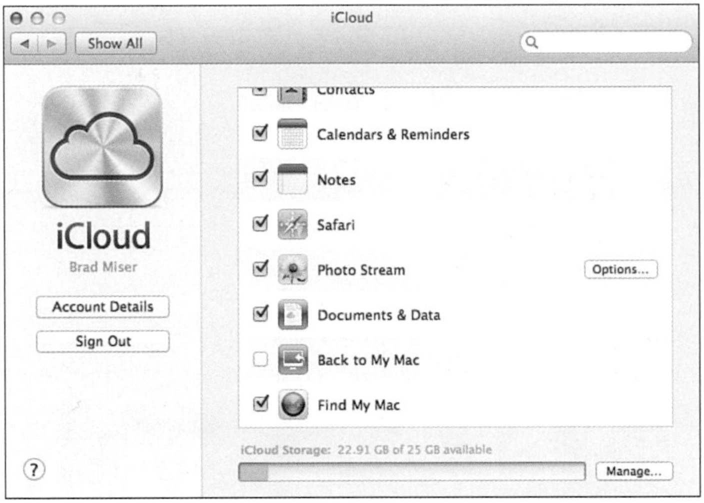

FIGURE 10.3

Use the iCloud pane of the System Preferences application to configure your iCloud services.

10. You can enable or disable the iCloud services you use by checking or unchecking their check boxes.

11. Ensure the **Photo Stream** check box is checked so you can work with Photo Stream, as explained in Part III, "iPads/iPhones/iPod touches."

12. Click **Options**.

13. Ensure that the **My Photo Stream** check box is checked.

14. Ensure that the **Shared Photo Streams** check box is checked.

15. Click **OK**. Your Mac is now using your iCloud account.

The following are a few pointers about working with the iCloud pane of the System Preferences application:

- You can disable any services you don't want to use at any time by unchecking their check boxes. You're prompted to keep the related information on your Mac or to delete it. You can enable or disable services as often as you'd like.

- The gauge at the bottom of the pane shows your current disk use. The more the bar is filled in, the more iCloud storage space you are currently using. If you click the **Manage** button, the Manage Storage sheet appears. In the left pane of the window, you see the services and applications that are currently using storage space and how much space each is using. When you select an application, you see the documents currently being stored for that application and how much space each document is consuming. You can select items and click the **Delete** button to remove them from the cloud. Click **Delete** to confirm. Click **Done** to close the sheet.

- If you open the Manage Storage sheet as described in the previous bullet and click **View Account**, you can log in to your iCloud account to see or change various information, such as your storage plan and payment information.

- If you click the **Account Details** button, a sheet showing your name and a description of your iCloud appears. You can change this information by editing it and clicking **OK**. This doesn't impact your account itself but does change how information about the account appears, such as the name shown in the From field on emails you send.

- You can sign out of your iCloud account by clicking **Sign Out**. If you enabled contacts to sync, you're prompted to keep them on or delete them from the Mac; other information you disable can only be deleted from the Mac. When you make your choice, you are logged out of your iCloud account. The iCloud pane returns to the version that allows you to sign into your account. You can sign back into your account or sign in to a different iCloud account.

Setting Up Automatic Store Downloads on a Mac

As described in various locations in this book, iTunes, the App Store, and iBookstore offer lots of great content you can enjoy on your Mac, Windows PC, and iOS devices. If you use an iOS device or a Windows computer along with your Mac, it is likely you'll download content from one of those stores on another device. You should set up iTunes so that any new music, book, or app downloads are automatically downloaded to your Mac as well.

Here's how:

1. Open iTunes.

2. Choose **iTunes**, **Preferences** or press ⌘-,.

3. Click the **Store** tab.

4. Check the **Music**, **Apps**, and **Books** check boxes as shown in Figure 10.4.

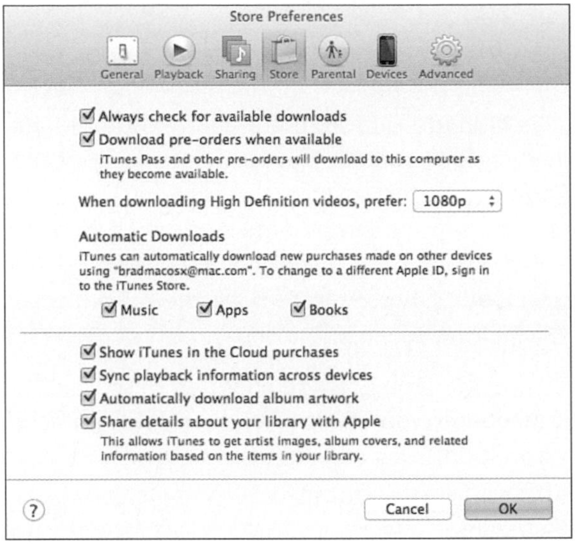

FIGURE 10.4

iTunes can automatically download music, apps, and books that you purchase on other devices.

5. If you don't want to see purchases you've made in the past in iTunes so that you can download them, uncheck the **Show iTunes in the Cloud purchases** check box. Most people should leave this checked so you can download any content that was purchased before you enabled automatic downloads as described in step 4.

6. To have your devices use the same playback position, such as your location in a song, on each device, ensure that the **Sync playback information across devices** check box is checked.

7. Click **OK**.

Configuring iCloud on a Windows PC

Configuring an iCloud account on a Windows PC enables you to access the great features iCloud offers. You need to download and install the iCloud control panel; then configure the iCloud services you want to use. Also, set up iTunes so that downloads from iTunes, the App Store, or iBookstore are downloaded to your computer automatically.

Download and Installing the iCloud Control Panel

To use iCloud with a Windows PC, you need to download and install the iCloud control panel. Here's how to do that:

1. Open a web browser and go to http://support.apple.com/kb/DL1455.

2. Click **Download**.

3. At the prompt, click **Run**. The software is downloaded to your computer, and the installer runs.

4. Click **Run** at the installer prompt.

5. Follow the onscreen instructions to complete the installation of the iCloud control panel. You must accept any actions when prompted by security dialogs to complete the process to allow the installer to make changes on your computer.

6. When the installation is complete, click **Finish**. You are ready to sign in to your iCloud account.

Signing In to an iCloud Account on a Windows PC

Sign in to your iCloud account by performing the following steps:

1. If the iCloud control panel is already open, skip to step 2; if not, open it by opening the **Windows** menu, clicking **Control Panel**, and then clicking **iCloud**.

2. Enter your Apple ID (see Figure 10.5).

FIGURE 10.5

Sign in to your iCloud account to use its services on your Windows PC.

3. Enter your Apple ID password.

4. Click **Sign In**. iCloud services become available, and you're ready to configure the specific services you want to use on the control panel, which now shows the services instead of the sign in tools as shown in Figure 10.6.

 NOTE   You might be prompted about allowing diagnostic and usage information to be sent to Apple. Click **Automatically send** or **Don't send** to clear the prompt.

FIGURE 10.6

These settings enable or disable information syncing and services for your iCloud account.

 NOTE   These steps and following information assume you have Outlook installed on your computer. If you don't, you see iCloud.com instead of Outlook in the iCloud control panel.

5. Ensure the **Show iCloud status in Notification Area** check box is checked if you want to be able to access the iCloud control panel or get iCloud help by clicking the iCloud icon on the System Tray.

6. Ensure the **Photo Stream** check box is checked.

7. Click **Options**.

8. Ensure the **My Photo Stream** check box is checked.

9. Ensure the **Share Photo Streams** check box is checked.

10. If you want to change the location where Photo Stream photos are stored, check the **Change** button; in most cases, the default locations are fine and you can skip to step 13.

11. Move to and select the folder in which you want Photo Stream photos to be automatically downloaded into and where you want to place photos to be uploaded automatically and click **OK**.

 TIP To create a new folder for Photo Stream, click **Make New Folder**.

12. Click **OK**.

13. Click **Apply**. Any changes you made are implemented.

 NOTE Depending on which options you enable or disable, you might be prompted to merge, delete, or keep various kinds of information.

14. Click **Close**. Your Windows PC starts using the iCloud services you enabled.

Here are some other pointers to keep in mind as you work with the iCloud control panel:

- When you disable information syncing and have Outlook installed, you're prompted to keep or delete the iCloud information that is currently stored on your computer. If you select the **Keep** option, the sync process is stopped, but the information that has previously been synced remains on your computer. If you select the **Delete** option, the information from iCloud is removed from your computer. If you don't have Outlook installed, the information is deleted from your computer.

- The gauge near the bottom of the control panel shows your current disk use. The more the bar is filled in, the more iCloud storage space you are currently using. If you click the **Manage** button, the Manage Storage dialog appears. In the left pane of the dialog, you see the services and applications that are currently using storage space and how much space each is using. When you select an application, you see the documents currently being stored for that application and how much space each document is consuming. You can select items and click the **Delete** button to remove them from the cloud. Click **Done** to close the dialog.

- If you open the Manage Storage dialog as described in the previous bullet and click **View Account**, you can log in to your iCloud account to see or change various information, such as your storage plan and payment information.

- If you click the **Account Options** button, a dialog appears. Click **Manage Apple ID** to change your account information using the Apple ID website.

- You can sign out of your iCloud account by clicking **Sign Out**. You're prompted to keep or delete the iCloud information currently on your computer (if you have Outlook installed). When you make your choice, you are logged out of your iCloud account. If Photo Stream was enabled, you see a prompt explaining that its photos have been saved and where they are saved. The iCloud control panel returns to the version that allows you to sign in to your account. You can sign back in to your account or sign in to a different iCloud account.

Setting Up Automatic Store Downloads on a Windows PC

As described in various locations in this book, iTunes, the App Store, and iBookstore offer lots of great content you can enjoy on your Mac, Windows PC, and iOS devices. If you use an iOS device or a Mac computer along with your Windows PC, it is likely you'll download content from one of those stores on another device. You should set up iTunes so that any new music, book, or app downloads are automatically downloaded to your computer as well by performing the following steps:

1. Open iTunes.

2. Open the iTunes menu and choose **Preferences** or press Ctrl+,.

3. Click the **Store** tab.

4. Check the **Music**, **Apps**, and **Books** check boxes as shown in Figure 10.7.

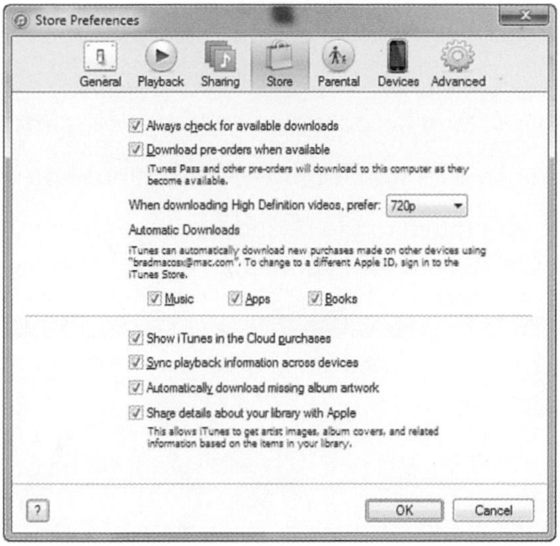

FIGURE 10.7

On a Windows PC, iTunes can automatically download music, apps, and books that you purchase on other devices.

5. If you don't want to see purchases you've made in the past in iTunes so that you can download them, uncheck the **Show iTunes in the Cloud purchases** check box. Leave this checked so you can download any content that was purchased before you enabled automatic downloads as described in step 4.

6. To have your devices use the same playback position, such as your location in a song, on each device, ensure that the **Sync playback information across devices** check box is checked.

7. Click **OK**.

Configuring iCloud on an iPad, iPhone, or iPod touch

iCloud was made for iOS devices and the iOS software has numerous iCloud features built in. To access these features, you need to sign in to and configure your iCloud account on the device; this includes configuring the device so your iTunes, App, and iBookstore purchases are downloaded to it automatically.

Signing In to an iCloud Account on an iPad, iPhone, or iPod touch

To configure your iCloud account on an iOS device, perform the following steps:

1. On the Home screen, tap **Settings**. The Settings app opens.

2. Tap **iCloud**. You move to the iCloud Settings screen. You're then prompted to enter your iCloud account information, as shown in Figure 10.8.

FIGURE 10.8

Sign in to your iCloud account on an iOS device to start using iCloud's great features.

3. Enter your Apple ID.

4. Enter your Apple ID password.

5. Tap **Sign In**, and your iCloud account is configured on your device.

6. If you're prompted about merging information already in your iCloud account, tap **Don't Merge** if you don't want the information already on the device to be moved into your iCloud account, or tap **Merge** if you do.

7. If prompted, tap **OK** to allow iCloud to access your device's location, or tap **Don't Allow** if you don't want this to happen. You need to allow this for some features, such as Find My iPhone, to work.

8. Set the slider to the ON position next to each kind of information you want to sync on your device, as shown in Figure 10.9; for example, if Mail is set to ON, email syncs between your iCloud account and the device. If you set a slider to the OFF position, that type of information won't sync between your iCloud account and the device.

FIGURE 10.9

Use the switches to determine which iCloud services are enabled on your iOS device.

9. Tap **Photo Stream**.

10. Ensure **My Photo Stream** is set to ON.

11. Ensure **Shared Photo Streams** is set to ON.

12. Tap **iCloud**. Your iCloud account configuration is complete.

You can start using iCloud as configured. However, it's good to be aware of additional options in case you'd like to tweak your account further. To see these, open iCloud Settings. The following are some of the additional configuration tasks you can do:

- At the top of the screen, you see your current account. Tap the account. In the iCloud Account Information section, you can change or reenter your password and change the description of your account; the default name is iCloud, but you might want to change it to your Apple ID or some other more personalized term.

  The Storage Plan section provides your current iCloud storage; the default is 5GB, so if you are new to iCloud, that is amount of space you have to work with. If you've upgraded your storage space or have additional space from an account that you converted to iCloud, you see your current amount and what your annual fee is for this amount. If you tap the storage space icon, you can change the amount of space allowed under your account. If you tap Payment Information, you can change the payment details for your account.

  If you tap Mail at the bottom of the screen, you can do advanced configuration of your iCloud email account.

- As you've already seen, you can use the controls in the center section of the iCloud Setting screen to enable or disable specific aspects of your iCloud account, such as whether you use its email.

- You can tap **Storage & Backup** to see how your iCloud storage is being used and to change your storage plan. You can also enable iCloud backup of your device.

- At the bottom of the iCloud Settings screen, you see the **Delete Account** button. Tap this if you want to stop using the account on the device.

Setting Up Automatic iTunes Store Downloads on an iPad, iPhone, or iPod touch

Ensure that any purchases you make in iTunes, the App Store, or iBookstore on any device are automatically downloaded to your iOS devices by performing the following steps:

1. Open **Settings**.

2. Tap **iTunes & App Stores**.

3. Ensure that the **Music**, **Apps**, and **Books** switches are in the ON position (see Figure 10.10). Any of these items downloaded on a Mac, Windows PC, or other iOS device are automatically downloaded to the device you are configuring.

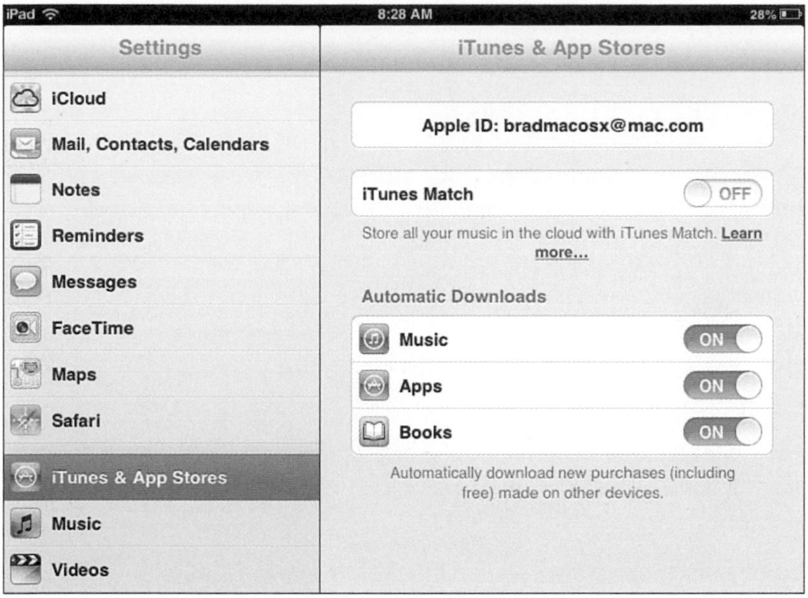

FIGURE 10.10

Enable your music, app, and book purchases to be downloaded to your iOS device automatically.

THE ABSOLUTE MINIMUM

In this chapter, you learned how iCloud can be useful to ensure you have your content available on all your devices. Important topics included the following:

- iCloud consists of online storage space and services. These services automatically send data to and retrieve data from the cloud on Macs, Windows PCs, and iOS devices. This keeps the information, apps, and content on your devices in sync with each other.

- To use iCloud, you must have an iCloud account. You can obtain a new iCloud account for free, or you might be able to use an existing account, such as an Apple ID that you use to shop in the iTunes Store in iTunes on a computer.

- Configure iCloud on a Mac to be able to sync data with the cloud and other devices. You use the iCloud pane of the System Preferences application to do this.

- You can use iCloud on a Windows PC by downloading and installing the iCloud control panel and configuring it to access your iCloud account.

- You can also use iCloud on iOS devices, enabling you to enjoy iCloud's features, many of which were designed specifically for iOS devices. You use the iCloud and iTunes & App Store Settings to configure your iCloud account on an iOS device.

11

PUTTING YOUR PHOTOS ON THE CLOUD WITH PHOTO STREAM

If you use more than one device to take, store, edit, or view photos, you'll find that Photo Stream is one of iCloud's most useful features. This is especially true if you use an iOS device to take photos. Photo Stream stores your photos in the cloud so that you can access them on any device through a Wi-Fi or an Ethernet connection to the Internet (Mac or Windows PC). The great news is that this happens automatically; you don't have to worry about syncing your photos among your devices because Photo Stream handles this for you.

With Photo Stream sharing, you can easily share your photos with others and enjoy photos being shared with you.

Understanding Photo Stream

Each of your devices can add photos to your Photo Stream (sender) and download photos from the Photo Stream (receiver) as shown in Figure 11.1. For example, you can take photos with your iPhone; the photos are automatically uploaded to your cloud. Those photos are then automatically downloaded, via Photo Stream, to all your devices on which Photo Stream is enabled. You don't have to sync any of the devices to work with your photos; Photo Stream brings photos to and receives photos from each device automatically.

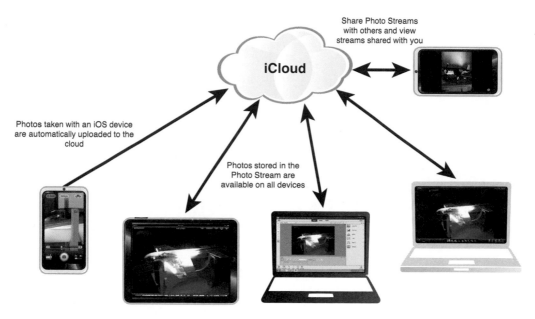

FIGURE 11.1

Each of your devices can receive photos from and send photos to your Photo Stream.

You can also use Photo Stream to share your photos with other Photo Stream users. You can create albums to share and then add photos to them to make them available to those who have accepted your shared Photo Stream. They can view your photos, add comments, and indicate they like the photos.

Likewise, you can view and comment on Photo Streams being shared with you.

To use Photo Stream, you must first configure it on each device. Then, how you work with your Photo Stream depends on the specific device. Throughout the rest of this chapter, sections describe how to work with Photo Stream on a Mac, a Windows PC, and iOS devices.

The following are general points that will help you understand and use Photo Stream more effectively:

- When you take photos on an iOS device, they are uploaded to Photo Stream when you are connected to a Wi-Fi network (Photo Stream doesn't move photos over a cellular data connection). If you take photos while a device is not connected to a Wi-Fi network, they are uploaded the next time you connect it to a Wi-Fi network.

- Up to 1,000 photos are stored in your Photo Stream for 30 days. Older photos are removed from your Photo Stream as needed to keep the number to 1,000 or fewer.

- Because Photo Stream is not a long-term storage location, you need to make sure any photos you want to keep are stored in a permanent location.

- If you use Photo Stream with a Mac or a Windows PC, photos are permanently stored for you automatically. When a photo is added to your Photo Stream, it is downloaded onto your Mac (iPhoto or Aperture) or Windows PC (designated download folder) automatically. So, as long as you have a Mac or Windows PC set up to use Photo Stream, you don't have to worry about losing any of your photos.

- When you add photos to iPhoto or Aperture on a Mac, or in the designated locations on a Windows PC, they are uploaded to your Photo Stream, too.

- On a Mac, iPhoto 11 (version 9.2 or later) or Aperture (version 3.2 or later) are required to use Photo Stream. To use Shared Photo Streams you must have iPhoto 9.4, Aperture 3.4, and OS X v10.8.2 or later.

- On a Windows PC, you need to be running Windows 7 or 8.

- On an iOS device, you can use Photo Stream with iOS 5 and later, but to use all the features, you need to have iOS 6 or later installed.

- Photos are stored in your Photo Stream at their full resolution. They also download to a Mac or Windows PC at the full resolution. When they are downloaded to an iOS device, the resolution is optimized for the device.

- Photo Stream supports the most common photographic formats, such as JPEG, TIFF, PNG, and RAW. Photo formats becomes a potential concern only when you add photos to a Mac or Windows PC that weren't taken with an iOS device or a digital camera, such as images you download from the Internet. These images have to be in a supported format to be uploaded to your Photo Stream.

- Photo Stream doesn't support video. If you take videos with an iOS device, they become available on other devices only when you sync the device to a computer and then move the video onto other devices through the sync process or share them in some other way, such as via YouTube or email.

PHOTO STREAM AND APPLE TV

An Apple TV can also access your Photo Stream to display photos on a TV. On the Apple TV, select the **Internet** menu and then select **Photo Stream**. If you aren't already signed into your iCloud account, select **Yes** at the prompt. If you want your Photo Stream photos to be the Apple TV's screensaver, select **Yes** at the prompt.

To view your Photo Stream, select **Internet**, **Photo Stream**. You can then use the Apple TV's remote to browse thumbnails of your Photo Stream photos. To view a photo, select its thumbnail. To view the photos in a slideshow, select **Slideshow** or click the **Play** button.

Using Photo Stream with a Mac

Photo Stream works great with a Mac. Like other devices, you need to first enable Photo Stream on the Mac. Then you can work with your Photo Stream photos in either iPhoto or Aperture. Both applications automatically download and save all your Photo Stream photos, and you can edit them, save them in albums, use them in projects, and perform all the other great tasks you can do with any of your other photos stored in those applications.

 NOTE To be able to use Photo Stream on a Mac, you access the iCloud pane of the System Preferences application to sign in to your iCloud account and enable Photo Stream. This task is explained in Chapter 10, "Obtaining and Configuring an iCloud Account."

Using Photo Stream with iPhoto

After you've enabled Photo Stream on your Mac, you can access it in the iPhoto application. iPhoto automatically downloads Photo Stream photos and saves them in your iPhoto Library. Any photos you add to iPhoto, such as by importing them from a digital camera, are automatically uploaded to your Photo Stream as well.

You can view and work with photos from the Photo Stream just like other photos in your iPhoto Library.

Enabling Photo Stream in iPhoto

First, enable Photo Stream in iPhoto by performing the following steps:

1. Launch iPhoto.

2. Choose **iPhoto**, **Preferences** or press ⌘-,.

3. Click the **Photo Stream** tab (see Figure 11.2).

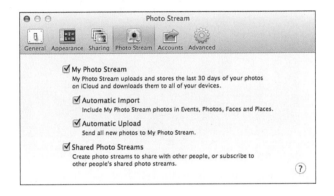

FIGURE 11.2

Set up Photo Stream in iPhoto so that your Photo Stream photos are automatically downloaded and saved on your Mac.

4. Check the **My Photo Stream** check box. This enables iPhoto to work with your Photo Stream.

5. Check the **Automatic Import** check box. This ensures that anytime a new photo is added to your Photo Stream, such as when you take a photo on an iOS device, it is automatically imported into your iPhoto Library.

6. Check the **Automatic Upload** check box. This causes iPhoto to upload any photos you import into your iPhoto Library to your Photo Stream.

7. Check the **Shared Photo Streams** check box. This enables you to both share your Photo Streams with others and view streams being shared with you.

8. Click the **Close** button to close the iPhoto Preferences dialog. In the source pane on the left side of the window, you see your Photo Stream in the Web section (see Figure 11.3).

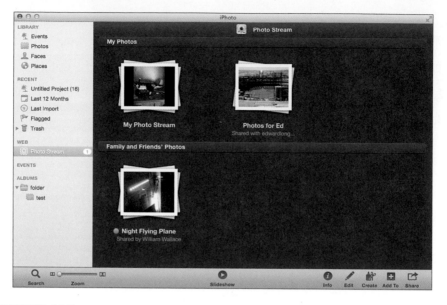

FIGURE 11.3

Set up Photo Stream in iPhoto so that your Photo Stream photos are automatically downloaded and saved on your Mac.

Working with Your Photo Stream in iPhoto

You don't have to move photos from the Photo Stream to your iPhoto Library to store them on your Mac. This happens automatically when iPhoto downloads photos from the Photo Stream. You can view the Photo Stream photos stored on your Mac by selecting Photos or any of the other sources in the library. For example, you can select the Photos category and you will see photos downloaded from your Photo Stream, just like those you've imported from a camera or other sources (see Figure 11.4).

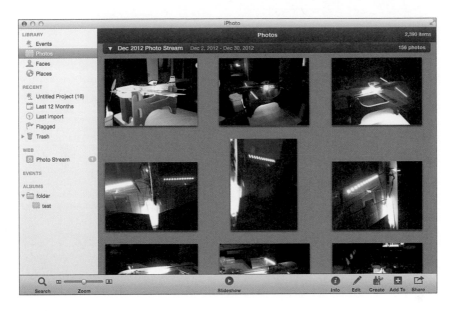

FIGURE 11.4

Here you see photos recently imported from my Photo Stream.

 NOTE   If there are a lot of photos in your Photo Stream when you first enable it in iPhoto, it can take a while for all of the photos to be downloaded to your Mac.

After they are downloaded from Photo Stream, you can use all of iPhoto's tools on them, too, just like photos you've added from other sources.

To see the photos in your Photo Stream, select **Photo Stream** in the WEB section on the Source list. You see two categories, labeled My Photos and Family and Friends' Photos, as shown in Figure 11.5 (if you haven't subscribed to any shared Photo Streams yet, you don't see the Family and Friends' Photos section). Those in the first group are the photos in your Photo Stream, which is called My Photo Stream (clever naming by Apple!), and the others are streams you are sharing with others (these are labeled with the names you give them).

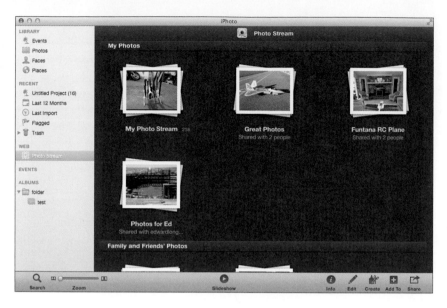

FIGURE 11.5

When you open the My Photo Stream source, you see the photos currently in your Photo Stream.

 NOTE   If you also import photos directly from an iOS device and from Photo Stream, you should be prompted about what you want iPhoto to do with the duplicates. Typically, you won't want to import the duplicate photos, but you can if you choose to. With Photo Stream, you don't need to manually import photos from an iOS device.

To browse and view the photos in your Photo Stream, double-click one of the albums you see. You can then browse, view, and work with photos similar to those in other sources.

However, because the photos are automatically stored in your iPhoto Library, you don't need to work with the My Photo Stream source; instead, work with the photos in the other sources that are stored in your iPhoto Library on your Mac. As you learn in the next two sections, you do want to access the Photo Stream to work with shared sources.

iPhoto periodically and automatically updates the Photo Stream source and imports any new photos in the Photo Stream. When this happens, you see the updating icon (a rotating circle made up of two curved arrows) next to the Photo Stream icon on the Source list. iPhoto updates the Photo Stream each time you launch the application, too.

Sharing Photo Streams in iPhoto

Photo Streams are great to share your photos with others. Any one who uses iCloud and has Photo Stream enabled on a device (Mac, Windows PC, or iOS) can view your photos, add commentary, and so on, within the related app on their device (such as the Photos app on an iOS device).

You can create and share a new Photo Stream on your device by performing the following steps:

1. Select the photos you want to share.

2. Click the **Share** button.

3. Choose **Photo Stream**.

4. Click **New Photo Stream**.

5. Enter the email addresses of the people with whom you want to share the photos.

6. Name the photo stream.

7. Check the **Public Website** check box if you want anyone to be able to view the photos using a web browser.

8. Click **Share** (see Figure 11.6). The new Photo Stream is created and the people with whom you share it receive notifications that enable them to access it (see the next section for details).

New Shared Photo Stream

Photo Streams let you share selected photos with other people.

To: William Wallace   Edward Longshanks

Name: Funtana

☑ Public Website
Allow anyone without an Apple device to view this Photo Stream on a public website.

Cancel   Share

FIGURE 11.6

Creating a new Photo Stream to share is easy, just complete this dialog.

When you select the Photo Stream source, you see the Photo Streams you are sharing in the My Photos section (see Figure 11.7).

FIGURE 11.7

I have shared two Photo Streams, Funtana and Photos for Ed.

You can add photos to an existing stream by doing the following:

1. Select the photos you want to add to an existing stream.

2. Click **Add To**.

3. Select **Photo Stream**.

4. Click the Photo Stream to which you want to add the photos. The photos are added to the Photo Stream. The people with whom you are sharing it receive notifications that new photos have been added.

The following are some more points to consider as you work with your shared Photo Streams:

- **Comments/Like**—People who can view your shared Photo Streams can add comments to them and indicate that they like them. You receive notifications when this happens, and the shared Photo Stream is marked with a blue circle. To see the comments, open the Photo Stream. Photos with unread commentary are marked with a blue quote bubble. Click the photo and you see the commentary along with information about who posted it and when. You also see who has liked the photo (see Figure 11.8).

FIGURE 11.8

Here you see that William Wallace likes this photo and has added commentary to it.

- **Share comments**—You can share your own comments about a photo by clicking **Add a comment**, typing your comments, and click **Post**. Others who are sharing the stream can read your comments so that you can have conversations about specific photos.

- **Get information**—To get information about a shared Photo Stream, select it and click **Info**. The Info pane opens (see Figure 11.9). Here you can add a description, see who you are sharing the Photo Stream with and if they have accepted it (you see a check mark by the person's name), turn Public Website sharing on or off, and visit the stream's website. You can remove a subscriber or resend the invitation by performing a secondary click on a person's name and choosing the action you want on the resulting menu.

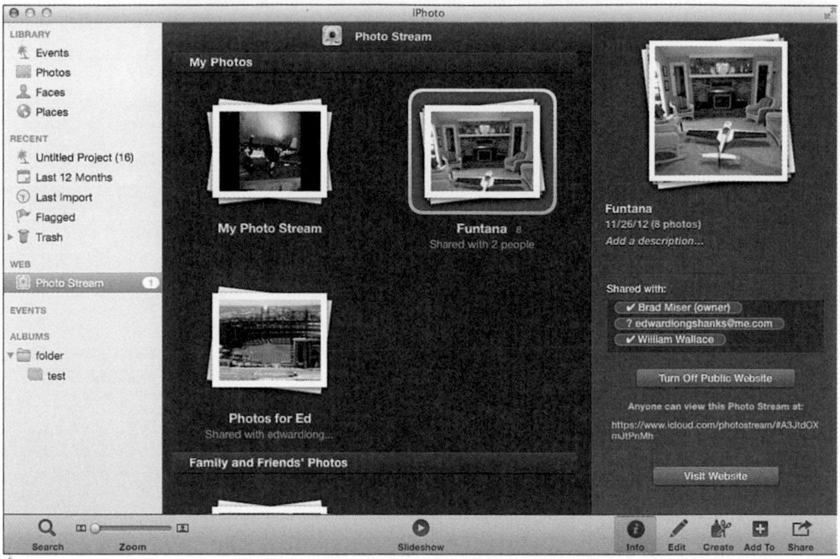

FIGURE 11.9

On the Info pane, you can see information about a shared Photo Stream.

- **Preview photos**—Move the pointer across the stream's thumbnail to preview the photos it contains.

- **Change the stream's name**—Select the name, edit it, and press Return to save the new name.

 NOTE A secondary click is sometimes known as a right-click. There are a number of ways to do this, such as by holding the Ctrl key down while you click, using a two-fingered gesture, clicking the right button on a mouse, and so on. The Ctrl-click option always works.

- **Remove a shared stream**—To delete a shared Photo Stream, perform a secondary click on it and choose **Delete Photo Stream**. When you delete a shared Photo Stream, it is no longer available to those who are subscribed to it. The photos remain in your iPhoto Library.

Working with Photo Streams Shared with You in iPhoto

When someone shares a Photo Stream with you, you see a notification, receive an email, and see the badge on the Photo Stream icon indicating you have new activity. To accept the shared stream in iPhoto, follow these steps:

1. Click **Photo Stream** in the WEB section on the iPhoto Source List. You see the new Photo Stream. You don't see a preview in the thumbnail because you haven't subscribed to it yet.

     TIP You can also click the **Show Me** button in the notification you receive or the **Join this Photo Stream** button in the notification email instead of performing step 1.

2. Hover over the Photo Stream's name. You see the Decline and Accept buttons.

3. Click **Accept** (see Figure 11.10). The subscription is added, and you can work with the shared Photo Stream.

FIGURE 11.10

When you click the Accept button, you are subscribed to a Photo Stream.

 TIP You can configure the notifications about shared Photo Streams by opening the Notifications pane of the System Preferences application and clicking **Photo Stream**.

Here are some things you can do with a shared Photo Stream:

*   **Preview photos**—Move the pointer across the stream's thumbnail to preview the photos it contains.

- **Browse and view its photos**—Double-click a shared stream to see the photos it contains. You can browse and view these photos just like those stored in your iPhoto Library.

- **Import photos to your iPhoto Library**—Select the shared stream, or open it and select the photos you want to add to your library, perform a secondary click, and choose **Import**. The photos are downloaded and become part of your iPhoto Library.

- **Comment/Like**—Click the **Quote** button in the lower-left corner of the photo on which you want to comment. The Info pane opens. Enter your comments and click **Post**. Click **Like** to indicate you like the photo.

- **Remove a shared stream**—To get rid of a shared stream, perform a secondary click on it and choose **Unsubscribe**.

 TIP Neither iPhoto nor Aperture imports photos from your Photo Stream unless they are open. You should periodically open the applications to ensure your Photo Stream photos are downloaded. You need to do this at least every 30 days, and more frequently if you add more than 1,000 photos to your Photo Stream in less time.

Using Photo Stream with Aperture

Aperture supports Photo Stream just like iPhoto does; however, the interface looks a bit different so there are some minor differences. Like iPhoto, you can enable automatic downloads and uploads, share your own photos in photo streams, and work with streams being shared with you.

To enable Photo Stream, choose **Aperture, Preferences**. Click the **Photo Stream** tab and configure the options as shown in Figure 11.11. These are the same options as those in iPhoto (see "Enabling Photo Stream in iPhoto" for details).

FIGURE 11.11

Enabling Photo Stream in Aperture is a matter of checking the check boxes you see here.

Also like iPhoto, after Photo Stream is enabled, you can select it on the Source list to view the photos there, as shown in Figure 11.12. Like iPhoto, because the Photo Stream photos are automatically stored in your library, you can work with them there rather than in the Photo Stream, but you can always see what's currently in your Photo Stream if that is of interest to you.

FIGURE 11.12

Working with shared Photo Streams in Aperture is similar to iPhoto.

You also see the streams you are sharing along with those to which you are subscribed.

Using Aperture to work with your Photo Stream and shared streams is similar to iPhoto. The user interface is a bit different in some cases. For example, the Quote button is located in the upper-left corner of shared photos' thumbnails instead of the lower left in iPhoto. And there isn't an Info button; instead, you click the Info tab to see information about shared streams, to make comments, and so on. But other than these minor differences, you can use the information in the section "Using Photo Stream with iPhoto" to take advantage of Photo Stream in Aperture.

Using Photo Stream with a Windows PC

Photo Stream on a Windows PC isn't integrated into specific applications as it is on Macs (at least it wasn't at press time; hopefully, this will change at some point). Instead, you designate a location for your Photo Stream photos to be stored and use a photo application to work with those photos.

 NOTE This section is based on Windows 7. If you use Windows 8, the details may be a bit different.

To use Photo Stream, you must be signed in to your iCloud account and have Photo Stream enabled (see Chapter 10 for the details). Included in this configuration is the selection of the location of your Photo Stream folder.

 TIP To see where your Photo Stream folder is located, open the iCloud control panel and click the **Options** button next to Photo Stream. You see the current location of the folder in the Photo Stream location section. You can use the Change button to change its location if you want to.

After you configure Photo Stream on your Windows PC, you can access its photos by opening the Photo Stream folder (one way to do this is by selecting your Pictures folder and then double-clicking the Photo Stream folder), as shown in Figure 11.13.

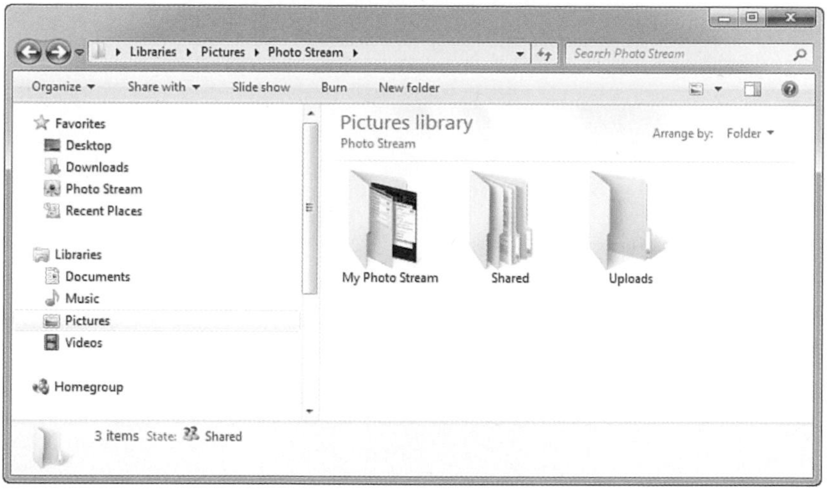

FIGURE 11.13

When you open the Photo Stream folder, you see the three subfolders shown here.

In this folder, you see the following three subfolders:

- **My Photo Stream**—This folder contains all the photos currently in your Photo Stream. When you open it, you see the photos organized according to the current option, such as by Month or Folder. You can browse and view these photos using Windows' standard tools. You can also open and use them in a photo application, such as Adobe Photoshop Elements.

- **Shared**—This folder contains Photo Streams you are sharing and those being shared with you. When you open the folder, you see each shared Photo Stream (see Figure 11.14). You can open any of these folders to work with the photos it contains.

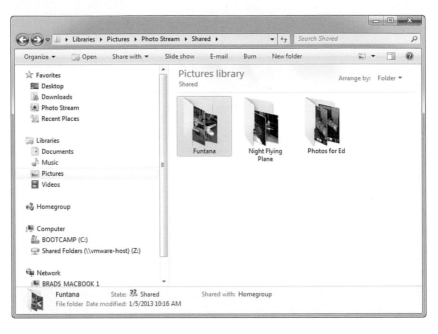

FIGURE 11.14

Each shared Photo Stream appears in the Shared folder.

- **Uploads**—Place photos in this folder that you want to upload to your Photo Stream.

You also can access your Photo Stream and shared streams by clicking **Photo Stream** in the Windows Favorites section. The resulting folder displays your Photo Stream along with those you are sharing and that are being shared with you (see Figure 11.15). For shared folders, you see the name of the person sharing the stream or "Me" if you are sharing it. You can open and work with any of these folders, the same as other folders containing photos.

FIGURE 11.15

Each shared Photo Stream appears in the Shared folder.

Sharing Photo Streams in Windows

You can share the photos in your Photo Stream with others by performing the following steps:

1. In the Favorites section of a Windows Explorer window, select **Photo Stream**.

2. Click **New Photo Stream**.

3. Enter the email addresses of the people with whom you want to share the photos.

4. Enter the name of the shared stream.

5. Check the **Create a public website to allow anyone to view this Photo Stream on icloud.com** check box if you want the photos to be publicly available on the Web.

6. Click **Next** as shown in Figure 11.16.

FIGURE 11.16

You can share photos from the Windows desktop by creating a new Photo Stream.

TIP   You can also create a new shared stream by selecting the photos you want to share, performing a right-click, choosing **Add to a Photo Stream**, and then clicking **New Photo Stream**. The dialog box shown in Figure 11.16 opens.

7. Click **Choose Photos**.

8. Use the resulting dialog to move to and select the photos you want to share, and click **Open**. The photos are added to the dialog along with space to add comments.

NOTE   You can share any photos on your PC. If they aren't already on your Photo Stream, they're uploaded and then shared.

9. Click **Add a comment** and type a comment for each photo (see Figure 11.17).

FIGURE 11.17

You can comment on photos you are sharing.

10. Repeat steps 7 through 9 until you've added all the photos you want to share.

11. Click **Done**. The Photo Stream is created and shared. Your invitees receive notifications and emails. You see the new, shared stream in your Photo Stream folder.

People with whom you shared the stream can view, use, and comment on or like your photos on their devices. When activity happens, such as someone accepting a stream you are sharing, you see a notification on the Windows desktop.

When a stream has new activity, it is marked with the blue dot icon. Open the stream. Any photos with new activity are marked with the blue quote bubble. Click the **quote bubble** or click the **Comments** button on the toolbar. The Comments pane opens; you can see comments from others and see who has clicked the photo's Like button (see Figure 11.18). You can converse about the photo by entering your own comments and clicking **Post**.

FIGURE 11.18

You can view the comments others have made and post your own.

To add photos to a shared stream, open it and click the **Add photos** button. Select and add photos the same as when you created the shared stream.

To change the stream, open the shared stream, and click the **Options** button. On the resulting dialog, you can do the following:

- Change the stream's name.

- See the status of current subscribers.

- Add or remove subscribers.

- Resend invitations.

- Change the status of the public website option.

To remove a shared stream, perform a right-click on it and choose **Delete**. Click **Delete** in the resulting dialog and the stream is removed. The photos remain on your computer—only the shared stream is impacted.

Working with Shared Photo Streams in Windows

When a stream is shared with you, you see a notification, and the stream appears in your Photo Stream folder (you don't see thumbnails unless you subscribe to it). You see the name of the stream and who wants to share it with you. Right-click the stream and choose **Accept** to subscribe to it or **Decline** if you don't want to subscribe. If you accept it, you are subscribed to the stream and it becomes active in your Photo Stream.

You can work with streams being shared with you in the following ways:

- **Browse and view its photos**—Double-click a shared stream to see the photos it contains.

- **Import photos to your photo application**—To add shared photos to your own photo application, open that application and import the photos in the shared stream the same as you would from any other location on your computer. The photos you import are downloaded from the shared stream and become like other photos you have added to that application.

- **Comment/Like**—Click the **Comments** button. The Comments area opens. Select the photo you want to comment on. Enter your comments and click **Post** (see Figure 11.19). Click **Like** to indicate that you like the photo.

FIGURE 11.19

You can comment on and like photos being shared with you.

- **Remove a shared stream**—To get rid of a shared stream, perform a right-click on it and choose **Unsubscribe**. Confirm the action at the prompt, and it is removed from your Photo Stream.

Using Photo Stream on iOS Devices

Photo Stream is a perfect match for iOS devices. To learn how to configure an iOS device to use Photo Stream, see Chapter 10. To learn how to work with Photo Stream on iOS devices, see Chapter 19, "Working with Photos and Video with the Camera and Photos Apps."

 TIP You can configure the notifications about shared Photo Streams on an iOS device by tapping **Settings**, **Notifications**, **Photos**. Then choose the type of notifications you want to receive, such as banners or alerts. You also can choose whether you receive a notification when anyone's Shared Photo Stream changes or only when Photo Streams shared by people in your contacts change.

Removing Photos from Your Photo Stream

Photos remain in your Photo Stream for 30 days. After that time, they are deleted automatically. Because photos don't count against your iCloud storage space, you don't need to delete photos from your Photo Stream. However, if you want to remove all your photos from your Photo Stream for some other reason, you can do so. There are two steps to this process. First, delete all the photos from the Photo Stream on the cloud. Second, delete the photos from the Photo Stream on each device on which they appear.

To remove photos from your Photo Stream on the cloud, perform the following steps:

1. Log in to your iCloud website by moving to icloud.com, entering your Apple ID and password, and clicking the right-facing arrow.

2. Click your name in the upper-right corner of the window. The Account pane appears.

3. Click **Advanced**.

4. Click **Reset Photo Stream**.

5. At the prompt, click **Reset**.

6. Enter your Apple ID password and click **OK**. All the photos in your Photo Stream are removed immediately.

7. Click **OK** to close the complete dialog.

To remove Photo Stream photos from all your devices, follow the steps in the corresponding bullet in the following list to remove them from each device:

- **iOS Devices**—Open the Settings app and tap **iCloud**. Tap **Photo Stream**. Slide the Photo Stream slider to the OFF position. The photos in the Photo Stream album are deleted and photos are no longer downloaded automatically. If you added photos from the Photo Stream into an album, you need to delete them from the album, too, because when you add a Photo Stream photo to an album, it is stored on the device.

- **Macs**—Disable Photo Stream in iPhoto or Aperture; this removes Photo Stream from those applications. Also disable Photo Stream on the iCloud pane of the System Preferences application. If photos were automatically downloaded from Photo Stream and you don't want them on your computer anymore, you also need to delete them from the iPhoto or Aperture Library.

- **Windows PCs**—Disable Photo Stream on the iCloud control panel by unchecking its check box. If you don't want any of the photos that were automatically downloaded from Photo Stream to remain on your PC, open the Photo Stream folder and delete the photos inside. If you imported photos into a photo application, you need to delete them from there as well.

THE ABSOLUTE MINIMUM

In this chapter, you learned how Photo Stream enables you to access your photos from Macs, Windows PCs, and iOS devices. Things you learned included the following:

- When you use Photo Stream, your photos are copied from each device onto the cloud via an Internet connection (Wi-Fi or Ethernet). Other devices can access those same photos through their Internet connections. This happens automatically so that you have access to your photos on each device whenever you want them.

- You can configure a Mac to work with Photo Stream using the iCloud pane of the System Preferences application. Photo Stream support is integrated into iPhoto and Aperture so that you can access Photo Streams directly in those applications.

- You can also use Photo Stream on a Windows PC. When you enable Photo Stream, you can use the Photo Stream folders to access your own Photo Stream, to share Photo Streams, and to subscribe to Photo Streams others share with you.

- Photo Stream really shines on iOS devices, especially when you use those devices to take photos, because Photo Stream can save them on a computer for you automatically.

- If you want to clear out your Photo Stream, you can do so from your iCloud website. You also need to remove photos from any devices they are stored on.

12

STREAMING YOUR MUSIC WITH ITUNES MATCH

iTunes Match is the iCloud service that makes all the music in your iTunes Library available on the cloud. You can then stream and download that music onto iOS devices and other computers so that you can listen to your music using any of these devices. This means you have all your iTunes music available to you regardless of which device you happen to be using at any point in time. It also eliminates the need to sync music onto iOS devices to be able to listen to it.

Understanding iTunes Match

Using iTunes Match, you can store up to 25,000 songs in the cloud (more if your iTunes Library includes songs that you purchased from the iTunes Store). You can access these songs on up to 10 devices, including Macs, Windows PCs, iPhones, iPads, iPod touches, and Apple TVs. iTunes Match connects all your devices to all your music via the Internet (see Figure 12.1). This makes your music available to you wherever you are (assuming you have an Internet connection on the device you are using).

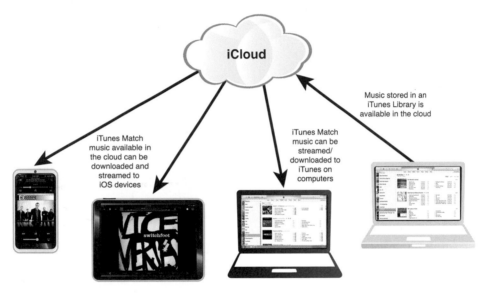

FIGURE 12.1

Using iTunes Match, your music is stored in the cloud so it can be streamed to any of your devices.

iTunes Match works for all the music in your iTunes Library, not just for music you've purchased from the iTunes Store (which, as you learn in Chapter 13, "Downloading Content onto iPads, iPhones, or iPod touches," you can download directly to any of your devices at any time). For example, if you've imported music from a CD into your library instead of buying that music in the iTunes Store, that music also becomes available in the cloud so that you can download it to your device. This eliminates the need to sync your music on your devices because you always have the music you want to hear at any point in time; you can see all the music in your iTunes Library on all the devices that are configured to use iTunes Match. If music you want to hear isn't currently stored on your device, just tap the Download button to add it to the device. You can also play music from the cloud; when the music starts to download, it also starts to play (streaming).

If you want to use iTunes Match, you must pay for the service; the cost is currently $24.99 per year in the United States (it may have a different price in other areas).

NOTE It may help to realize that iTunes Match is tied to your Apple ID, not to a specific iTunes Library. If you enable iTunes Match on more than one computer, all the music from each computer is uploaded to the cloud, and each can also download and play music from the cloud.

Whether you benefit from iTunes Match depends on your specific circumstances. If you have music only from the iTunes Store in your iTunes Library, you don't need iTunes Match because you can download any purchased music to your devices at any time already for no additional cost. If your devices have enough space to store all the music in your iTunes Library along with all the other content you want on the device, you don't need iTunes Match because you can use the sync process to store your music on the device. However, if you have a lot of music from sources other than the iTunes Store in your library, and your iOS device doesn't have enough space to store it all, iTunes Match may be right for you.

NOTE iTunes Match music is delivered in the Advanced Audio Coding (AAC) format encoded at 256kbps. If music in your iTunes Library is not already in this format, a temporary version in this format is created and then uploaded to the cloud. This format may actually be higher quality than the music that is permanently stored in your iTunes Library.

There are two basic steps to enabling iTunes Match. Step one is to activate iTunes Match for your iCloud account and enable it in iTunes on at least one computer; this puts your music in the cloud. Step two is to configure your devices to use iTunes Match.

When you have completed these two steps, you can use iTunes Match to download and listen to any of your music on your devices at any time.

Setting Up iTunes Match in iTunes on Computers

To get started with iTunes Match, you need to add the iTunes Match service to your iCloud account. Then iTunes Match configures your cloud with the music in the iTunes Library on the computer you use.

You can configure other computers to use iTunes Match so that you can download your music to iTunes on those computers too.

You can also use iTunes to manage your iTunes Match music.

Adding iTunes Match to Your iCloud Account

To add the iTunes Match to your iCloud account, perform the following steps:

1. In iTunes on a computer, choose **Store**, **Turn On iTunes Match**. You move to the iTunes Match screen.

2. Click **Subscribe for $24.99 Per Year** (see Figure 12.2).

FIGURE 12.2

To enable iTunes Match, click the Subscribe button.

3. Enter your Apple ID (if the correct one isn't entered for you automatically) and password.

4. Click **Subscribe**.

5. Follow the onscreen instructions to review or update your payment or other information as required.

   iTunes Match starts the upload process, which has three steps. During step 1, iTunes collects information about your iTunes Library. During step 2, iTunes matches songs in your library with those available in the iTunes Store; these songs immediately become available in the cloud to download or stream on your devices.

   During step 3, iTunes uploads songs in your library that aren't in the iTunes Store; this part of the process can take a while depending on the number of songs involved. You can use iTunes for other things during this process. When the process is complete, you see how many songs are available to you in the cloud.

 NOTE The music in your iTunes Library falls into one of two categories. One is that the music is available in the iTunes Store; any music that falls into this category is immediately available on the cloud whether you purchased it in the iTunes Store or not. The other possibility is that the music is not available in the iTunes Store; in this situation, the music is uploaded to the cloud from your computer.

6. If you are prompted when the process is complete, click **Done**. Your music is in the cloud and ready for you to listen to it from any of your devices. In iTunes, you see the cloud icon next to the Source selection menu indicating that iTunes has connected to iTunes Match (see Figure 12.3).

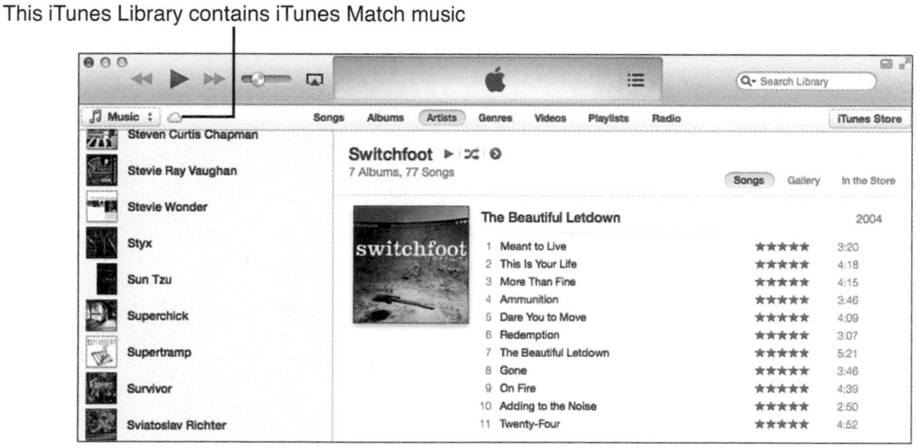

This iTunes Library contains iTunes Match music

FIGURE 12.3

The cloud icon indicates that iTunes is using iTunes Match.

 NOTE iTunes Match uploads up to 25,000 songs, not counting those you have purchased from the iTunes Store. Song files over 200MB won't be uploaded to the cloud. Songs protected with Digital Rights Management (DRM) won't be uploaded unless your computer is authorized to play those songs.

Adding a Computer to iTunes Match

To be able to access your cloud music from a computer, configure iTunes Match in iTunes by performing the following steps:

1. In iTunes, log in to the iTunes Store by clicking the **iTunes Store** button and sign in using the Apple ID for which you enabled iTunes Match (you might be signed in already, in which case you can move to step 2). If a different Apple ID than the one you are using for iTunes Match is shown in the upper-left corner of the iTunes Store screen, click the account shown and click **Sign Out**. Then click **Sign In** and sign in again using the **Apple ID** for which iTunes Match is enabled.

2. Choose **Store, Turn On iTunes Match**.

3. Click **Add This Computer** (see Figure 12.4).

FIGURE 12.4

Enabling iTunes Match in iTunes on a computer enables it to join the cloud.

4. Enter your account's password.

5. Click **Add This Computer**. iTunes starts the three-step iTunes Match process. Any music that is in the current computer's iTunes Library but isn't in the cloud is added to your music collection on the cloud. If this computer doesn't have much music stored on it, the process is completed fairly quickly.

6. When the process is completed, click **Done** (see Figure 12.5). You're ready to listen to music from the cloud.

FIGURE 12.5

This computer can access music on the cloud.

Managing iTunes Match in iTunes

The following are some tips to help you manage iTunes Match:

- If you add new music to your library, such as importing a CD, you can manually refresh your music on the cloud by choosing **Store**, **Update iTunes Match**. iTunes Match goes through the three-step process again, which adds any new music in your iTunes Library to the cloud.

 NOTE   Periodically, iTunes Match automatically scans your iTunes Library and adds new music to the cloud so that you don't need to refresh it manually. If you want the new music to be available on the cloud immediately, manually refreshing it makes it so.

- When iTunes Match is active, icons next to songs indicate their status. When you don't see any icon in this column, it means the song is available on the computer. The **Download** button indicates that the song is available on the cloud and can be downloaded and streamed (see Figure 12.6). A cloud with a slash through it indicates the song isn't eligible for iTunes Match for some reason; for example, digital booklets that you get with some music can't be added to the cloud. A cloud with an exclamation point means there was an error uploading the song; use the **Update iTunes Match** command to try to fix the problem. Two clouds with a slash through them indicates a duplicate; duplicates are not uploaded to the cloud.

FIGURE 12.6

Songs with the Download button are available on the cloud.

- If you want to stop using iTunes Match, choose **Store, Turn Off iTunes Match**. Your music remains on the cloud, but the music in the iTunes Library is no longer matched, nor can you download any music from the cloud.

- To reenable iTunes Match, choose **Store, Turn On iTunes Match**. You move back to the iTunes Match screen. Click **Add This Computer** and complete the sign-in process. iTunes Match goes through the three-step process of matching music again.

Setting Up iTunes Match on iPads, iPhones, or iPod touches

Set up an iOS device to use iTunes Match by completing the following steps:

1. Tap **Settings**. The Settings app opens.

2. Tap **Music**.

3. Set the **iTunes Match** switch to ON.

4. Tap **Enable** at the prompt explaining that the music content on the device will be replaced.

5. If you want all the music available to you to be shown in the device, set **Show All Music** to ON as shown in Figure 12.7; if you set this to OFF, only music that has been downloaded to the device is shown. The music available in the cloud is available in the Music app.

Settings	Music	
Maps		
Safari	Sound Check	OFF
	EQ	Off >
iTunes & App Stores	Volume Limit	Off >
Music	Group By Album Artist	ON
Videos		
Photos & Camera	iTunes Match	ON
iBooks	Show All Music	ON
Podcasts	All music that has been downloaded or that is stored in iCloud will be shown.	
	Home Sharing	
Twitter	Apple ID: bradmacosx@mac.com	
Facebook		

FIGURE 12.7

This iPad is ready to use iTunes Match.

 TIP To configure an Apple TV to access your iTunes Match music, open the Settings screen, choose iTunes Store, and sign in to the account for which iTunes Match is enabled. Turn on iTunes Match. When you want to listen to music, choose the Music option on the main menu, and you can listen to any music on the cloud.

Listening to iTunes Match Music

When iTunes Match is enabled on a device, you can use it to download and listen to music from the cloud. You do this with iTunes on a computer or the Music app on iOS devices.

Listening to Your iTunes Match Music on a Computer

Listening to music from the cloud on a computer is a snap. In iTunes, browse and find music as you normally would. Do any of the following to listen to music:

• If songs aren't marked with an icon, they are stored on the computer already and are ready to play whether the computer is connected to the Internet or not.

- Songs marked with the Download button are available on the cloud. To play a song without downloading it, select and play the song as you normally would. The song plays via streaming from the Internet, but is not stored on the computer. The next time you play it, it plays via streaming again. The computer has to be connected to the Internet to stream music.

- To download a song, click its cloud icon. The song is downloaded to the computer and stored in the iTunes Library. You can play it without being connected to the Internet.

- Likewise, album covers without the Download icon are stored on your computer. Those marked with the Download icon (in the upper-right corner) are available on the cloud (see Figure 12.8). You can download albums by clicking their Download icons; you see this in various views, such as when you are viewing your music by Album.

FIGURE 12.8

You can download an entire album by clicking its Download button.

Listening to Your iTunes Match Music on an iOS Device

Listening to iTunes Match music on an iOS device is similar to listening to music available on the device through the iTunes sync process with one exception. That is, if the music is not currently stored on the device, it has to be downloaded before it can be played. Fortunately, it can stream so that it plays while it downloads, causing little delay in the music starting even if it isn't currently stored on the device. Working with iTunes Match music in the Music app is covered in detail in Chapter 15, "Listening to Music with the Music App."

 NOTE Be aware that when you use iTunes Match on an iOS device, it must have an Internet connection to be able to stream and download music. If the device doesn't have a connection (or using iTunes over a cellular network has been disabled and that is the only type of network available), you can listen only to music that is currently stored on the device. (If the Show All Music setting is enabled, you can still see music, even though you can't download and play it). When you aren't going to be able to connect to a network for a while, make sure before you disconnect from the network that you've downloaded all the music you want to be able to listen to.

THE ABSOLUTE MINIMUM

In this chapter, you learned how iTunes Match can put your music on the cloud so that you can listen to it on any of your devices. The topics included the following:

- iTunes Match stores all the music in your iTunes Library on the cloud so that you can download and listen to that music on multiple devices, including Macs, Windows PCs, iPhones, iPads, iPod touches, and Apple TVs. Once configured, iTunes Match works automatically so that you don't have to worry about syncing music; you can just choose the music you want to hear and iTunes Match takes care of the rest for you.

- To use iTunes Match, add it to your iCloud account. Then configure it and manage it on each of your computers.

- You use the Music Settings on an iOS device to enable iTunes Match. Music on the cloud becomes available in the Music app.

- When iTunes Match is enabled, you can listen to your music on computers and iOS devices. Playing iTunes Match music is similar to playing music stored on a device.

13

DOWNLOADING CONTENT ONTO IPADS, IPHONES, OR IPOD TOUCHES

One of the reasons that iOS devices—iPads, iPhones, and iPod touches—are so useful is because of all the great apps you can use for entertainment, such as music, movies, and TV shows, and also to work with documents such as text documents or presentations. To be able to access the content you want to work with, you must have the content stored on your device (except for content that is available via the cloud, such as music you can get through iTunes Match). You also must have the app related to the activity you want to do. For example, to use the Pandora music streaming service, you must have the Pandora app installed on your device.

In this chapter, you learn how to use the iTunes app to download music, movies, and TV shows onto your iOS device. You also learn about the App Store app that you can use to download apps onto your device. This chapter also covers downloading content from other sources so that you can add it to your device by syncing it with iTunes (which is covered in detail in the next chapter).

CONNECTION REQUIRED

To use the various apps covered in this chapter (or any app for that matter) to download content, your device must be connected to the Internet. All iOS devices can connect to the Internet through Wi-Fi networks; iPhones and some iPad models can also use cellular data networks. You need to be aware of the type of Internet connection you have because some of the content you download comes in large files, such as music and movies.

Most cellular data plans have a limit on how much data you can download each month. If you exceed this amount, you are usually charged a large overage fee. If your data plan has a limit, you should ensure that your iOS device is configured so that it downloads music and video content only when it is connected to a Wi-Fi network. To do this on an iPhone, tap the **Settings** app, and then tap **General**, **Cellular**; on the Cellular screen, slide the iTunes switch to **OFF**. To do this on an iPad, tap the **Settings** app, and then tap **Cellular Data**; on the Cellular Data screen, slide the iTunes switch to **OFF**. With this setting off, the iTunes app downloads content only when you have a Wi-Fi connection, thus avoiding the chance of exceeding your data limit because of downloading iTunes content.

Setting iTunes and App Store Preferences

One of the great things about music, apps, and books that you download through iTunes, the App Store, and iBooks is that you can configure your devices so that any time you download new content, it is downloaded to all your devices automatically. For example, you can download an album onto your iPhone and it is also downloaded to your iPad and into your iTunes Library on your computer automatically. To ensure your content is downloaded onto all your iOS devices automatically, perform the following steps on each device:

1. Tap the **Settings** app.

2. Tap **iTunes & App Stores**.

3. Set the **Music**, **Apps**, and **Books** switches to **ON** (as shown in Figure 13.1).

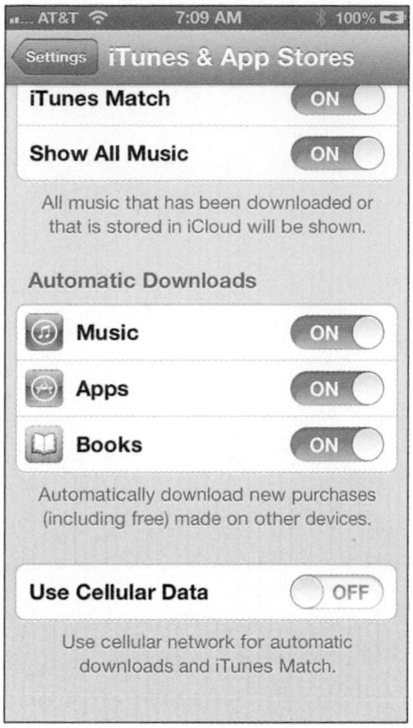

FIGURE 13.1

When the Automatic Downloads switches are in the ON position, any content you download from the iTunes or App Stores is downloaded to the device automatically.

4. If the device is able to connect to a cellular network and your data plan has a limit on the amount of data you can download per month (see the previous sidebar), set the **Use Cellular Data** switch to **OFF**.

 TIP   To configure iTunes on a computer to automatically download content, open Preferences and click the **Store** tab. Ensure that the **Music**, **Apps**, and **Books** check boxes are checked and then click **OK**. Anytime you download content from iTunes, the App Store, or iBookstore on any device, it will be added to your iTunes Library, too.

Using the iTunes App to Download Music

The iTunes app enables you to download music, movies, TV shows, and audiobooks onto your iOS device. (If you've configured the automatic settings described in the previous section, any music you download is also downloaded to your other devices automatically.) If you have used iTunes on a computer to download music from the iTunes Store (see Chapter 3, "Building Your iTunes Library"), you will see that using the iTunes app is similar.

You can find content to download in two basic ways: by browsing or by searching. After you've found music you are interested in, you can preview it to decide if it is for you. If you want to add the music to your music library, downloading it is a snap.

 NOTE The figures in this section show the iTunes app on an iPad mini. Using the iTunes app on iPhones/iPod touches or iPads is similar, except the amount of screen space differs. On iPhones/iPod touches, the smaller screen size means that some of the options are a bit hidden. You'll read about significant differences in the text so that you can follow the steps on one of these devices just as easily. You might notice very minor differences, but these differences won't cause you any trouble as you follow along with these steps. For example, when you view the contents of an album on an iPhone/iPod touch, you won't see the Popularity column that you see on an iPad.

To get started with the iTunes app, move to the Home screen and tap the **iTunes** icon. If it isn't highlighted already, tap the **Music** button on the toolbar at the bottom of the screen. On the toolbar, you choose how you want to look for content by tapping one of the following buttons (see Figure 13.2):

- **Music** enables you to download music.

FIGURE 13.2

The iTunes app enables you to download lots of great content directly onto iOS devices, such as this iPad mini.

- **Movies** takes you to movies in the iTunes Store so you can browse, preview, and download them.

- **TV Shows** does the same for TV programming.

- **Audiobooks** provides a catalog of audiobooks that you can download. On iPhones/iPod touches, tap the **More** button to see this option.

- On iPads, you can use the **Top Charts** button to see various charts of "top" content. On iPhones/iPod touches, you tap the **Charts** tab at the top of the screen to do the same.

- On iPhones/iPod touches, you can move to the Tones (ringtones and alerts) Home page by tapping the **More** button and then tapping **Tones**. From there, you can preview and download music and other sounds that you can use for ringtones and alerts on your device.

- **Genius** uses the iTunes genius feature to present content in the store based on compatibility or similarity to content already in your library. To see genius recommendations on an iPhone or iPod touch, tap the **More** button and then tap **Genius**.

- **Purchased** takes you to content you have already downloaded from the store so that you can download it again if needed. On iPhones/iPod touches, tap the **More** button to see this option.

- On iPhones/iPod touches, tap the **More** button and tap **Downloads** to work with content you are downloading from the store.

- **Search** enables you to search for specific content in the store. On an iPad, the Search tool appears in the upper-right corner of the screen, whereas on iPhones/iPod touches, you see the Search button on the toolbar at the bottom of the screen.

The general steps to download music using the iTunes app on an iOS device are similar to those for downloading it using iTunes on a computer:

1. Find content of interest to you. You can do this by browsing or searching.

2. Preview content.

3. Download content you want to add to your library.

4. Manage the download process as needed.

Each of these general steps is explained in the following sections.

Browsing for Music with the iTunes App

Browsing for music in the iTunes Store can be fun, and it can be a great way to discover music that might not be familiar to you. One of the good things about browsing is that it is really easy to do because just about everything you see on the iTunes app's screen is "tappable," which means you can move to groups of content or specific content by tapping its icon. There are lots of ways to choose the content you want to browse. For example, you can use the Genre option to browse music by genre, you can use the Charts tools to browse music by various charts, or use the Genius feature to browse music based on its similarity to music you already have in your library.

The downside of browsing is that it can take a while to get to content you want to download. If you have some idea about music you want, searching for it is much more efficient.

The following steps show you how to browse music by genre (using one of the other options is similar):

1.   In the iTunes app, tap the **Music** button if it isn't selected already.

 TIP   If you want to browse the Pop or Rock genre on an iPad, tap **Pop** or **Rock** instead of the More button in step 2, and then skip to step 5.

2.   On an iPad, tap the **More** button at the top of the screen; on an iPhone/iPod touch, tap the **Genres** button. You see a list of the genres available in the store.

3.   Swipe up and down the genre list to browse all the genres available (see Figure 13.3).

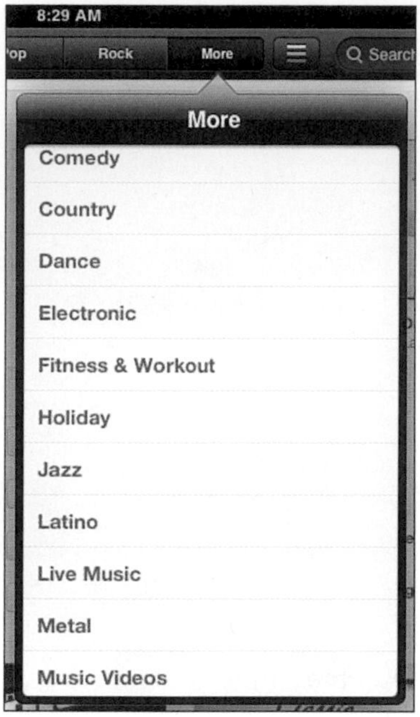

FIGURE 13.3

Here you see some of the music genres available in the iTunes Store.

4. Tap the genre that you want to browse. The genre's Home page appears (see Figure 13.4).

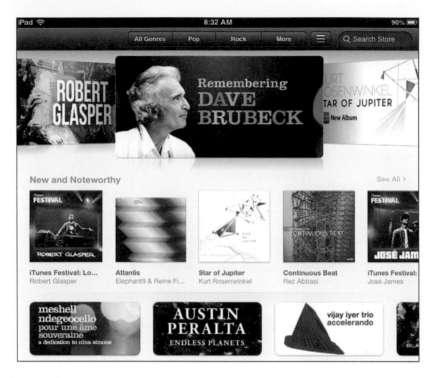

FIGURE 13.4

When you select a genre to browse, you move its Home page.

5. Swipe around the screen to browse the various categories and albums available to you.

6. Tap an item of interest to you. If you tap an artist, you move into the collection of music from that artist. If you tapped a group of some type, such as a music related to a theme, you see the albums or songs in that grouping. If you tapped an album, you see the album's content and can skip to step 9.

7. Browse the group's page by swiping around the screen.

8. When you get to an album you want to explore, tap its cover.

9. Swipe up and down the album's screen to see its tracks and other information (see Figure 13.5).

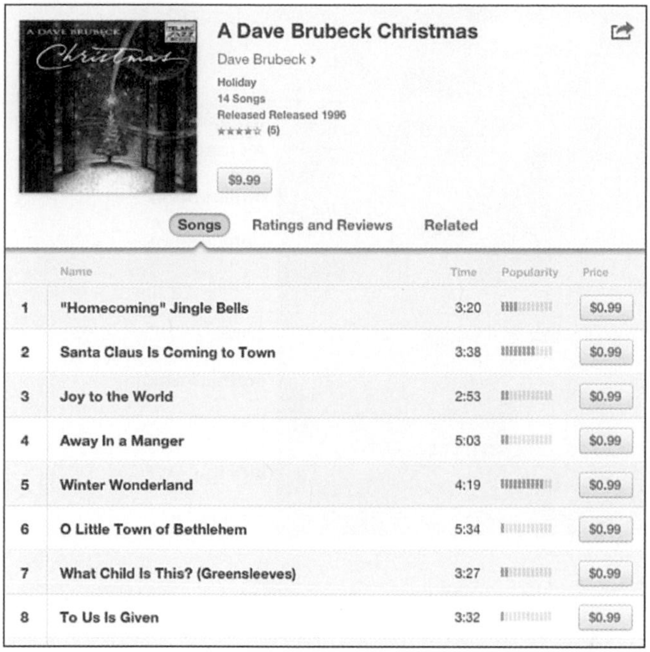
A Dave Brubeck Christmas
Dave Brubeck ›
Holiday
14 Songs
Released Released 1996
(5)
$9.99
Songs
Ratings and Reviews
Related
Name
Time
Popularity
Price
1 "Homecoming" Jingle Bells 3:20 $0.99
2 Santa Claus Is Coming to Town 3:38 $0.99
3 Joy to the World 2:53 $0.99
4 Away In a Manger 5:03 $0.99
5 Winter Wonderland 4:19 $0.99
6 O Little Town of Bethlehem 5:34 $0.99
7 What Child Is This? (Greensleeves) 3:27 $0.99
8 To Us Is Given 3:32 $0.99

FIGURE 13.5

An album's page enables you to explore its content.

10. Preview the album's tracks and review its information (see the section, "Previewing and Downloading Music with the iTunes App").

Searching for Music with the iTunes App

If you have some idea about the music you want, searching is a more efficient way to find it. You can search for artists, songs, and so on. Here's how:

1. In the iTunes app on an iPad, tap in the Search Store box located in the upper-right corner of the screen and skip to step 3; on an iPhone/iPod touch, tap the Search button in the toolbar.

2. Tap in the Search bar.

3. Type a search criterion, such as an artist's name or song title. As you type, content that matches your search appears under the Search bar (see Figure 13.6). The first line of the results shows you what you are searching for.

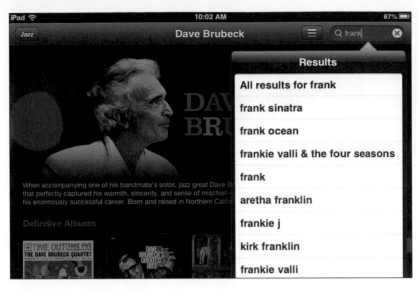

FIGURE 13.6

Here I'm searching for music associated with "frank."

4. When you see something of interest on the results list, tap it. For example, tap an artist's name. You see a list of content related to your search, organized by albums or songs.

5. Swipe up, down, right, and left to browse the search results, which are organized into categories, such as Albums, Songs, Ringtones, Music Videos, and so on (see Figure 13.7).

FIGURE 13.7

I tapped on Frank Sinatra on the results list shown in Figure 13.6; here you see the results of that search.

6. To explore the contents of an album, tap it. When you tap an album, at the top of the screen you see the album's general information, such as when it was released and how many songs it contains. In the lower part of the window, you see the tracks on that album.

 NOTE If you tap a different kind of content, such as a music video, you see options appropriate for that type.

7. Swipe up and down the album's screen to see its tracks and other information (refer back to Figure 13.5).

8. Preview the album's tracks and review its information (see the next section).

The iTunes app remembers your search so it will still be there the next time you work with the Search tool. To remove a search, tap the Clear button (**x**).

Previewing and Downloading Music with the iTunes App

You can preview any song or music video in the store to help you decide if you want to add it to your collection. On an album's screen (see Figure 13.8), you can also get information about the music, such as its description and reviews from other people. On an album's screen, you can do the following:

Nothing But the Best (The Frank Sinat... ↗

Frank Sinatra ›

Vocal
25 Items
Released May 12, 2008
★★★★★ (107)

$14.99

Songs   Ratings and Reviews   Related

	Name	Time	Popularity	Price
⏹	Come Fly With Me	3:13	▮▮▯▯▯▯▯▯▯▯	$1.29
2	The Best Is Yet to Come (With Count Basie and His ...	2:55	▮▮▮▮▯▯▯▯▯▯	$1.29
3	The Way You Look Tonight	3:22	▮▮▮▮▯▯▯▯▯▯	$1.29
4	Luck Be a Lady	5:14	▮▮▯▯▯▯▯▯▯▯	$1.29
5	Bewitched	2:59	▮▮▮▯▯▯▯▯▯▯	$1.29
6	The Good Life (With Count Basie and His Orchestra)	2:27	▮▮▯▯▯▯▯▯▯▯	$1.29
7	The Girl from Ipanema (With Antonio Carlos Jobim)	3:14	▮▮▮▯▯▯▯▯▯▯	$1.29
8	Fly Me to the Moon (In Other Words)	2:27	▮▮▯▯▯▯▯▯▯▯	$1.29

FIGURE 13.8

Here, you see that I'm previewing the song, "Come Fly with Me."

- **Preview a song**—Tap the number of the track in the first column. A preview plays; the length of the preview depends on the content you tapped. Most previews are between 30 and 90 seconds. While a song plays, the Stop button replaces the track number; the amount of the circle around that button that fills with blue indicates how much of the preview has played. You can tap the Stop button to stop the preview.

- **Read reviews**—Tap the **Ratings and Reviews** tab on an iPad or the **Reviews** tab on an iPhone/iPod touch. Swipe up and down the screen to read all the review information. At the top, you see an overview of the reviews, indicated by the star ratings. Toward the bottom of the screen, you can read the individual reviews.

- **Add your own review**—Tap **Write a Review**. Complete the resulting form, which requires you to sign in to your iTunes Store account, to record your feedback.

- **Browse related content**—Tap the **Related** tab to see content that is "related to" the content you are exploring. This shows you more content by the same artist, content that was purchased by people who downloaded the content you are browsing, and so on. You can tap content on this tab to explore it.

- **Share your interests**—Tap the **Share** button (see Figure 13.9) at the top of iTunes screens to share the content you are exploring. You can share by email, message, Twitter, and Facebook. The messages you send contain a link to the item you are viewing. You can tap **Copy Link** to copy the item's link to the Clipboard, which you can use to paste the link into other areas, such as a document. You can tap **Gift** to send a link to someone that enables them to download the music (you must pay for it, of course).

- **Buy an album or song**—To purchase and download an album, tap the button showing the item's price at the top of the album's screen. To buy a song on any screen, tap its Price button. The Price button becomes the BUY button (see Figure 13.9). Tap the **BUY** button. If prompted to do so, enter your Apple ID password and tap OK. The album or song starts to download to your device.

FIGURE 13.9

When you are ready to add an album or song to your library, tap its Buy button.

- **Monitor downloads**—You can monitor the downloads on an iPad by tapping the **Downloads** button that appears on the toolbar while content is downloading; the badge on the button indicates the number of items to be downloaded. You can do the same on an iPhone/iPod touch by tapping the **More** button (its badge indicates how many items are downloading) and then tapping **Downloads**. On the resulting screen, you see the status of each item being downloaded (see Figure 13.10). You can pause a download by tapping its **Pause** button. When the process is complete, the Downloads screen becomes empty. This indicates that the music you purchased has been added to the device and is available for your listening enjoyment. By the way, monitoring downloads is optional, the process works just as well if you don't monitor it. In fact, you can keeping shopping in the iTunes Store while content downloads, if you like.

FIGURE 13.10

While you are downloading content, you can use the Downloads tab to monitor the progress of the download process.

 NOTE The BUY button changes to reflect the status of an item. For example, when you are downloading it, the button reflects that it is being downloaded. After a song has been downloaded to your device, the BUY button is replaced by the PLAY button.

- **Move off an album screen**—To close an album's screen, tap the **Done** button. You return to your previous location, such as the search results screen.

- **Move from Song to Album**—When you browse a list of songs, tap a song twice to move to the album that the song comes from.

- **Go back in time**—You can view a list of content you have previewed by tapping the **History** button (which looks like a list and is located to the left of the Search tool on an iPad or just under the battery icon on an iPhone/iPod touch). You can preview one of these items by tapping its art. You can return to the source of the item (such as the album a song comes from) by tapping its title. If you haven't purchased the item, you can tap its Price button to download it. To clear your history list, tap **Clear**, and then tap **Clear History**. To close the History screen, tap **Done**.

- **Moving downloaded content onto other devices**—If you've configured each device for automatic downloads, this is done automatically. If not, you can download purchased content onto a different device, as explained in the next section. The next time you sync the device with iTunes on a computer, purchased content will be moved from the device into your iTunes Library if it wasn't downloaded there automatically.

 TIP When you are viewing album information on an iPad, swipe to the left or the right above or below the album screen to move to the next or previous album in the group, respectively. Tap a cover to view an album's details.

Managing Purchased Music with the iTunes App

You can manually download music you have purchased in the iTunes Store on another device or redownload music on a device if something happens to that music (such as the device's memory being erased). For example, suppose you downloaded music on your computer before you had your iPad set up to automatically download purchases. You can use the iTunes app to download that content. Doing this on an iPad is a bit different from doing it on an iPhone/iPod touch.

To manage purchased content on an iPad, tap the **Purchased** button on the iTunes app's toolbar. Tap the **Not on This iPad** tab. You see a list of all the content you've downloaded that is not currently on the device.

You can choose how the list is organized by tapping the drop-down list in the upper-right corner of the screen and choosing Songs by Name, Albums by Name, and so on. The list of content is reorganized according to your selection. You can swipe up or down the list to browse its contents. When you see something of interest, tap it. Its content appears in the right part of the window. For example, if you tap an artist, all the music by the artist that you have purchased but that is not currently stored on the device is shown (see Figure 13.11). To download the content, tap its **Download** button, which is the cloud with an download arrow on it. You can download all the content by an artist by tapping the **Download All** button at the top of the list. The content is downloaded to the device, but you aren't charged for it.

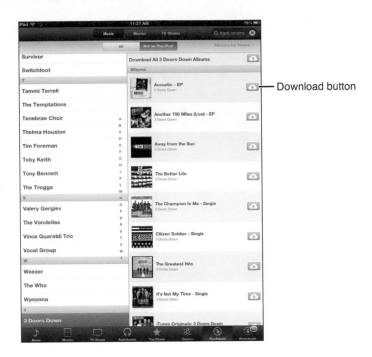

FIGURE 13.11

Tap the Download button to download content that you've previously purchased from the iTunes Store onto a device.

On an iPhone/iPod touch, tap the **More** button on the toolbar and then tap **Purchased** followed by **Music**. Tap **Not on This *Device***, where *Device* is the type of device you are using. You see a list of the available music for download, organized by artist name. Tap an artist. You see the music available for download from that artist. Tap an item's **Download** button to download it to the device.

Using the iTunes App to Download Movies and TV Shows

You can use the iTunes app to download movies and TV shows just as easily as you can for music. The screens look a bit different, but the process is similar. The following are the highlights:

1. Tap the **Movies** or **TV Shows** button. You move to the Home page for the type of content you selected.

2. Use the browse or search techniques you learned for music to locate content in which you are interested. For example, the screen in Figure 13.12 shows the screen for Season 4 of the TV series *Star Trek*: "Deep Space Nine."

FIGURE 13.12

You can preview and download any episode in a TV show's season or the entire season.

3. Preview content by tapping its **Play** button. If you are viewing a TV show, you see a preview in the Videos app. For a movie, you can watch trailers and teasers.

 NOTE   If your device's memory is full or nearly full, you might not have the space to be able to store content on it, especially movies because they are large files. To see how much space is available on an iOS device, open the **Settings** app and tap **General**. Tap **About**. The amount shown in the Available row is how much room you have on the device to add more content. If this amount is small, you might need to delete some content before you add more.

4. To download content, tap its price button, and then tap the **BUY** button. This process works the same as it does in music. If you are downloading a movie or a TV show, you might have the option to buy or rent the movie and choose from different quality options (such as HD). Like other tasks, you are prompted to sign in to your iTunes account as needed.

5. Monitor the download process. Video files are much larger than audio files, so downloading them takes quite a bit longer. You can use your device for other tasks while the content is downloading.

 NOTE   Movies that you rent from the iTunes Store have more limitations than other types of content. For instance, rented content can be on only one device at a time. In addition, rented content expires and is automatically deleted from your device either 30 days after you have downloaded it or 24 hours (48 outside of the United States) after you have started watching it.

Using the App Store App to Download Apps

The App Store, which is an app in itself, enables you to find apps and download them directly onto your iOS device. The App Store app works similarly to the iTunes app. For example, you can browse apps by different categories or search for specific apps. Tap **App Store** on the Home screen to get started.

Like the iTunes app, there are buttons on the toolbar at the bottom of the screen and at the top of the screen. These include the following:

- **Featured**—This button takes you to apps featured in the App Store. This screen organizes apps in several categories. New and Noteworthy shows you apps that are new to the store. What's Hot lists apps that have been downloaded frequently.

- **Top Charts**—This option takes you to lists of the top apps. This screen has three options: Paid shows you the top apps for which you have to pay a license fee. Free shows you a similar list containing only free apps; and Top Grossing shows the apps that have been downloaded the most (rather than those that have made the most money).

- **Genius**—The Genius option locates apps for you based on apps that you have already downloaded. The idea is that if you downloaded one kind of app, you'll probably be interested in other apps of that type. This works similarly to the Genius feature for music.

- **Search**—On an iPad, the Search field is located in the upper-right corner of the screen. On an iPhone/iPod touch, the Search button is located on the toolbar. In either location, this tool enables you to search for apps. You can search by name, developer, and other text.

- **Purchased**—This button, located on the toolbar on an iPad or on the Updates screen on an iPhone/iPod touch, enables you to download apps you have previously downloaded from the App Store on the same or a different device. This feature works just like downloading music you have downloaded previously.

- **Updates**—Use this to update apps stored on your device. It is explained later in this chapter in the section, "Managing Apps with the App Store App."

- **Categories**—On an iPad, you see category tabs at the top of the screen; these are All Categories, which shows you all apps; Games, which takes you to games; Education, which takes you to educational apps; and More, which shows the list of all other categories. On an iPhone/iPod touch, you can use the Categories button at the top of the screen to see the category list. In all cases, when you select a category, the apps you see are those associated with the category you selected.

Downloading Apps with the App Store App

Because you know how to use the iTunes app, you also know how to use the App Store app. A quick example will confirm this. These steps show you how to browse by categories to find and download the Remote app so that you can remotely control iTunes on a computer (which will be explained in Chapter 15, "Listening to Music with the Music App"):

1. On an iPad, tap the **More** button at the top of the App Store app's screen; on an iPhone/iPod touch, tap **Categories**.

2. Tap **Entertainment**. You move the Home page for apps in the Entertainment category.

3. Swipe up and down to browse the groupings of apps, such as New and Noteworthy, Essentials, and so on.

 TIP A faster way to get to a specific app is to search for it. Tap in the search tool and type the app's name. Then tap the app on the search results.

4. Tap the **Remote** icon. This may be on its own on the Home page; if not, it is in the Essentials section. You move to the app's Info screen (see Figure 13.13).

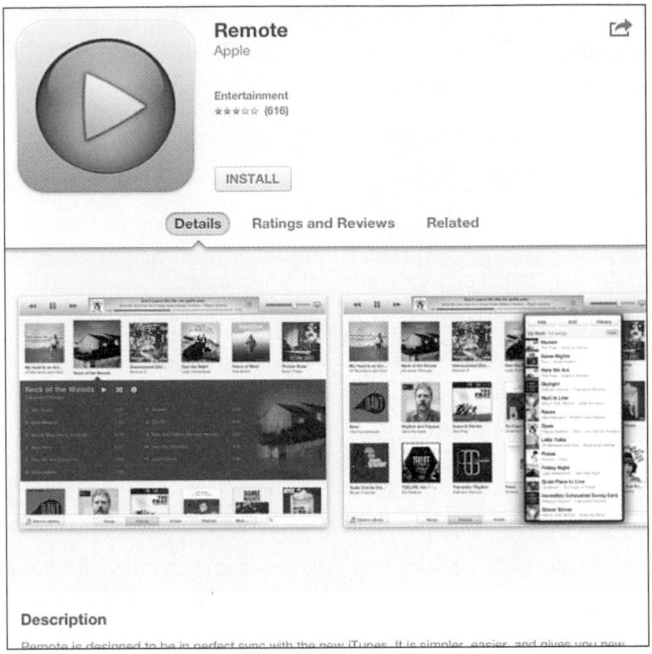

FIGURE 13.13

The Remote app enables you to remotely control iTunes on a computer, which is useful when you are streaming content to other devices via AirPlay (see Chapter 9, "Streaming Music and Video through an AirPlay Network").

5. To explore the app, perform steps 6 through 12; to download it, skip to step 13.

6. Review the name, average user rating, and cost (displayed in the app's Download button). If you've downloaded the app before, the DOWNLOAD button will be the INSTALL button. If not, the button will read FREE if it is a free app or will show the app's price if it has a license fee.

7. To read a description, swipe up on the screen.

8. Swipe down on the screen to view the screenshots above the description. If the app is landscape oriented, rotate the device so the screenshots make sense. (Note that the screen you view doesn't reorient like most screens do, but at least the screenshots themselves look better.)

9. Swipe on the screenshots to see them all.

10. Tap **Ratings and Reviews** (iPad) or **Reviews** (iPhone/iPod touch). (If you've rotated the device, you'll want to move it back to the Portrait orientation.)

TIP   To let someone else know about the app, tap the **Share** button and then tap how you want to let them know, such as Mail, Messages, Twitter, and so on.

11. Read the user reviews for the app; you'll have to swipe up to see them all.

12. Tap the **Details** tab.

13. Tap the Download button. Tap **FREE** if it is a free app, or tap the price to download the app if it has a license fee. The button then becomes INSTALL APP, if it is a free app, or BUY APP, if it has a license fee. If the Download button was INSTALL, the app is immediately downloaded and installed, and you can skip steps 14 and 15.

14. Tap **INSTALL APP** or **BUY APP**.

15. If prompted to do so, enter your Apple ID password and tap **OK**.

You can see the progress of the process in the app's icon and the Installing status message. You don't have to wait for the app to download. You can start the process and then use your device normally. When an app is being installed, you see its icon and status on the Home screen.

When the process is complete, in the App Store app the status information is replaced by the Open button; tap **Open** to launch the app.

When the installation is complete, on the Home screen, you see the app's icon marked with the New banner to show you that you haven't opened it before, and it is ready for you to use.

 TIP   After you install a new app, move to the Settings screen and look for the app's icon. If it is there, the app has additional settings you can use to configure the way it works. Tap the app's icon and use its Settings screen to configure it.

Managing Apps with the App Store App

iOS apps are regularly updated to fix bugs or add features and enhancements. When updates are available for apps installed on your device, the badge on the App Store icon indicates how many updates for your installed apps are available. To update your apps, perform the following steps:

1. In the App Store app, tap **Updates**. The number of apps for which updates are available is shown in the badge the Updates tab. On the Updates screen, you see all the installed apps for which an update is available (see Figure 13.14).

FIGURE 13.14

You should update your apps to benefit from bug fixes and new features.

2. If many updates are available, swipe up and down the screen to see them.

 TIP To download and install all available updates, tap **Update All** in the upper-left corner of the Updates screen.

3. Tap the **More** (iPads) or **What's New** (iPhone/iPod touch) for an app.

4. Read about the update.

5. If the update is free (most are), tap **UPDATE**; otherwise, tap the button showing the price of the update.

6. If prompted to do so, enter your Apple ID password and tap **OK**.

The update process works just like the installation process does. As the update is installed, you see the progress in the app's icon and the Installing status. When complete, the Status button is replaced by the Open button, which you can tap to open the updated app.

If an app or an update to an app is large, to conserve data flow over a cellular connection, your device may have to be connected to a Wi-Fi network before installing the update. If that's the case, you'll be informed via onscreen messages. You'll need to wait until you have a Wi-Fi network to install it.

NOTE You can use the App Store app's Purchased function to redownload apps. On an iPad, tap the **Purchased** button on the toolbar. On an iPhone/iPod touch, tap **Updates** and then tap **Purchased** at the top of the screen. This works just like downloading purchased music.

Downloading Content from Other Sources

Although the iTunes and App Stores offer you lots of content and apps for your iOS device, they are by no means the only sources you might want to use. In most cases, you download content to a computer, add that content to iTunes, and add the content to your iOS device through the sync process. For example, you can download songs from Amazon.com and have those automatically added to your iTunes Library. You can move this music onto your device by syncing music with iTunes. (The details for this specific source are provided in Chapter 3, "Building Your iTunes Library," and Chapter 14, "Synchronizing iTunes Content with an iOS Device.") Likewise, you can add movies that you've converted from DVD to iTunes and then move those movies onto your device through the sync process (also covered in Chapters 3 and 14).

 NOTE Using the iBooks app to download books is described in Chapter 18, "Reading Books with the iBooks App."

THE ABSOLUTE MINIMUM

In this chapter, you learned how to download music, movies, TV shows, and apps onto an iOS device. The highlights were the following:

- You can configure an iOS device to automatically download music, apps, and books through the iTunes & App Store preferences. This ensures that any of the content you download on one device is installed on the others automatically.

- You can use the iTunes app to browse or search for music. You can preview music you are interested in and read what others think of it. Downloading music from the store requires just a couple of taps.

- You can also use the iTunes app to download movies and TV shows. The process is very similar to downloading music. One difference is that movies and TV shows aren't automatically downloaded to other devices. You can redownload them manually on other devices without paying for them again (except for movies you rent, which can be downloaded only once).

- The App Store app enables you to browse and search for apps to download to your iOS device. You can choose from many thousands of apps. Downloading them to your iOS device also requires just a few taps.

- The iTunes and App Stores are the most convenient sources of content because content available there downloads directly onto your iOS devices. However, you can add content from other sources to your device by first adding it to your iTunes Library and then using the sync process to add it to your iOS devices.

14

SYNCHRONIZING ITUNES CONTENT WITH IOS DEVICES

In Chapter 13, "Downloading Content onto iPads, iPhones, or iPod touches," you learned how to download music, movies, TV shows, and apps directly onto iOS devices using the iTunes and App Store apps. However, you may have content in your iTunes Library on your computer that isn't available in the iTunes or App Stores. For example, you may have music that you've imported into iTunes from audio CDs or movies that you've converted from DVD. To get this type of content onto an iOS device, you can sync the device with your iTunes Library.

Understanding the Sync Process

During the sync process, iTunes moves content that you designate from the iTunes Library on your computer onto the iOS device. Likewise, content that is on the iOS device but not currently in the iTunes Library is moved into the iTunes Library on your computer. So, the sync process moves content in both "directions."

Syncing can be done by connecting an iOS device directly to a computer using a USB cable, or it can be done wirelessly over a Wi-Fi network.

To be able to sync content, that content must be stored in the iTunes Library. You then use iTunes Sync settings to identify the specific content that you want to move onto the iOS device. With the sync settings configured, you can sync the iOS device to move content onto it.

You need to change the sync settings only when you want to change the content on the iOS device.

 NOTE For information about adding content that you want to sync to your iTunes Library, see Chapter 3, "Building Your iTunes Library."

Configuring Sync Options

When iTunes can communicate with an iOS device (whether it is connected with a USB cable or via a Wi-Fi network), you can use the Sync settings screens to configure the sync options for various types of content, such as Music, Movies, and so on.

To configure sync settings, first connect the iOS device to your computer—the first time you sync, you need to use a USB cable. If you configure the device to allow for Wi-Fi syncing (you learn how in the next section), you can perform subsequent syncs whenever the iOS device and computer are the on the same Wi-Fi network.

To connect an iOS device, plug in the USB connector on its cable to a USB port on the computer. Connect the other end to the Lightning or Dock connector on the bottom of the device. You hear a tone from the device indicating that it is connected, and the charge symbol appears briefly on its screen.

NOTE All iOS devices have a single port on the bottom of their cases. On current-generation iOS devices, this is the Lightning port, which has a small, thin rectangular shape that matches the connector on one end of the USB cable that came with the device. On older iOS devices, this is the Dock port, which is also rectangular but quite a bit longer and wider than the Lightning port. There are technical differences between the two types, but the most significant difference is that it doesn't matter which side is up on the Lightning connector, whereas the Dock connector can be correctly plugged in with the top side "up."

When you connect the iOS device to the computer, iTunes should open automatically; if it doesn't, open it manually. When at least one iOS device is connected to your computer, iTunes has the Sync screen available, which you access by clicking the button that appears. To move to the Sync screen when you have one iOS device connected, click the button labeled with the device's type, such as **iPad**, located just under the Search tool. To move to the Sync screen when you have more than one iOS device connected, click the *X* **Devices** button, where *X* is the number of devices you have connected, and choose the device you want to sync on the list that appears by clicking it (see Figure 14.1).

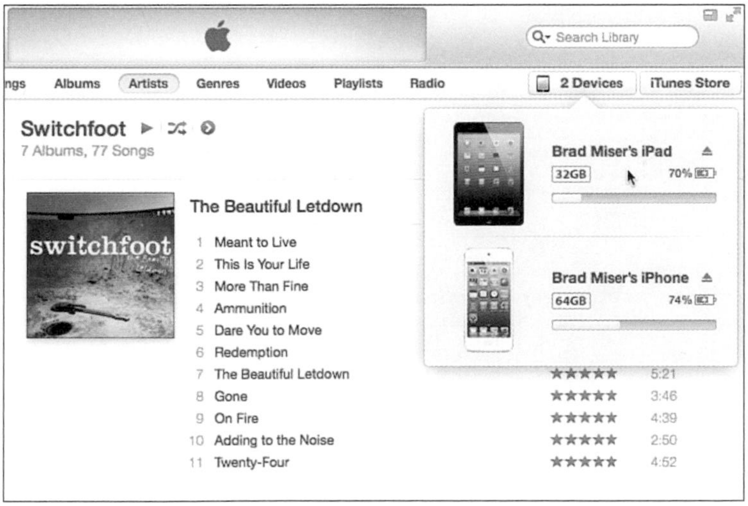

FIGURE 14.1

When you have more than one iOS device connected to your computer, click the Devices button and then click the device that you want to configure.

The Sync screen for the selected device appears. Along the top of the screen, you see the tabs you can use to configure sync settings for various types of content. You're ready to configure each area of the sync process.

Configuring Summary Options

The Summary sync settings are general in nature, meaning they are used to configure options that change how the device works, such as whether it can sync via Wi-Fi, where its information is backed up, and so on. To configure the summary settings, do the following:

1. With the Sync screen open, click the **Summary** tab. Here you set the general sync parameters for the device (see Figure 14.2).

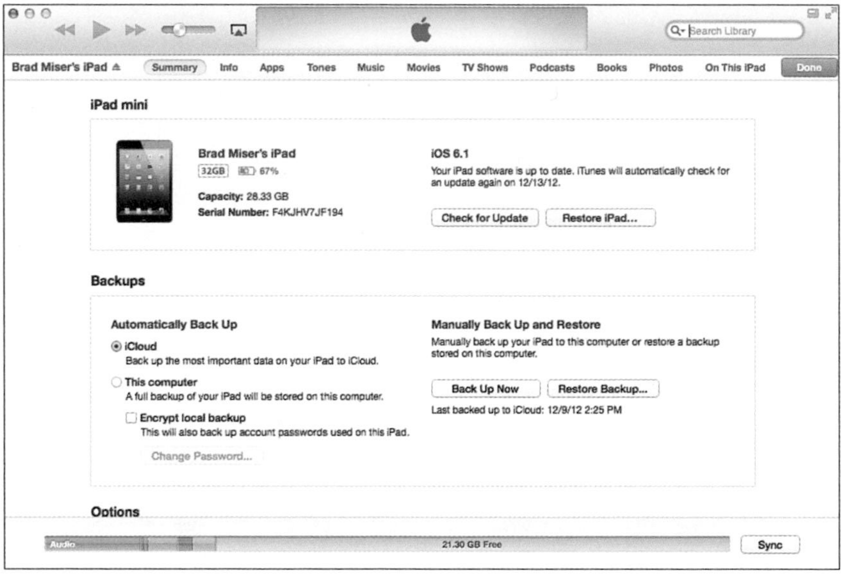

FIGURE 14.2

Use the settings on the Summary tab to configure the general sync settings for a device.

2. If you have an iCloud account configured on the device and want to back up its "important" contents on the cloud, click the **iCloud** radio button. The benefit of using iCloud for backing up is that the device can be backed up anytime it can connect to the Internet. The downsides are that less information is backed up than when you back up to a computer and that you probably have less storage space on the cloud than you do on your computer.

3. If you want to back up to your computer, click the **This computer** radio button. The downsides of backing up to the computer are that the device must be

able to communicate with the computer (using a cable or a Wi-Fi network) to be backed up, and if something happens to all the data on your computer, you could lose your iOS backup too. (Of course, you should always back up the contents of your computer's hard drive so you can recover all its data if a major problem happens.) However, you get a more complete backup with this option.

4. If you back up to your computer and want to protect the backup of your devices' data with encryption, check **Encrypt local backup**, create and verify a password, and click **Set Password**; this password will be required to restore the backed up information onto the device.

> **TIP** You can manually back up the device to the computer by clicking the Back Up Now button (even if you select the iCloud backup option). This stores the device's data on the computer. If you need to recover your data, click **Restore Backup**.

5. Scroll down to the **Options** section (see Figure 14.3).

Options

- ☑ Open iTunes when this iPad is connected
- ☑ Sync with this iPad over Wi-Fi
- ☑ Sync only checked songs and videos
- ☐ Prefer standard definition videos
- ☐ Convert higher bit rate songs to   128 kbps :   AAC
- ☐ Manually manage videos
- [Reset Warnings]
- [Configure Universal Access...]

Audio   22.41 GB Free   [Revert]   [Apply]

FIGURE 14.3

The Options settings include the option to sync over Wi-Fi.

> **NOTE** Because I'm providing information that applies to all iOS devices, I use the generic term "device" in these steps. The actual text on the screen reflects the type of device you are working with. For example, if you are configuring an iPad, the name of the check box in step 6 is **Open iTunes when this iPad is connected**. Also, you see different options for the various types of devices, as explained in the steps.

6. If you are configuring an iPad, ensure that the **Open iTunes when this iPad is connected** check box is checked. This causes iTunes to open every time you connect your device to your computer, which is convenient for syncing purposes.

7. If you are configuring an iPhone or iPod touch, ensure that the **Automatically sync when this Device is connected** check box is checked. Whenever you connect the iPhone to the computer, it is synced.

8. Check **Sync with this Device over Wi-Fi** if you want to be able to sync your device via the Wi-Fi network. This is useful because you don't have to physically connect your device to your computer to sync it. You can enable this option and also connect your device to your computer to sync, so there's really no reason not to allow Wi-Fi syncing.

9. If you don't want content that you have configured iTunes to ignore to be moved onto the device, check the **Sync only checked songs and videos** check box. You configure iTunes to ignore content by unchecking the check boxes next to songs or other content that you want to be ignored. Enabling this sync setting mirrors those selections when it comes to moving the content onto the device because any content whose check box is not checked won't be moved onto the device during the sync process.

10. If you want to move only the standard definition of videos onto the device, check the **Prefer standard definition videos** check box; this saves space because the HD versions are larger files.

11. To cause iTunes to convert songs that have been encoded so they are high quality (larger file sizes) to files that have smaller sizes (so more content fits onto the device), check the **Convert higher bit rate songs to** check box and select the conversion you want to use, such as 128kbps, on the menu. (You aren't likely to hear the difference when playing this content with your device.) This is useful if you've included audio encoded to a higher quality setting to save some storage space on your device. If you've imported audio from CDs using the settings as described in Chapter 3 or downloaded it from the iTunes Store, you don't need to set this because your content is already using an efficient format.

12. If you check the **Manually manage music and videos** check box, you can place content on the device by dragging songs, movies, and other content onto the device. (If you are using iTunes Match, this check box is **Manually manage videos** because you manage all your music through iTunes Match.)

NOTE The Reset Warnings button causes iTunes to reset various warnings that it uses to communicate with you so that any you've told the software not to display again appear on the screen the next time the related event occurs. For example, if you try to sync content that no longer exists on your hard drive, you see a warning message. You can click the Don't show this message again check box so that the same message no longer appears. If you click the Reset Warnings button, it would appear again the next time you try to sync missing content.

13. To apply the settings to the device and sync it, click **Apply**, or if you are going to configure other areas, you can click this button later. (If you've never configured the device before, this button might be Sync instead of Apply; if so, click the **Sync** button). When you have applied the settings to a device, this button becomes the **Sync** button you can click to sync the device. More on this later.

 NOTE The **Configure Universal Access** button takes you to a dialog where you can enable features designed for hearing- or seeing-impaired people. For example, you can enable VoiceOver to cause interface elements to be spoken, change to a black and white display, and so on.

IOS SOFTWARE

At the top of the Summary settings, you see information about the current version of the iOS software the device is running (refer to Figure 14.2). You can see if updates are available by clicking **Check for Update**. If an update is available, you can install it by clicking the **Update** button (which appears instead of the Check for Update button). To "start over" and reinstall the iOS software on the device, click **Restore Device**, where *Device* is the name of the device you are working with.

Configuring Music Syncing

To be able to listen to music with the Music app, you need to have music available to that app. You store music on the device by syncing the music you want to have available. To configure the music that you want on your device, perform the following steps:

NOTE iTunes Match enables you to stream music from the cloud onto an iOS device. If you use iTunes Match, you don't sync music onto the device, so you can skip this section. See Chapter 12, "Streaming Your Music with iTunes Match," to learn how to use this service to stream your music.

1. Click the **Music** tab.

2. Check the **Sync Music** check box.

3. If you have enough room on the device to store all the music content in your library, click the **Entire music library** radio button. Unless you have a relatively small amount of music and other content in your Library, you'll probably need to click the **Selected playlists, artists, albums, and genres** option button instead; this enables you to select specific music to move onto the device. The rest of these steps assume this option is selected. When you select it, the Playlists, Artists, Albums, and Genres selection tools appear.

 TIP As you select music, movies, and other content to move onto your device, the Capacity gauge at the bottom of the iTunes window is updated to show you exactly how much of your device's storage the current sync settings will use. The gauge is segmented by type of content, including audio, video, photos, and so on. If you have more content selected than will fit, the gauge is full, it becomes marked with hash marks, and you see the overcapacity message that shows how much you've gone over the available space. You'll need to remove content from the sync to be sure of the content that will be moved onto the device (if you sync anyway, some of the content won't be moved onto the device or the sync process won't finish).

4. Ensure the **Include music videos** check box is checked if you want music videos in your collection to be moved onto the device.

5. Ensure the **Include voice memos** check box is checked if you use the Voice Memos or other app to record audio notes and want those memos to be moved from the device into your iTunes Library.

6. If you want any free space on the device to be filled with music that iTunes selects, check the **Automatically fill free space with songs** check box.

7. In the Playlists section, expand or collapse a folder to see or hide the playlists it contains by clicking the triangle next to its name (see Figure 14.4).

FIGURE 14.4

Choose the music you want to have on a device by configuring the Music sync settings.

> **NOTE** Each section on the Music tab has its own scrollbar that you can use to browse the content in that section; for example, you can scroll up and down the Artists list. You also can use the iTunes scrollbar to move up and down the tab, which you might need to do to see all its contents.

8. To include a playlist in the sync so that all the items that playlist contains are moved onto the device, check the check box next to it on the Playlists list.

9. To move all the items within a folder of playlists onto the device, check the folder's check box.

10. To move all the songs by specific artists onto the device, check the artist's name on the Artists list.

> **NOTE** When you make changes to the sync settings, the Revert button appears. Click this button to undo any changes to the sync settings that you've made since the last time you synced the device.

11. Click the check box next to each genre whose contents you want to move onto the device. For example, to move all the music in the **Blues** genre, check its check box.

12. Check the check boxes for albums you want to move onto the device.

13. To apply the settings to the device and sync it so the select music is copied onto it, click **Apply,** or if you are going to configure other areas, you can click this button later.

 NOTE You can manually place content, such as songs, movies, and so on, onto a device. When you do this, a section for manually placed content appears at the bottom of the related tab, such as the Music tab, where you see the Manually Added Songs section.

Configuring Movie Syncing

To move your movies onto your device, perform the following steps:

1. Click the **Movies** tab (see Figure 14.5). In the Rented Movies section, you see the movies you are currently renting. (If you don't have any rented movies in your library, you don't see this section.) The rented movies currently stored in your library are shown in the box on the left, whereas the rented movies on the device are shown in the box on the right.

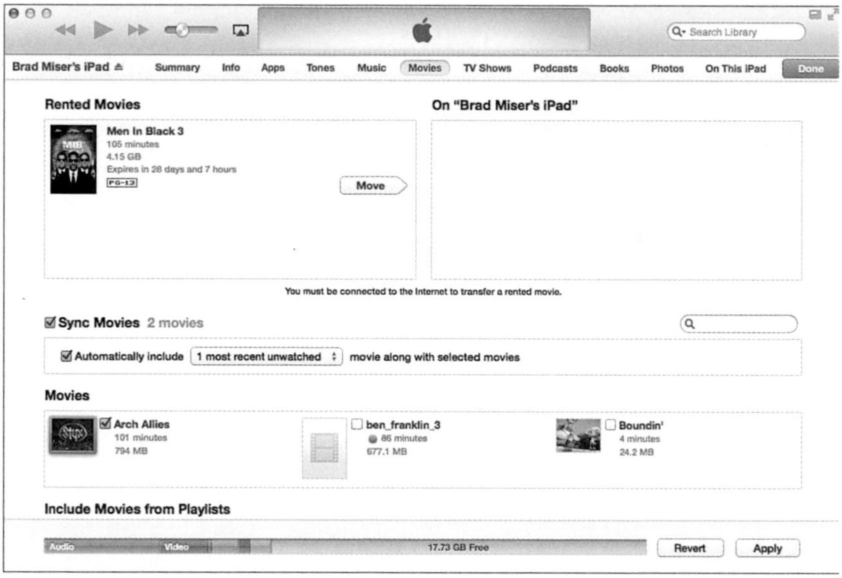

FIGURE 14.5

Because of their large file size, you usually need to be selective about the movies you include in the sync process.

2. Click a rented movie's right-facing **Move** button to move it from the iTunes Library onto the device. The movie's icon moves to the right pane of the window, which indicates it will be moved onto the device during the next sync.

TIP To move a rented movie from the device back into the iTunes Library, click the left-facing Move button next to the movie you want to move. During the next sync, it is removed from the device and placed back into the iTunes Library.

3. Check the **Sync Movies** check box.

4. To automatically copy movies onto the device, check the **Automatically include** check box and choose which movies you want to copy on the pop-up menu. For example, to automatically include the three movies you most recently added to your library, but haven't watched yet, choose the **3 most recent unwatched** option.

5. To move only specific movies onto the device, uncheck the **Automatically include** check box.

6. Check the check box next to each movie you want to copy onto the device.

7. To remove a movie from the device, uncheck its box.

8. Scroll down to see the Include Movies from Playlist section. (If you don't have at least one movie in a playlist, this section doesn't appear on the screen.)

9. Use the playlist check boxes and folder triangles to choose playlists containing movies you want to move onto the device; these work just like the music playlist section tools.

10. To apply the settings to the device and sync it so the selected movies are copied onto it, click **Apply,** or if you are going to configure other areas, you can click this button later.

FORMATS MATTER

Movies can be in many formats; some can be played on your device and others can't. Unfortunately, you can't tell if a movie is in the correct format on the Movies tab. Any movies you obtain from the iTunes Store are in the correct format, but if you add movies from other sources, they might not be. If you try to include a movie not in a compatible format, you see an error dialog during the sync process that shows you which movies aren't formatted correctly. You can create a device-formatted version by selecting the movie in the iTunes Library, opening the **File** menu, choosing **Create New Version**, and then choosing **Create iPod or iPhone Version** or **Create iPad or Apple TV Version,** depending on the type of device you want to play the movie on. This creates a copy of the movie in the correct format; you should name this copy so that you know which is which. Then, select the device-formatted version on the Movies tab to include it in the sync.

Configuring TV Show Syncing

Having TV shows on your device is cool because you can watch them anywhere. To choose the TV shows you want to be available to you, do the following:

1. Click the **TV Shows** tab.

2. Check the **Sync TV Shows** check box.

3. To have iTunes automatically select shows to move onto your device, check the **Automatically include** check box; if you want to manually select shows to include on the device, uncheck this check box and manually select the episodes you want to move onto the device, as explained in steps 8 through 11.

4. On the first pop-up menu, choose how you want iTunes to select the shows to move. For example, to choose the newest three shows you most recently added to your library, but haven't watched yet, choose the **3 newest unwatched** option.

5. On the second pop-up menu, choose **all shows** to include all your shows in the sync or **selected shows** to include only certain shows in the sync. If you have only a few shows in your library, you might be able to use the all shows option, but in most cases, you'll need to use the selected shows option because of the storage space limit on your device.

6. If you use the automatically include with selected shows option, check the check box next to each series whose shows you want to include in the sync. The episodes to move will be selected based on your choice in step 5.

7. Select the series containing episodes you want to move onto the device (see Figure 14.6). In the right pane, you see the episodes of that series in your library, organized by season. You can do this even if you have used the automatically include option; the episodes you select will be added to those included along with those added because of the automatic option.

FIGURE 14.6

You can add specific episodes of a TV series to your iOS device by checking their check boxes on this screen.

8. To expand a season to see all the episodes it contains, click its triangle; to collapse it, click the triangle so it points to the right.

9. To include an entire season, check the season's check box.

10. To include specific episodes, check their check boxes.

 NOTE Movies or TV shows that you haven't watched are marked with a blue circle next to their names. If you've watched part of a movie or show, its circle is partially filled. If you've watched all of a movie or TV show, it doesn't have a circle.

11. If you have playlists containing TV shows, use the controls in the **Include Episodes from Playlists** section to include those in the sync; these work just like the other playlist selection tools.

12. To apply the settings to the device and sync it so the selected movies are copied onto it, click **Apply,** or if you are going to configure other areas, you can click this button later.

NOTE   You can use the Info tab to synchronize contacts, calendars, email accounts, bookmarks, and other options. However, in most cases, you're better off syncing this information with iCloud, Exchange, or other cloud-based accounts because you can sync anytime you have an Internet connection.

Configuring Podcast Syncing

To listen to podcasts on an iOS device, you use the Podcasts app. If you use only that app to subscribe to and listen to podcasts, you don't need to sync podcasts onto your device because the Podcasts app downloads podcast episodes for you directly onto the device (and so you don't need to sync podcasts to move them from the computer onto the device). (See Chapter 16, "Listening to Podcasts with the Podcasts App," for information about using the Podcasts app.)

NOTE   If the Podcasts app isn't installed on the iOS device, you might not see the Podcasts tab on the Sync screen. The Podcasts tab appears after you have installed the app.

If you listen to podcasts on your computer too, it's a good idea to sync podcasts so you are able to listen in either place without repeating or missing episodes. To sync your podcasts, perform the following steps:

1.   Click the **Podcasts** tab (see Figure 14.7).

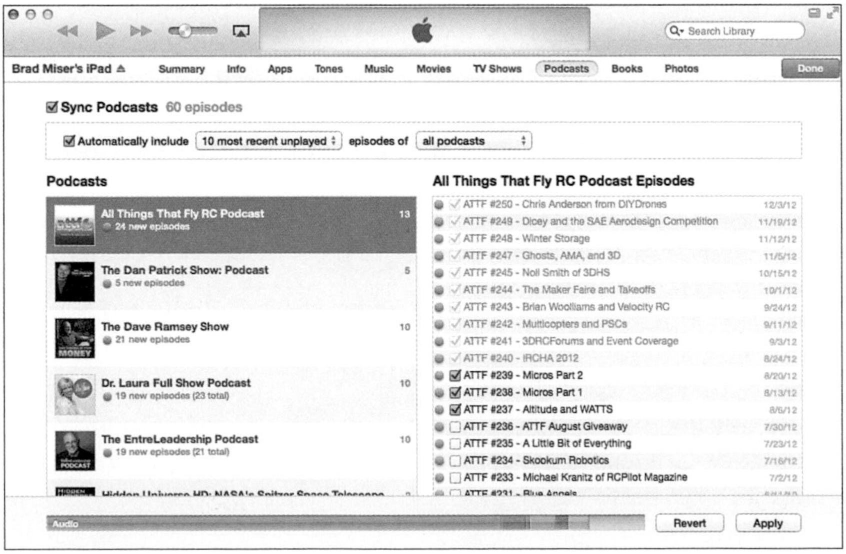

FIGURE 14.7

Use the Podcasts tab to keep your podcasts in sync on your computer and iOS devices.

2. Check the **Sync Podcasts** check box.

3. To have iTunes automatically sync podcasts, check the **Automatically include** check box; if you want to manually select podcasts to sync, uncheck this check box and skip to step 7.

4. On the first pop-up menu, choose the number and type of episodes you want to include in the sync, such as the **10 most recent unplayed**.

5. On the second pop-up menu, choose **all podcasts** to include all your podcasts in the automatic sync or **selected podcasts** to choose specific podcasts.

6. If you choose selected podcasts in step 5, check the check box next to each podcast you want to include in the sync.

7. Select the podcast containing episodes you want to move onto the device.

8. Check the check box next to each episode you want to sync; if you've selected the automatically include option, you can select additional episodes to include in the sync.

9. If you have podcast episodes in playlists that you want to sync, select the playlists by checking their check boxes in the Include Episodes from Playlists section.

10. To apply the settings to the device and sync it so the selected podcasts are copied onto it, click **Apply,** or if you are going to configure other areas, you can click this button later.

Configuring Book Syncing

You can move books onto your device using steps similar to those you use to move other content.

1. Click the **Books** tab.

2. Check the **Sync Books** check box.

 NOTE If the iBooks app isn't installed on the iOS device, you might not see the Books tab on the Sync screen. The Books tab appears after you have installed the app.

3. To move all your ebooks onto the device, click **All books** and skip to step 9; to choose specific books to move, click **Selected books**.

4. To include both PDFs and books in the sync, select **Books and PDF files**; you can choose **Only Books** or **Only PDF files** if you want to limit the sync to one of those types of content.

5. Choose how you want the content sorted by selecting **Sort by Title**, **Sort by Author**, or **Sort by Date**.

6. Check the check boxes for the books and PDF documents you want to move onto the device (see Figure 14.8).

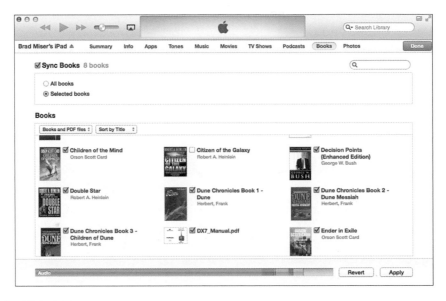

FIGURE 14.8

When you sync books onto an iOS device, you can use the iBooks app to read them.

7. To apply the settings to the device and sync it so the selected podcasts are copied onto it, click **Apply,** or if you are going to configure other areas, you can click this button later.

AUDIOBOOKS

You can also use iTunes to store audiobooks (available from the iTunes Store and many other sources), and then add them to the device using the Sync Audiobooks selection tools located below the Sync Books section. These tools work similarly to the music selection tools; you can choose specific books, specific parts of books, or audiobooks in playlists to include in the sync.

Configuring Photo Syncing

As you learn in Chapter 19, "Working with Photos and Video with the Camera and Photos Apps," your iOS device is a great way to view your photos while you are on the go. You can move photos from a computer onto a device so that you can view them individually and as slideshows. The steps to move photos from a computer to your device are slightly different on Windows PCs and Macs. See the section that applies to your computer.

 NOTE If you have more than one iOS device connected to your computer, the Photos tab doesn't appear. Disconnect one of the devices to cause the Photos tab to appear.

Moving Photos from a Windows PC onto an iOS device

You can use iTunes to move photos you're storing in the My Pictures or other folders on your PC, or those you are storing in Adobe Photoshop Album 2.0 or later or Adobe Photoshop Elements 3.0 or later. The options you see differ slightly when you move photos from a folder versus moving them from an application, but the general steps are the same. The following example shows syncing photos from a folder.

 NOTE Like other types of content, you can only sync photos with one source on your computer. If you change the source of photos with which you are syncing, the photos in the new source replace the photos from the previous source that are stored on the iOS device.

1. Click the **Photos** tab.

2. Check the **Sync Photos from** check box.

3. On the pop-up menu, choose the folder or application containing the photos you want to move onto your device, such as the **My Pictures** folder or **Photoshop Elements**.

 TIP To sync photos stored in any folder on your computer, select **Choose folder**, and then navigate to and select the folder containing the photos you want to sync. Then click **Select Folder**.

4. If you want all the photos in the selected source to be moved onto your device, click the **All folders** or **All photos and albums** radio button and skip to step 8. (The options you see depend on the choice you made in step 3. This example shows the My Pictures source to be synced.)

5. If you want only selected folders or albums to be moved onto the device, click the **Selected folders** or **Selected albums** radio button (see Figure 14.9).

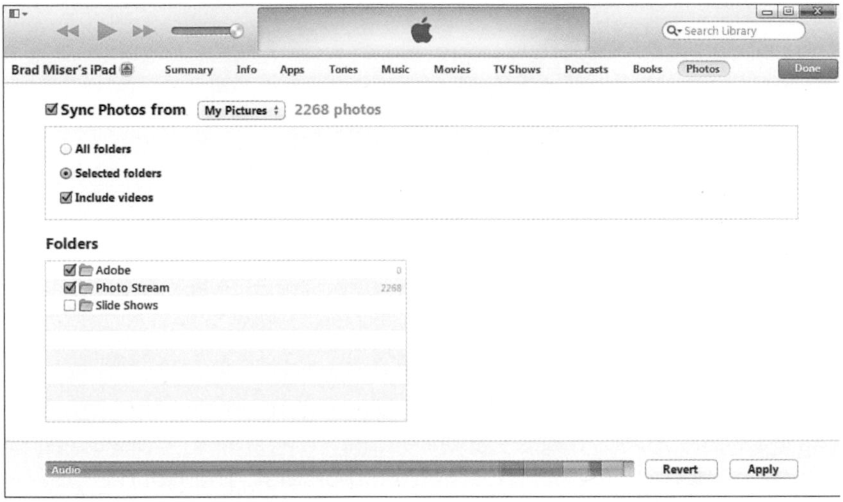

FIGURE 14.9

Use the Photos tab to copy (sync) photos from a Windows computer onto an iOS device.

6. To move videos in the selected source onto the device, check the **Include videos** check box.

7. Check the check box next to each photo album or folder that you want to sync with the device.

8. To apply the settings to the device and sync it so the selected photos are copied onto it, click **Apply,** or if you are going to configure other areas, you can click this button later. If you have previously synced photos from a different source, you see a warning explaining that the existing photos will be removed and replaced by the ones currently included in the sync. Click **Yes** or **OK** to complete the sync so photos from the source you selected in step 3 are moved onto the device.

Moving Photos from a Mac to an iOS Device

iTunes is designed to work seamlessly with iPhoto or Aperture. You can move all your photos or selected photo albums from iPhoto or Aperture to your device by syncing. You can also move photos you've stored in a folder on your Mac almost as easily. The following steps show syncing with iPhoto; syncing with Aperture works the same way.

1. Click the **Photos** tab.

2. Check the **Sync Photos** from check box.

3. On the pop-up menu, choose **iPhoto**.

4. If you want all the photos in iPhoto to be moved onto your device, click the **All photos, albums, events, and faces** radio button and skip to step 11.

5. To choose specific photos to move onto the device, click the **Selected albums, events, and faces, and automatically include** option button.

6. On the pop-up menu, choose which events you want to include in the sync automatically, such as the **10 most recent events**.

7. To include videos in the sync, check the **Include videos** check box.

8. Choose the albums you want to move onto the device by checking their check boxes (see Figure 14.10). Like other content, you can expand folders, browse albums, and so on.

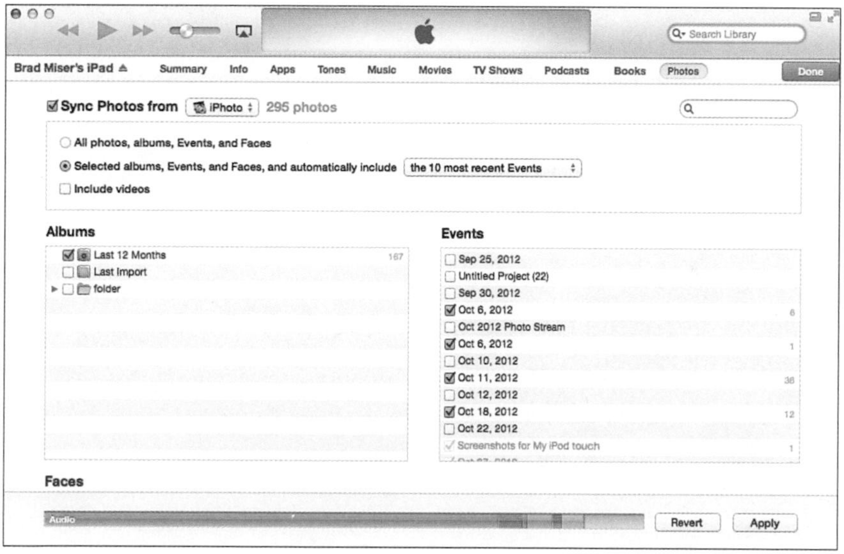

FIGURE 14.10

Use the Photos tab to copy (sync) photos from a Mac onto an iOS device.

9. Choose the events whose photos you want to include by checking their check boxes; these will be in addition to the automatic events included based on your menu choice in step 6.

10. Choose the people who have been identified with the Faces feature whose photos you want to have available on the device by checking the check boxes next to their names.

11. To apply the settings to the device and sync it so the selected photos are copied onto it, click **Apply,** or if you are going to configure other areas, you can click this button later.

Managing the Sync Process

When you've selected the content you want to move onto your device by configuring the sync settings, you need to sync it to move that content onto the device.

If you've made changes to the sync settings, click **Apply**; iTunes saves the sync settings for the device and starts the sync process, which copies the selected content from the iTunes Library onto the device. If there's enough space on the device, the process continues until all the content has been copied. If you've selected more content than there is room for on the device, you see a warning dialog explaining how much content you selected versus how much is available. (You can tell this is a problem before the sync process if there is a warning message in the Capacity gauge.)

If you have selected too much content, you need to decrease the amount of content you are moving from the library to the device, such as by including fewer movies, and perform the sync again by clicking **Apply**.

During the sync process, you see information about what iTunes is doing in the Information area at the top of the iTunes window. When the sync is complete, the sync process information disappears from this area.

 NOTE When an iOS device is connected to your computer, you see the Eject button near the device's name at the top of the Sync screen and on the Device button when you are viewing your iTunes library. Technically speaking, you should click this button before you disconnect a device to ensure that all processes have stopped. However, in practice, as long as the sync process isn't running, you can just disconnect the device. If you disconnect the device during the sync process, it might not complete correctly, so you should make sure the sync process is complete before disconnecting the iOS device.

When the process is complete, you can disconnect the device from the computer (unless you want to charge its battery); of course, if you are syncing wirelessly, you don't need to disconnect it.

If you haven't made changes to the sync settings, you can click the **Sync** button to perform a sync with the current settings. Although this uses the same sync settings as the previous sync, the content that gets moved may be different. For example, if you have listened to podcast episodes, those episodes may be removed from the device and episodes you haven't listened to yet are moved onto the device.

To exit the sync screens, click **Done**. If you have changed sync settings and haven't synced the device, click **Apply** to save the settings and sync the device, or click **Revert** to revert to the previous settings.

Whenever you connect the iOS device to your computer, the sync process starts automatically (unless you've disabled the related setting for an iPhone).

On an iOS device on which you've enabled Wi-Fi Syncing, move to the Settings app, tap **General**, tap **iTunes Wi-Fi Sync**, and tap **Sync Now** (see Figure 14.11). The sync process occurs using the current settings. It's great to be able to sync via Wi-Fi because you don't have to connect your device to your computer. Just tap the Sync Now button and sync on the go. (If you move to the iTunes Wi-Fi Sync screen and don't do anything for a few moments, the sync process starts automatically.)

FIGURE 14.11

You can start the sync process over a Wi-Fi network by tapping Sync Now.

You can also change the sync settings when you are syncing over Wi-Fi, too; select and configure the sync in the same way as when it is connected to the computer. (If you don't see your device, connect it to your computer and ensure that the Sync over Wi-Fi setting is enabled, and apply the settings to enable Wi-Fi syncing.)

SYNCING ISSUES

Not having enough space on the device to complete the sync is just one type of warning you might see during the sync process. If you've included content that can't be synced for some reason, such as a movie that isn't in the correct format, you also see a warning. Or if you want to sync content from more than five iTunes Store accounts, that content won't be moved onto the device. In most cases, the sync process continues, but the content with the problem is not copied onto the device. Click **OK** to clear any warnings and the sync process continues.

THE ABSOLUTE MINIMUM

In this chapter, you learned how to move content onto an iOS device by syncing it with iTunes.

- When you sync a device, iTunes copies content you select from the iTunes Library or other sources (such as a photo application) onto the iOS device so you can use that content. For example, you can copy music from iTunes onto a device so you can listen to it with the Music app.

- When iTunes can communicate with an iOS device, with a USB cable or over a Wi-Fi network, you can use the Sync screen to determine which content is included in the sync process. There is a tab for each type of content, including Music, Movies, and so on. Select a tab and use the resulting controls to configure the sync settings for that type of content.

- There are a number of ways to sync a device, such as clicking the Sync button in iTunes or the Sync Now button on the iTunes Wi-Fi Sync screen on an iOS device. If there is a problem with the sync process, iTunes will let you know, or you see a message on the iOS device's screen.

15

IN THIS CHAPTER

- Setting music preferences
- Finding music you want to listen to
- Listening to music
- Working with the Genius
- Listening to music with AirPlay

LISTENING TO MUSIC WITH THE MUSIC APP

The original purpose of the iPod (which was the first iOS device) was to enable you to listen to your music anytime and anywhere. Through all the generations of iPods, iPod touches, iPhones, and iPads, this function has remained one of the best things about an iOS device. With the Music app, you can enjoy your music wherever and whenever you are. In this chapter, you learn how to make the most of this great app.

The Music app looks and works a bit differently on iPads and iPhones/iPod touches. Throughout this chapter, you see figures and information on both types of devices, pointing out the differences. Although the Music app looks a bit different on the different types of devices, after you use it on one device, you won't have any trouble using it on the others.

Setting Music Preferences

Before you get into your music, take a few moments to configure the Music settings on your iOS device:

1. Tap **Settings**. You move into the Settings app.

2. Tap **Music** (see Figure 15.1).

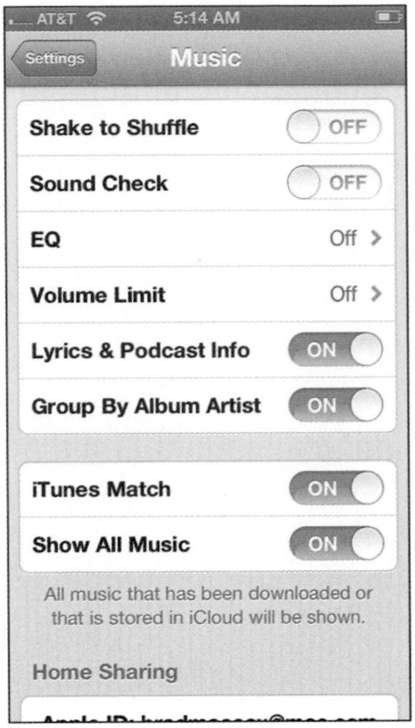

FIGURE 15.1

Here are the Music settings on an iPhone/iPod touch; fewer settings are available on iPads.

3. If you don't want the Music app to shuffle to the next song when you shake an iPhone/iPod touch, slide the **Shake to Shuffle** switch to OFF. Slide the switch to ON to enable shuffling by shaking again. iPads don't have this setting.

4. Slide the **Sound Check** switch to ON if you want the Music app to attempt to even the volume of the music you play so that all the songs play at about the same relative volume level.

5. To set an equalizer, tap the **EQ** bar.

6. Swipe up and down the screen to see all the equalizers available to you.

7. Tap the equalizer you want the Music app to use when you play music; the current equalizer is indicated by the check mark. To turn the equalizer off, tap **Off**.

8. Tap **Music**.

9. To set a limit to the volume level on your iOS device, tap **Volume Limit**.

10. Drag the **volume slider** to the point that you want the maximum volume level to be.

11. Tap **Music**.

12. To hide lyrics and podcast information on the Now Playing screen on iPhones/iPod touches, slide the **Lyrics & Podcast Info** switch to OFF. When this switch is disabled, you always see the album art for whatever is playing. To show this information again, slide the switch to ON again. iPads don't have this setting.

13. If you don't want music to be grouped by the album artist, slide the **Group By Album Artist** switch to OFF. When you set the switch to OFF, songs are always grouped by the artist associated with the songs instead of the album those songs come from. For example, if you have an album that has music with several artists on it, the grouping is done by the artist for each song instead of the artist associated with the album.

14. To enable the device to stream music from the cloud, set the **iTunes Match** switch to ON and perform step 15; to disable iTunes Match, set the switch to OFF and skip to step 16.

NOTE To use iTunes Match, you must have activated the iTunes service for your iTunes Library. See Chapter 12, "Streaming Your Music with iTunes Match," for details about setting up iTunes Match.

15. To show all music available in the Music app, whether it has been downloaded to the device or is only on the cloud, set the **Show All Music** switch to ON; if this switch is set to OFF, only music that has been downloaded to the device is shown in the Music app.

TIP If you use iTunes Match and the device is going to be without an Internet connection while you are listening to music, setting the **Show All Music** switch to OFF is useful because you see only music you can actually listen to. When set to ON, you see all your music. If you can't stream music because you don't have an Internet connection, you won't be able to play music that hasn't been downloaded, even though you can see it in the Music app.

16. To enable streaming content from iTunes libraries and other sources over a local network, tap the **Apple ID** in the Home Sharing section.

17. Enter the Apple ID associated with the music you want to share; in most cases, this should be your Apple ID.

18. Enter the password for the account you entered in the previous step.

19. Tap **Done**. The keyboard closes and you're done configuring Music settings.

Finding Music You Want to Listen To

There are two fundamental steps to listening to music and other audio content. First, find the content you want to listen to by using one of the many browsing and searching features the Music app offers. You can find music you want to listen to by using the Cover Flow Browser, browsing artists, searching, and so on. Second, after you find and select what you want to hear, use the Music app's playback controls to listen to your heart's content. The same controls are available to you no matter how you selected the music you are playing.

To get started, move to the device's Home page and tap the **Music** app's icon. The app launches and you can start enjoying your tunes.

Using the Cover Flow Browser to Find Music (iPhone/iPod touch)

When you use the Music app on an iPhone/iPod touch, the Cover Flow Browser simulates what it's like to flip through a stack of CDs; you can quickly peruse your entire music collection to get to the right music for your current mood. iPads don't have this browser, so if you only use an iPad, you can skip this section.

1. Rotate your iPhone/iPod touch so it is in landscape orientation; the Cover Flow Browser appears (see Figure 15.2). Each cover represents an album from which you have at least one song in your music collection. The album cover displayed in the center of the screen is the one currently in focus.

FIGURE 15.2

On an iPhone/iPod touch, you can use the Cover Flow Browser to "flip" through your music collection.

2. To browse your tunes, swipe a finger to the right to move ahead in the albums or to the left to move back; the faster you swipe, the faster you "flip" through the albums. When you stop so that an album is in focus, under its cover (from top to bottom) you see the name of the artist, the album title, and, if a song from the album is currently playing, the name of the song.

 TIP Tap any album cover you see on the Cover Flow Browser screen to quickly bring that album into focus.

3. To see a list of the songs on an album, move it into focus and tap its cover or tap the Info button (the **i** located in the lower-right corner of the screen). The song list screen appears.

4. To browse the list of songs, swipe your finger up or down the screen.

5. To play a song, tap it on the song list. The song plays and is marked with a blue Play button arrow on the list of songs.

6. To pause a song, tap the **Pause** button. The music pauses, and the Play button replaces the Pause button.

7. To play a different song, tap it.

8. To return to the album's cover, tap its title information at the top of the list, tap the Info button, or just tap outside of the album cover.

9. While you're listening, you can continue browsing to find more music you want to listen to. (When the Music app starts playing the next song in the album you are currently playing, the cover for that album jumps back into focus.)

10. Rotate the iPhone/iPod touch 90 degrees to see the Now Playing screen.

11. Use the Now Playing screen to control the music (covered in detail in the section, "Using the Now Playing Screen (iPhone/iPod touch)," later in this chapter).

 NOTE   If you leave the Cover Flow Browser alone for a moment or two, the album from which music is currently playing snaps into focus.

Using Playlists to Find Music

As you learned in Chapter 7, "Creating and Using Playlists," playlists are a great way to create your own collections of music you want to listen to. When synced onto your device or when available via iTunes Match, playlists are a great way to find music on your iOS device.

1. Tap the **Playlists** button on the Music app's toolbar. The playlists on your iOS device appear. Playlists look a bit different on an iPad (see Figure 15.3) compared to an iPhone/iPod touch (see Figure 15.4).

FIGURE 15.3

On an iPad, playlists are represented by album covers associated with the music they contain.

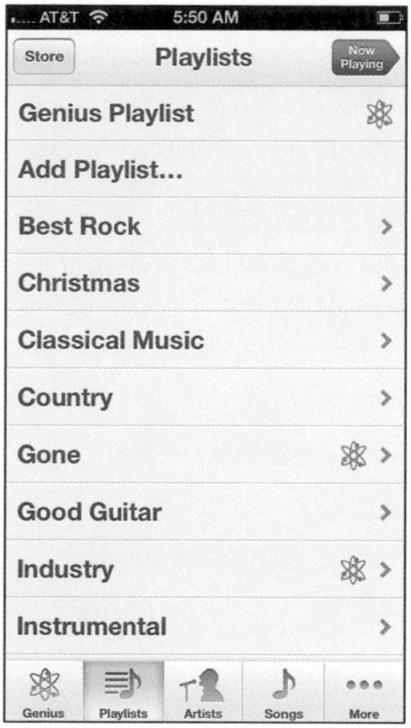

FIGURE 15.4

On an iPhone/iPod touch, the Playlists screen isn't as visually appealing; however, it works just as well.

These playlists are organized just as they are on the Source list in iTunes; if you use folders to organize your playlists, you see those folders on the Playlists screen. For example, if you have a folder in iTunes called Rock, a playlist titled Rock appears on the Playlists screen and contains all the playlists in the Rock folder in iTunes. Genius playlists are marked with the Genius icon.

NOTE You can put Genius playlists on your iOS device by syncing the playlists in your iTunes Library onto the device. Creating and managing Genius playlists are covered in Chapter 7, while the sync process is explained in Chapter 14, "Synchronizing iTunes Content with iOS Devices."

NOTE If you don't see the Genius button on the Music app's toolbar, enable the iTunes Genius in iTunes by choosing **Store**, **Turn On Genius** (see Chapter 7), and then resync your device (see Chapter 14).

2. Swipe your finger around the screen to browse your playlists.

3. Tap a playlist or folder that you'd like to explore. The list of songs in that playlist or the list of playlists within the folder appears with the title of the playlist or folder at the top of the screen.

4. If you moved into a folder, browse the playlists within that folder.

5. Tap the playlist you want to see. You see the songs contained in the playlist.

6. Swipe your finger up and down to browse the songs the playlist contains. (You can also search a playlist by browsing up until you see the Search bar; learn how in the section "Searching for Music" later in this chapter.)

7. When you find a song you want to listen to, tap it. The song begins to play.

8. Use the Music app's playback controls to control the music (covered in detail in the "Listening to Music" section later in this chapter).

NAVIGATING THE MUSIC APP

You can use the Back and Forward buttons to navigate among the various screens in the Music app. These are labeled to indicate the name of the screen you'll move to when you tap the button. The Back button is always located in the upper-left corner of the screen, and the Forward button is located in the upper-right corner. For example, when you are viewing the albums for a specific artist, the Back button is labeled Artists because it takes you back to the Artists screen. However it is labeled, the Back button always takes you to the screen you most recently viewed. Likewise, the Forward button moves you "ahead" one screen.

Using Artists to Find Music

You can find music by browsing artists whose music is stored on the iOS device. Like the other options, the Artists screen looks a bit different on iPads versus iPhones/iPod touches, but it works similarly.

1. Tap **Artists** on the Music app's toolbar. The list of all artists whose content is on the iOS device appears. On an iPad, you see a thumbnail for each artist with a representative album cover (see Figure 15.5). On an iPhone/iPod touch, you see a text list of the artists. In either case, artists are grouped by the first letter of their first name or by the first letter of the group's name (not counting "The" as the first word in a name).

FIGURE 15.5

The Artists option enables you to quickly find music by a specific artist.

 NOTE If you don't see the Artists button on the toolbar, tap **More** and then tap **Artists**.

2. Swipe your finger up and down the list to browse all available artists. (At the top of the screen, you see the Search tool, which enables you to search for specific artists. See "Searching for Music," later in this chapter, for more information.)

3. To jump to a specific artist's music, tap the letter on the index along the right side of the screen for the artist's or group's first name; to jump to an artist or group whose name starts with a number, tap **#** at the bottom of the index.

 NOTE If you don't have a lot of music on your device, you won't see the Index along the right side of the screen. It appears as the content on your device grows beyond a certain point.

4. Tap an artist whose music you'd like to explore. A list of songs by that artist appears. On an iPad, you see the songs organized by album; skip to step 7. If you are using an iPhone/iPod touch and have more than one album by the artist, you see a list of the albums by that artist; if you have only one album by the artist, you see a list of the songs and can skip step 7.

5. Swipe your finger up and down the screen to browse the artist's albums.

TIP On an iPhone/iPod touch, if you have songs from more than one album by a particular artist, an All Songs option appears at the top of the artist's screen. Tap it to see all the artist's songs on all the albums in your collection.

6. To see the contents of an album, tap it. The track list appears with the album's title, album art, and information (such as playing time) at the top of the screen.

7. Swipe your finger up and down the screen to browse all the songs by the artist (iPad) or on a specific album (iPhone/iPod touch).

8. When you find the song you want to listen to, tap it. The song begins to play.

9. Use the Music app's playback controls to control the music (covered in detail in the "Listening to Music" section later in this chapter).

TIP To rapidly move up and down an index, drag your finger up or down the index. As you drag, the index is shaded and the contents of the screen change very quickly.

Using Other Ways to Find Music

In the previous sections, you learned in detail about some of the ways to find music. You can use a number of other options to find music you want to listen to. Depending on the device you are using, you may not see all these options on the Music app's toolbar. If not, tap the **More** button to see any options not shown on the toolbar.

The other options for finding music include the following:

- **Songs**—The Songs browser enables you to browse and search your music by individual song, similar to the Albums browser. Tap **Songs**. You see all the songs currently available to the Music app. You can swipe up or down the screen to browse the list or use the index to jump to a specific song. Tap a song to play it.

- **Albums**—The Albums options presents your music based on the albums your collection contains. Browse for or use the index to find the album you want to listen to. Tap an album to see the list of tracks it contains. Tap a song on the album to play it.

- **Composers**—This option organizes your music by the composer associated with it (the composer is the person or people who wrote the music, in contrast to the artist that performs it). The Composers tool is very similar to the Artists tool.

- **Genres**—This one presents your music based on its genre, such as Rock, Classical, and so on.

- **Shared**—This option enables you to browse for and play music that is being shared on other devices on your local network.

- **Compilations**—This category (on iPhones/iPod touches) organizes music based on the album on which it is compiled. For example, if you have an album consisting of music from various other albums, this option keeps the music organized by the compilation. Other options, such as Artist, will separate the contents of the compilation based on that option.

 TIP   On an iPad, tap **More** to see the **Sort By Artist** switch. Set this switch to **ON** if you want lists to be sorted by artist name, or set it to **OFF** if you want lists to be sorted by track title.

 NOTE   You can search the contents of any content screen (Artists, Albums, and so on) you are browsing. More on this in "Searching for Music," later in this chapter.

CONFIGURING THE MUSIC TOOLBAR ON AN IPHONE/IPOD TOUCH

The five buttons at the bottom of the Music app's screen on an iPhone/iPod touch enable you to get to specific content quickly. You can choose four of the buttons that appear on the screen to make accessing content by the categories that are most useful to you even easier and faster.

1. Tap **More** to move to the More screen.

2. Tap **Edit**. The Configure screen appears.

3. Drag a button you want to add to the toolbar to the location of one of the buttons currently there; lift your finger when the button is in the location where you want to place it. The button you dragged replaces the button over which you placed it. The original button is moved onto the Configure screen.

4. Repeat step 3 until the four buttons you want to have on the toolbar are there. (The fifth button is always the More button.)

5. Drag the buttons to the left or right on the toolbar until they are in the order you want.

6. Tap **Done**. The app's toolbar contains the buttons you placed on it along with the More button.

Downloading iTunes Match Music

iTunes Match is useful because you don't have to worry about syncing the music in your iTunes Library to your iOS device; any music in your iTunes Library is available on your iOS device automatically. If the music you want to hear isn't already stored on the iOS device, when you select it, it gets downloaded and begins to play. (To learn how to set up iTunes Match, see Chapter 12.)

Finding music available via iTunes Match works as described in the previous sections. The difference is that before you can listen to the music, it must be downloaded to your device. However, iTunes Match music streams to your device, meaning that you can play it while it downloads.

You can tell if music has been downloaded to your device by the Download button, which is the one with a cloud containing a downward-facing arrow (see Figure 15.6).

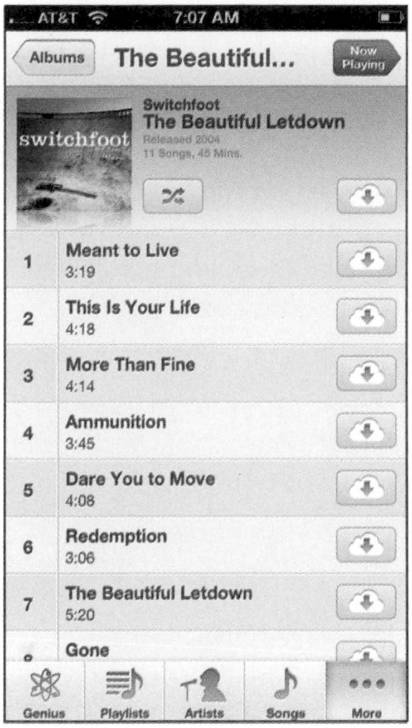

FIGURE 15.6

This album is available via iTunes Match, but it hasn't been downloaded to the device yet.

To download a song without playing it, tap the **Download** button. The song downloads, and the progress indicator replaces the Download button; the circle in that indicator fills with blue as the song is downloaded. When the song is downloaded, the indicator disappears, which shows you that the song has been downloaded to the device.

To stream a song, tap the song's title. The song starts to download; as soon as enough of it has downloaded so it will be able to play without interruption, it starts to play.

To download all the songs on an album, tap its **Download** button. Each song downloads and the progress indicator appears next to each as it does so. When the process is complete, all the indicators disappear.

Here are some more points to ponder when it comes to using iTunes Match:

- If you have a slow Internet connection, it may take a moment for a song that is downloading to start playing after you tap it.

- If content is grayed out and doesn't have the Download button next to it, it is not available in the cloud, so you can't download and play it. This is likely because it just hasn't been uploaded by iTunes Match yet. If you come back to the content at a later time, it will probably be available.

- If a device can use a cellular data network and you have enabled the setting to allow it, you can download content when you are connected to the cloud via that network. However, music files are large, and if your data plan has a limit, you may exceed that limit if you download a lot of music. If this is the case for you, be aware of when you are downloading music; it's better to download when you are connected to Wi-Fi.

- If you are going to be without an Internet connection for a while, make sure you download the music you want to listen to before you lose your connection. Without an Internet connection, you are limited to playing only the music that has been downloaded to your device.

Searching for Music

Browsing is a useful way to find music, but it can be faster to search for specific music in which you are interested. You can search most of the screens that you browse, and when a category contains many items, such as Songs, searching can get you where you want to go more quickly than browsing. Here's how:

1. Tap a category of music that you want to search. The category you choose determines what fields will be searched. For example, if you tap **Artists**, the search is performed on the artist's name. If you tap **Songs**, the search is performed on song titles.

2. On an iPhone/iPod touch, swipe down the screen so that you move up the screen until you see the Search tool, or tap the magnifying glass icon at the top of the screen's index; on an iPad, the Search tool is always visible in the lower-right corner of the screen.

    NOTE If your device doesn't have a lot of music on it, you might not see the Index along the right side of the screen. The Search tool always appears at the very top of the screen, so you can get to it by swiping down the screen.

3. Tap in the Search tool. The onscreen keyboard appears.

4. Type the text or numbers for which you want to search. As you type, the items that meet your search criterion are shown; the more you type, the more specific the results become. Below the Search tool, you see the results organized into categories, such as Albums and Songs.

5. When you think you've typed enough to find what you're looking for, tap **Search** in the keyboard on an iPhone/iPod touch, or tap the Keyboard key on an iPad. The keyboard disappears. You see the results of the search, organized by type, such as songs, playlists, music videos, and so on.

6. Browse the results (see Figure 15.7).

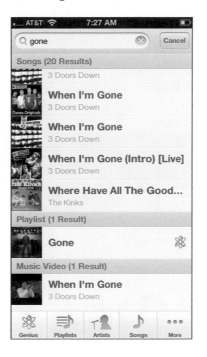

FIGURE 15.7

Here, I searched for the song "gone" and found a number of results.

7. Tap songs, albums, or other items on the results list to get to the music you want to play.

You can clear a search by tapping the x that appears on the right end of the Search tool when it contains text or numbers. You can edit the search text just like you edit any other text.

Listening to Music

After you've found the music you want to listen to, the screens and controls you use on iPhones/iPod touches are a bit different from those on an iPad.

Playing Music on an iPhone/iPod touch

When you play music on an iPhone/iPod touch, the Now Playing screen appears if the iOS device is in portrait orientation (if it is landscape orientation, you see the Cover Flow Browser instead). This screen provides information along with many controls and options for playing music, as you see in Figure 15.8 and in the following list:

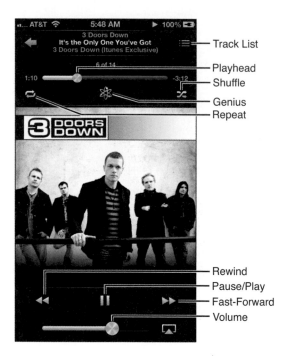

FIGURE 15.8

The Now Playing screen provides lots of ways to control the tunes.

- **Information about the music**—At the top of the screen, you see the artist. The song title is shown in bold; underneath that is the album from which the song comes.

- **Timeline**—Just under the song information is the timeline bar that has the elapsed time on the left side and the remaining time on the right end. The

Playhead shows the current location in the track. You can drag the Playhead to the left to move back or to the right to move forward.

 TIP On iPhone 4S and earlier and on iPod touches, 3rd Generation and earlier, the Timeline bar can be shown or hidden. If you don't see the Timeline bar, tap the screen to make it appear. Tap the screen again to hide it.

- **Repeat**—To repeat the current source, such as playlist or genre, until you stop playing it, tap the Repeat button. When the source is set to repeat indefinitely, the Repeat button turns orange. To repeat the source one time, tap the Repeat button again; the button remains orange and contains a small 1. To turn off repeat, tap the button again so it becomes white.

- **Genius**—Tap to activate the Genius. This is covered in detail in the section, "Working with the Genius."

 NOTE If you haven't enabled the Genius in iTunes with which the device is synced, you might not see the Genius button. See Chapter 7 for the details of enabling the Genius in iTunes.

- **Shuffle**—Tap to have the Music app to randomly select the next song to play. The Music app selects a song from the source you were browsing and plays it; you move to the Now Playing screen. After that song plays, the Music app selects another one and plays it. This continues until all the songs in the source have played.

 TIP If you enabled the Shake to Shuffle setting as described earlier, you can cause the Music app to randomly shuffle to the next song by gently shaking the device back and forth.

- **Album art**—In the center of the screen, you see the art associated with the current song. On older iPhones and iPod touches, you can tap the album art to show or hide the Timeline bar and lyrics.

- **Rewind**—Tap to return to the start of the current track, tap and hold to rewind, or tap twice to move to previous track.

- **Pause/Play**—Tap to pause while music is playing. When music is paused, tap to play.

- **Fast Forward**—Tap to skip to the next track, or tap and hold to fast-forward.

- **Volume**—Drag to the right to increase volume, or drag to the left to decrease it.

If you tap the Track List view button, the album art is replaced by the track list (see Figure 15.9). Here you see the list of all tracks on the album from which the current song comes, even if you aren't listening to the album itself (such as when you are listening to a playlist that contains the current song). You see the order of tracks on the album along with their names and playing times. Swipe your finger up and down to browse through the tracks in the album. You can tap a song to play it. Rate the song currently playing by tapping one of the dots just below the song information. Stars fill up to the dot you tapped to give the song a star rating between one and five.

FIGURE 15.9

The track list shows the list of songs on the album from which the song currently playing comes.

When you play a song from the Track List view screen, you jump to Album mode. From that point on, you work only with the album from which the current song came. For example, if you play a playlist, switch to the Track List view, and play a different song on the same album, you change the source to be only that album, so the next song that plays is the next one on the album, not the next one in the playlist. If you only view the song's information or give it a rating in Track List view, when you move back to the Cover view, you still work with the original source, such as a playlist.

To return to the Album Art view, tap the button showing the album art that is located to the right of the song information.

If you are using an iPhone 5 or iPod touch, 5th generation or later, the Timeline bar is always displayed. If you are using an older device, the Timeline bar can be hidden; if it is not currently displayed, tap the screen once to display it. Tap it again to hide it.

You can add lyrics to songs in iTunes. To see the lyrics for the current song, tap the album art. If the song has lyrics, they appear. You can swipe up and down the screen to read them.

TIP On iPhone 4S or iPod touch, 4th generation, or earlier, lyrics appear when the Timeline bar is visible. If you can see the Timeline bar but don't see any lyrics, the song doesn't have lyrics associated with it.

The Now Playing screen remains in the state in which you last viewed it. For example, if you display lyrics and move away from the Now Playing screen, lyrics will display the next time you move back. Likewise, if lyrics are hidden when you move away, they remain hidden when you return.

To move back to the music selection screens, tap the Back button located to the left of the song information. You move back to the screen you were most recently viewing, such as the track list for an album.

You can get back to the Now Playing screen by tapping the Now Playing button located in the upper-right corner of the screen.

NOTE When music is playing, the Play icon appears next to the battery icon at the top of the screen.

Playing Music on an iPad

Playing music with the Music app on an iPad is a bit different than on an iPhone/iPod touch because iPads don't show a Now Playing screen like the other types of devices do. Instead, when you select and play a source of music, such as a playlist, you remain on that source's screen while the music plays (see Figure 15.10). Working with other sources, such as albums, looks a bit different, but the controls and information are similar.

FIGURE 15.10

When you choose and play a source of music, such as the music for an artist as shown here, there are lots of ways to control the tunes.

To play a song, tap it. It begins to play and is marked with the speaker icon. While music is playing, you can swipe up and down the screen to browse the current source. The information and controls that are available include the following:

- **Information about the music**—At the top of the screen, you see the artist, song, and album from which the song comes. These items are colored differently to separate them; for example, the artist may be in white, the song in black, and the album in white.

- **Timeline**—Just under the song information is the timeline bar that has the elapsed time on the left side and the remaining time on the right end. The Playhead shows the current location in the track. You can drag the Playhead to the left to move back or drag to the right to move forward.

- **Rewind**—Tap to return to the start of the current track, tap and hold to rewind, or tap twice to move to previous track.

- **Pause/Play**—Tap to pause while music is playing. When music is paused, tap to play.

- **Fast Forward**—Tap to skip to the next track, or tap and hold to fast-forward.

- **Album Art**—Tap to move to the Album Art screen; more on this shortly.

- **Repeat**—To repeat the current source, such as playlist or genre, tap the Repeat button. When the source is set to repeat indefinitely, the Repeat button turns black. To repeat the source one time, tap the Repeat button again; the button remains black and contains a small 1. To turn off repeat, tap the button again so it becomes white.

- **Genius**—Tap to activate the Genius. This is covered in detail in the section, "Working with the Genius."

 NOTE If you haven't enabled the Genius in iTunes with which the device is synced, you might not see the Genius button. See Chapter 7 for the details of enabling the Genius in iTunes.

- **Shuffle**—Tap to have the Music app randomly select the next song to play. The Music app selects a song from the source you were browsing and plays it; you move to the Now Playing screen. After that song plays, the Music app selects another one and plays it. This continues until all the songs in the source have played.

- **Volume**—Drag to the right to increase volume or drag to the left to decrease it.

- **Source**—The button for the current source is highlighted. Tap any of the source buttons to view that source.

To see the Album Art screen (see Figure 5.11), tap the **Album Art** button. The artwork associated with current screen replaces the track list.

FIGURE 15.11

You can view the art associated with the current song, which tends to be more visually interesting than the list of tracks.

To see the list of songs on the album containing the currently playing song, tap the **Track List** button, which is located in the bottom-right corner of the screen. The album art is replaced by the track list. Here you see the list of all tracks on the album from which the current song comes, even if you aren't listening to the album itself (such as when you are listening to a playlist that contains the current song). You see the order of tracks on the album along with their names and playing times. Swipe your finger up and down to browse through the tracks in the album. You can tap a song to play it. Rate the song currently playing by tapping one of the dots just below the song information. Stars fill up to the dot you tapped to give the song a rating between one and five stars.

To return to the source's screen, tap the left-facing arrow just to the left of the source buttons at the bottom of the screen.

Controlling Volume

Volume is one of the most important controls for music. You can use a number of options to change the volume at which music is playing.

If you are on the Now Playing screen on an iPhone/iPod touch or on any of the screens in the Music app on an iPad, you can use the Volume slider as described previously.

You can also use the volume buttons on the upper-left side of the device. Press the upper button to increase volume or the lower one to decrease it. If you aren't viewing a Music app screen while you are press a volume button, a volume indicator appears on the screen to show you the relative volume level as you press the keys.

If you are listening to music using Apple's earbuds, press the upper part of the switch on the right earbud's wire to increase volume or the lower part to decrease it.

Playing Music While You Do Something Else

The Music app plays in the background when you switch to a different app, which is a good thing. You can control the tunes by going back to the Music app. One way to do this is to press the Home button once to move back to the Home screen and then tap the Music button, but if you don't have the Music app placed at the bottom of the Home screen, you might have to move to a different Home screen to tap it.

This works fine, but you can use the Multitasking bar to jump directly to the Music app, regardless of where its icon is stored. Press the Home button twice; the Multitasking bar appears. Swipe to the right on the toolbar and tap the Music app's icon to move into the app; you return to the screen you were on the last time you used it.

You can also control audio directly from the Multitasking bar. Press the Home button twice to show the Multitasking bar. Swipe to the right on the toolbar until you see the Playback controls. The playback tools appear along with the name of the song currently playing (see Figure 15.12). Use the Playback controls to control the audio.

 NOTE When you see the Playback controls on the Multitasking bar on an iPhone/iPod touch, you must swipe to the right again to see the Volume slider.

FIGURE 15.12

Using the Playback controls on the Multitasking bar (this is an iPad) can be faster than moving back into the Music app.

Controlling Music When a Device Is Locked

When audio is playing and your iOS device sleeps and locks, it would be a hassle to move back to the Music app to control that audio; you'd have to tap the Home button or Sleep/Wake button to wake the iOS device up, slide the Unlock slider, and then move to the Music app (which can require several steps, depending on what you were doing last). There is a faster way.

Wake the iOS device by pressing the Sleep/Wake or Home button. The title of the song currently playing and the associated album art appear. Press the Home button twice; the Music app controls appear (see Figure 15.13). Use the playback tools to control the tunes. These work the same as they do in the Music app.

FIGURE 15.13

Controlling music from the Locked screen is much faster than moving back to the Music app.

After a period of time passes without your using them, the playback tools are hidden and you see only the album art. To restore the tools, press the Home button twice. You can also hide the tools by pressing the Home button twice. For example, if you keep the device in your pocket, you might want to hide the tools before you put it back in there to prevent the tool's buttons from activating accidentally.

 NOTE   When you wake up an iOS device and audio is not playing, you see the Locked screen's wallpaper. If audio is playing, you see the album art for that audio instead. In either case, if you press the Home button twice, the playback tools appear. If no audio is currently playing, you can start the most recently selected content again; to change the source of content, you need to go back into the Music app.

Using Siri to Play Music

If you have a Siri-capable device (iPhone 4S or later; iPod touch, 5th Generation or later; iPad 3 or later; iPad mini), you can play music by speaking commands.

Press and hold the Home button, or the center part of the buttons on the earbuds, until you hear the Siri chime; or tap the Microphone icon if Siri is already active. The "What can I help you with?" text appears along with the microphone icon, which is shaded in purple. This indicates Siri is ready for your command.

Speak the search phrase for the music you want to listen to. There are a number of variations in what you can say. Examples include "Play album *Time of My Life*," "Play song 'Gone' by Switchfoot," "Play playlist Jon McLaughlin," and so on. Siri provides a confirmation of what you asked and begins playing the music.

There are a number of commands you can speak to find, play, and control music (and other audio):

- "Play artist" plays music by the artist's name you speak.

- "Play album" plays the album you name.

 NOTE   If a name you speak includes the word "the," you need to include "the" when you speak the command.

- "Shuffle" randomly plays a song.

- "Play more like this" uses the Genius to find songs similar to the one playing and plays them.

- "Previous track" or "next track" does exactly what they sound like they do.

- To hear the name of the artist for the song currently playing, say "Who sings this song?" This works even when the music doesn't have any lyrics.

- You can shuffle music in an album or playlist by saying "Shuffle playlist *playlistname.*"

- You can stop the music, pause it, or play it by speaking those commands.

CAUTION   Voice commands work pretty well, but they aren't perfect. Make sure you confirm the command by listening to the feedback Siri provides when it repeats your command. Sometimes, a spoken command can have unexpected results, which can include making a phone call to someone on your Contacts list. If you don't catch such a mistake before the call is started, you might be surprised to hear someone answering your call instead of hearing music you intended to play. You can press and hold the Home button down to activate Siri, and then say "no" or "stop" to stop Siri if a verbal command goes awry.

CONTROLLING MUSIC BY VOICE ON OLDER DEVICES

If you have a device that is not Siri capable, you aren't left out in the cold when it comes to speaking commands. You can speak the name of a playlist, album, or artist to find and play the associated music. Activate voice-command mode by pressing and holding the Home button or the center part of the button on the earbud headset until you hear the voice command chime or see the Voice Control screen. Speak the voice command. For example, to find and play a playlist, say, "play *playlistname*," where *playlistname* is the name of the playlist you want to find and play. You'll hear the iOS device repeat the command it thinks it heard and then perform it.

Working with the Genius

The Genius feature finds music and builds a playlist based on songs that "go with" a specific song. How the Genius selects songs that "sound good" with other songs is a bit of a secret, but it works amazingly well. You can have the Genius build a playlist for you in a couple of ways and then listen to or update it.

To have the Genius create a playlist for you, do the following:

1. Find and play a song using any of the techniques you learned earlier in this chapter.

2. Tap the **Genius** button. While the music continues to play, the Genius playlist is created. If you are using an iPad, move to step 3. On an iPhone/iPod touch, you move to the Genius Playlist screen where you see the songs that the Genius selected. The song that is currently playing is at the top of the list and is marked with the Genius and speaker icons. Skip to step 4.

3. On an iPad, tap the **Playlists** source button and then tap the **Genius** playlist. You move to the Genius Playlist screen where you see the songs that the Genius selected. The song that is currently playing is at the top of the list.

4. Tap any song on the playlist to start playing it.

5. To have the Genius change the playlist, tap **Refresh** (see Figure 15.14). Songs may be added, and the order in which they are listed may be changed.

FIGURE 15.14

Genius playlists are a great way to keep your music fresh by listening to it in different ways.

6. To save the playlist, tap **Save**. The name of the playlist changes from Genius to be the name of the song on which the playlist was based.

TIP On an iPhone/iPod touch, you can create a new Genius playlist by moving to the Playlists screen, tapping **Genius Playlist**, and then tapping the song on which you want the new playlist based.

Genius playlists that you have saved appear in the Playlists source just like other playlists you have created, except they are marked with the Genius icon. You can play Genius playlists just like others on the Playlists screen, and you can edit them. Genius playlists are also moved into your iTunes Library on your computer the next time you sync your iOS device.

You can update a genius playlist by tapping it. The Genius playlist's screen appears. Tap **Refresh**. The Genius builds a new playlist based on the same song. The resulting playlist might have the same or different songs, and they might be in a different order. The refreshed playlist replaces the previous version.

TIP You can remove songs from or change the order in which songs play in a Genius playlist by moving to its screen and tapping **Edit**. Drag songs up or down the list to change the order in which they play. Remove songs by tapping the button containing a red circle with a hyphen in it and then tapping **Delete**. When you have made all the changes you want, tap **Done**.

On an iPhone/iPod touch, you can delete a genius playlist by moving to its screen, tapping **Delete**, and then tapping **Delete Playlist**. The playlist is deleted. (The songs on your iOS device are not affected.)

Listening to Music with AirPlay

With AirPlay, you can stream your music and other audio to other devices so that you can hear it using a sound system instead of the iOS device's speakers or earbuds. For example, if you have an Apple TV connected to a home theater system, you can stream audio to the Apple TV so it will play via the home theater's audio system. You can also stream to an AirPort Express base station to which you've connected speakers. Or you can stream to AirPlay-compatible speakers that are designed to receive AirPlay signals directly.

To use AirPlay, your iOS device needs to be on the same Wi-Fi network as the devices to which you are going to stream your audio. After you have set up the devices you are going to use, such as an AirPort Express base station and speakers, you can stream to them using the following steps:

1. Play the music or audio you want to stream.

2. Tap the **AirPlay** button (see Figure 15.15). (If your iOS device isn't on a Wi-Fi network with AirPlay devices, this button doesn't appear). The AirPlay menu appears; the iOS device, AirPlay devices, and Bluetooth speakers it can communicate with are shown (see Figure 15.16). The device marked with the check mark is the one through which the iOS device is currently playing music.

FIGURE 15.15

Use the AirPlay button to stream your music onto AirPlay and other devices.

FIGURE 15.16

Tap a device to stream music to it.

3. Tap the device to which you want to stream the music you are playing. The AirPlay menu closes and the iOS device starts playing music on the selected device. The AirPlay button becomes orange, indicating that your iOS device is playing music via the AirPlay network.

4. Use the Music app's controls to control music playback.

5. To return audio playback to the iOS device, tap the **AirPlay** button.

6. Tap the **iOS device**. You return to the Now Playing screen and hear the audio on your iOS device's speakers or headphones.

THE ABSOLUTE MINIMUM

In this chapter, you learned about the Music app that enables you to take control over your music.

- There are a few music settings you can configure to tweak how the Music app works. For example, you can use the Sound Check setting to have the Music app level out the relative volume levels of your music.

- The first step to listening to music is finding the music to which you want to listen. There are many sources of music, including playlists, artists, albums, songs, and so on. You can browse for music within these sources, or you can search for specific music to find it quickly.

- The Music app provides lots of controls for your music. The Music app looks and works a bit differently on iPads and iPhones/iPod touches, but the functionality you will enjoy is similar on both types of devices. You can also control music playback from the Multitasking bar and from the Locked screen. Siri enables you to control music with voice commands.

- The Genius is a great way to mix up your music because it creates playlists for you that contain songs that "go with" the song you are playing. This can give you a unique music experience each time you listen because you can refresh the contents to change the songs a playlist contains and the order in which they play.

- You can use AirPlay to listen to your music on other devices, such as an Apple TV connected to a home theater system or to an AirPort Express base station to which speakers are connected.

IN THIS CHAPTER

- Configuring the Podcast app's settings
- Building your podcast library
- Listening to audio podcasts

LISTENING TO PODCASTS WITH THE PODCASTS APP

Podcasts offer all sorts of content to which you can listen or watch. Most podcasts are episodic, with each episode being released periodically, such as daily, weekly, and so on. You can choose from a huge number of podcasts. Some are the same as shows on the radio, whereas others are produced by other types of organizations, such as those associated with hobbies, special interest groups, and the like. Podcasts exist on just about every kind of topic you can imagine (and maybe more than a few that you can't!).

Using the Podcasts app, you can subscribe to podcasts (most podcasts are free) so that new episodes are downloaded to your iOS device automatically. You can then listen to episodes using the playback tools the app offers (these are somewhat different from those provided in the Music app). The app also provides tools you can use to manage your podcasts, such as to determine when episodes are removed from your device.

Podcasts to which you subscribe and listen can also be synced among your devices through your Apple ID/iCloud account. This means you can listen to an episode on one device, such as an iPhone, and when you change devices, such as to an iPad, you can pick up where you left off on the first device. Syncing also works (see the later sidebar) with iTunes so that you have the same podcasts in the same state on iOS devices and computers.

 NOTE If the Podcasts app isn't installed on your iOS device, use the App Store app to download and install Apple's Podcasts app. The App Store app is covered in Chapter 13, "Downloading Content onto iPads, iPhones, or iPod touches."

Configuring the Podcast App's Settings

You should configure the Podcast app's settings to determine how it handles your podcasts. Here's how:

1. Move to the **Settings** icon and tap it.

2. Tap **Podcasts** (see Figure 16.1); you might have to swipe up the screen to see this option.

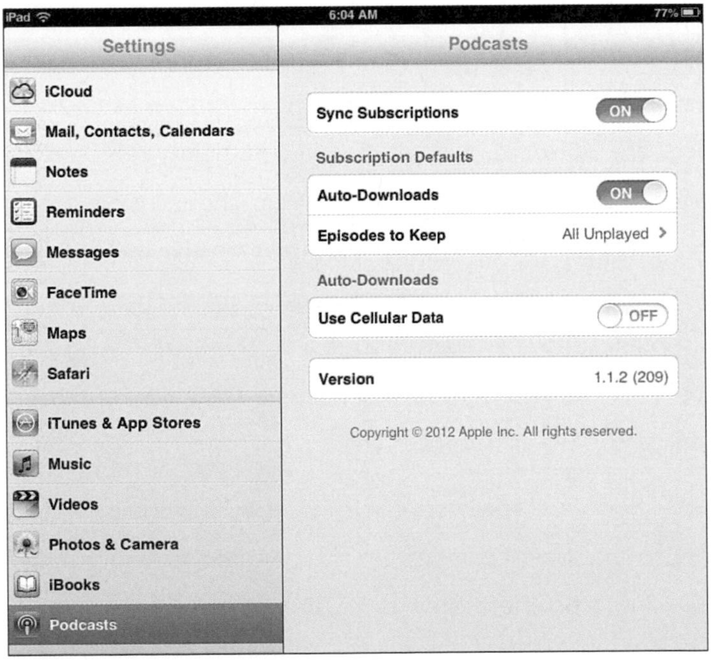

iPad 📶	6:04 AM	77% 🔋
Settings	**Podcasts**	

Settings	Podcasts	
☁ iCloud		
✉ Mail, Contacts, Calendars	**Sync Subscriptions**	ON
▢ Notes	**Subscription Defaults**	
▤ Reminders	**Auto-Downloads**	ON
▢ Messages	**Episodes to Keep**	All Unplayed >
◉ FaceTime	**Auto-Downloads**	
▦ Maps	**Use Cellular Data**	OFF
▨ Safari		
◎ iTunes & App Stores	**Version**	1.1.2 (209)
♫ Music	Copyright © 2012 Apple Inc. All rights reserved.	
▥ Videos		
▨ Photos & Camera		
▢ iBooks		
◉ Podcasts		

FIGURE 16.1

Use the Podcasts settings to configure how the Podcasts app should work.

3. To have your podcasts subscriptions synced on all your devices, set the **Sync Subscriptions** switch to ON. This causes podcasts to which you have subscribed on any iOS device to be subscribed to on the current device. For example, when you subscribe to a podcast on an iPhone and this setting is enabled on an iPad, the podcast to which you are subscribed also appears in the Podcasts app on the iPad. Your playback position is also synced so when you change devices, you play a podcast at the same position in the episode you were listening to on a different device.

4. To have episodes of your podcasts downloaded to the device automatically, set the **Auto-Downloads** switch to ON.

5. Tap **Episodes to Keep**.

6. Determine when you want episodes to be kept on the device. For example, to keep only episodes to which you've listened, tap **All Unplayed Episodes**. If you want to keep only a specific number of episodes, tap **Last** X **Episodes**, where X is the number you want to keep on the device.

7. Tap **Podcasts**.

8. If you have a cellular data connection and have a limit on the amount of data you can download, set the **Use Cellular Data** switch to OFF. If you do this, new episodes are downloaded only when you are connected to the Internet using a Wi-Fi network.

PODCASTS APP AND ITUNES

At press time, the Podcasts app and podcasts in iTunes don't sync reliably; sometimes they are in proper sync and the state of podcasts is the same on all devices; at other times, they appear to get out of sync. This means the content state (such as if you've listened to episodes or not, and where you are listening in a specific episode) may not be the same in your iTunes Library as it is in the Podcasts app. This can be very annoying because you may find yourself listening to content that you've already heard or missing episodes you haven't listened to. Hopefully, Apple will continue to improve podcast syncing between the Podcasts app and iTunes, especially in how it syncs among all devices, including iOS devices and iTunes on computers. Until that happens, be aware that there can be differences in the state of your podcasts on iOS devices and iTunes.

Building Your Podcast Library

The Podcasts app enables you to create a library of podcasts to which you can listen or watch. You can browse or search for podcasts and preview them. If you decide you want to subscribe to a podcast, it just takes a tap to add it to your library. You can also use the app to configure the settings for individual podcasts, delete podcasts in which you are no longer interested, and so on.

Browsing for Podcasts Using Top Stations

The Top Stations option presents you with a selection of podcasts (to access all the podcasts available, use the Store option, as explained in the next section). To use the Top Stations option, perform the following steps:

1. Tap the **Podcasts** app.

2. Tap the **Top Stations** tab at the bottom of the screen.

3. To browse audio podcasts, set the switch at the top of the screen to the speaker position (the icon on the left); to browse video podcasts, set it to the video position (the icon on the right). The rest of these steps are for the audio option; however, the video option is similar.

4. Swipe to the left or right on the bar at the top of the screen to choose the category of content you want to browse. The top line in this bar shows the high-level categories of content, such as Education or Games & Hobbies. Under this, you see the current subcategory, such as Aviation or Hobbies. As you swipe on the bar, you see various podcasts in the current category and subcategory (see Figure 16.2).

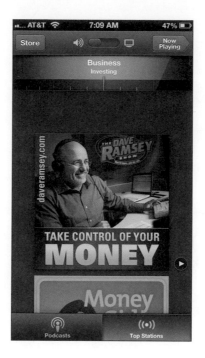

FIGURE 16.2

Here I'm browsing the Business, Investing category.

5. Swipe up and down the screen to browse all the podcasts in the current subcategory.

6. When you find a podcast of interest, tap it. You see the podcast's screen (see Figure 16.3).

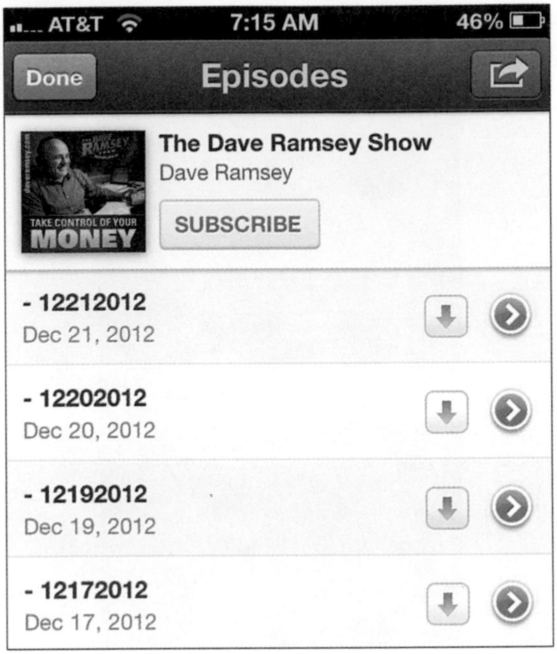

FIGURE 16.3

From a podcast's screen, you can preview it, and if you want to have it in your library, subscribe to it.

7. To learn how to preview and subscribe to a podcast, refer to the section, "Previewing and Subscribing to Podcasts," later in this chapter.

Browsing or Searching for Podcasts in the Store

The Top Stations option provides only a small subset of the available podcasts. The Store enables you to access many more podcasts. You can browse the store, or if you have specific show or topic in mind, you can search for it.

Browsing for Podcasts in the Store

Browsing the store is a great way to discover podcasts on a wide range of topics.

1. Tap the **Podcasts** app.

2. Tap the **Store** button (at the bottom of the screen on an iPad or at the top on an iPhone/iPod touch). You move into the store.

3. Tap one of the options at the bottom of the screen to select the category of podcasts you want to browse. For example, the **Featured** option shows you

podcasts that are currently being featured, and the **Top Charts** shows you podcasts based on popularity. One of the more useful options is to browse by category, which is the focus of the rest of these steps. On an iPad, tap the **More** button to see the list of categories. On an iPhone/iPod touch, tap the **Categories** button to see the list.

 TIP On an iPad, you see two categories, Arts and Business, at the top of the screen next to the More button. If you want to browse one of those categories, tap it instead of the More button.

4. Swipe up and down the list to browse all the available categories (see Figure 16.4).

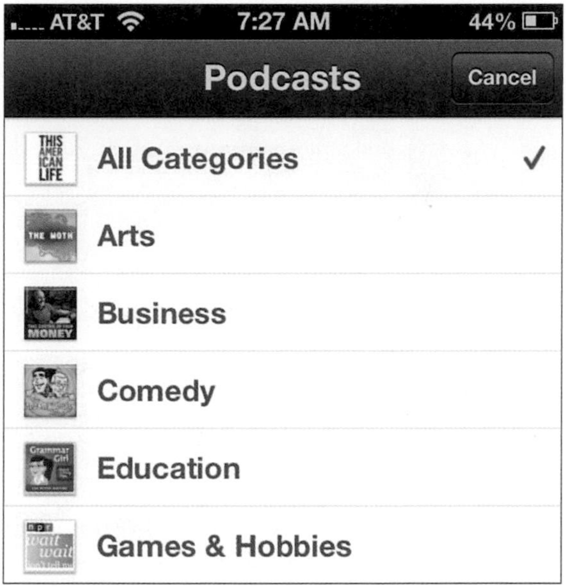

FIGURE 16.4

You can browse many categories of podcasts. .

5. Tap the category you want to browse, such as **Business**. You see the podcasts in that category organized into various subcategories, such as New & Noteworthy, What's Hot, and so on. You can browse the podcasts in each section by swiping to the left or right on the icons in that section.

6. To see all the podcasts in a subcategory you want to browse, tap **See All** in that subcategory's section (see Figure 16.5).

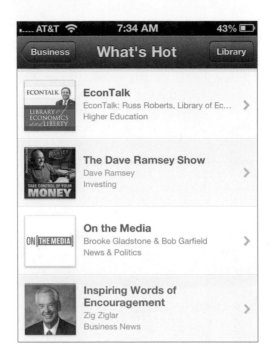

FIGURE 16.5

Here I'm browsing all the podcasts in the What's Hot subcategory in Business podcasts.

7. Swipe up and down the screen to browse all the podcasts in the subcategory.

8. To get more information about a podcast, tap it. You see the podcast's screen from where you can preview, read about, and subscribe to it.

9. To learn how to preview and subscribe to a podcast, refer to the section, "Previewing and Subscribing to Podcasts."

Searching for Podcasts in the Store

If you know specific information about a podcast, you can find it quickly by searching for it. You can search based on a variety of information, most commonly either the name of the person with which a podcast is associated or the title (or part of the title). To search for a podcast, do the following:

1. Tap the **Podcasts** app.

2. Tap the **Store** button (at the bottom of the screen on an iPad or at the top on an iPhone/iPod touch). You move into the store.

3. On an iPad, tap in the **Search** bar in the upper-right corner of the screen; on an iPhone/iPod touch, tap the **Search** button located at the bottom of the screen and then tap in the **Search** bar that appears.

4. Type the content for which you want to search. As you type, you see results that match what you are typing.

5. Continue typing until you see what you want on the results list (see Figure 16.6).

FIGURE 16.6

Searching for a podcast enables you to find specific podcasts quickly and easily.

6. Tap the result you want to explore. You see a list of podcasts that meet the result you tapped.

7. Swipe around the screen to explore all the results.

8. To get more information about a podcast, tap it. You see the podcast's screen from where you can preview, read about, and subscribe to it.

9. To learn how to preview and subscribe to a podcast, refer to the following section, "Previewing and Subscribing to Podcasts."

Previewing and Subscribing to Podcasts

When you've found a podcast of interest, you can preview it, read about, and if you decide you want to add it to your library, subscribe to it (see Figure 16.7).

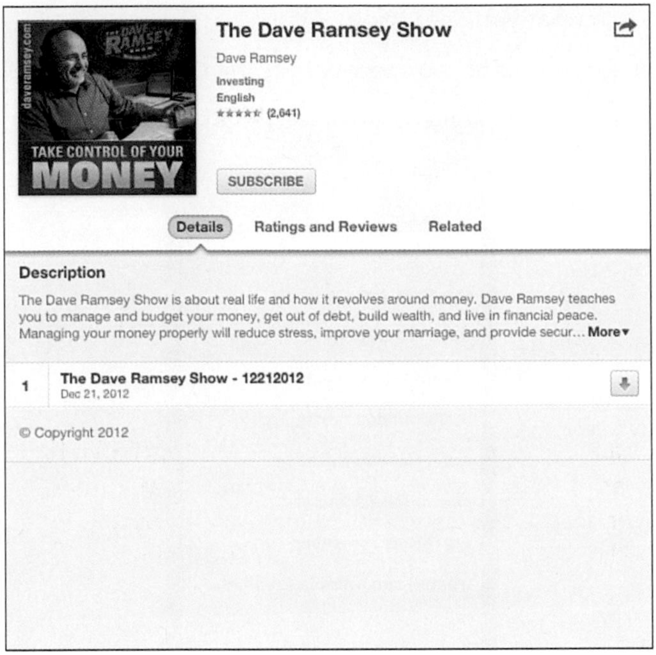

The Dave Ramsey Show

Dave Ramsey

Investing
English
★★★★☆ (2,641)

[SUBSCRIBE]

(Details)   Ratings and Reviews   Related

Description

The Dave Ramsey Show is about real life and how it revolves around money. Dave Ramsey teaches you to manage and budget your money, get out of debt, build wealth, and live in financial peace. Managing your money properly will reduce stress, improve your marriage, and provide secur... **More▼**

1   **The Dave Ramsey Show - 12212012**
     Dec 21, 2012

© Copyright 2012

FIGURE 16.7

You can learn about a podcast and subscribe to it to add it to your library.

On a podcast's screen, you can do a number of tasks, including the following:

- **Read about it**—On the Details tab, you see a description of the podcast above the list of episodes that are currently available for it. To see all of the description, tap **More**.

    NOTE If you get to a podcast's screen using the Top Stations option, you have fewer options than when you get to it through the store. You can listen to the podcast by tapping an episode. You can get information about an episode by tapping the information button (on an iPad, this is the "i" button; on an iPhone/iPod touch, it is the right-facing arrow located along the right side of the screen). You can also subscribe to the podcast.

- **See ratings and reviews**—Tap the **Ratings and Reviews** tab on iPads or **Reviews** tab on an iPhone/iPod touch to see what other people think about the podcast.

- **See related podcasts**—To see podcasts that are related (usually because they are on a similar topic or by the same person), tap the **Related** tab. You can browse the related podcasts and tap one to get to its screen.

- **Share the podcast**—Tap the **Share** button in the upper-right corner of the screen to send a link to the podcast via Mail, Message, Twitter, or Facebook. You can copy a link to the podcast to paste into a document by tapping **Copy Link**.

- **Preview it**—To listen to a podcast, tap the episode you want to listen to. On an iPhone/iPod touch, the episode immediately begins to play and you can use the app's playback controls to listen to it. On an iPad, you see the Episodes icon appear; tap the **Play** button in the icon to listen to it. See "Using the Podcast App's Now Playing Screen" for the details.

- **Download it**—To download an episode, tap its **Download** button (downward-pointing arrow). The episode is downloaded to your device. When the process is complete, the Download button is replaced by the text "DOWNLOADED" to indicate the episode is now stored in your library from where you can listen to it. This option is useful when you want to try listening to individual episodes of a podcast, but if you aren't sure if you want to subscribe to it yet.

- **Subscribe to it**—To add the podcast to your library so that new episodes are automatically available there, tap **SUBSCRIBE**. You move into your library and see the podcast to which you are subscribed. All the available episodes for the podcast become available in your library and you can download and listen to them.

 TIP To move back to your library from the store, tap the Library button. If you are browsing in categories or on some other screens, you may need to tap the Back button to get back to a screen with the Library button on it.

Working with Your Podcast Library

All the podcasts to which you are subscribed or for which you've downloaded at least one episode are stored in your library. Here you can browse your podcasts and choose which ones you want to play.

Browsing Your Podcasts

To access your library, tap the **Podcasts** app on the Home screen. Tap the **Podcasts** tab at the bottom of the screen. You see each podcast to which you've subscribed along with those of which you've downloaded at least one episode (see Figure 16.8). The badge (blue circle with a number in it) indicates how many episodes of the podcast are available to you that you haven't listened to yet. If there are more podcasts than can be displayed on the screen, you can swipe up and down the screen to browse them. To view the episodes of a podcast, tap its icon (this is covered in the section called "Listening to Audio Podcasts," later in this chapter).

FIGURE 16.8

In your podcast library, you see each podcast that is available for your listening (or watching) enjoyment.

You can switch between views of your podcasts. The default Icon view shows each podcast as a large thumbnail, as shown in Figure 16.8. (On an iPhone/iPod touch, these buttons are located on the right side of the top of the screen; you might have to swipe down the screen to move to the top where they are located.) If you tap the List view button, you see the podcasts listed with small icons; the number of episodes to which you haven't listened is indicated by the number to the right of the podcast's name (see Figure 16.9 to see this view on an iPad and Figure 16.10 to see it on an iPhone/iPod touch). You can swipe up and down the screen to browse all your podcasts.

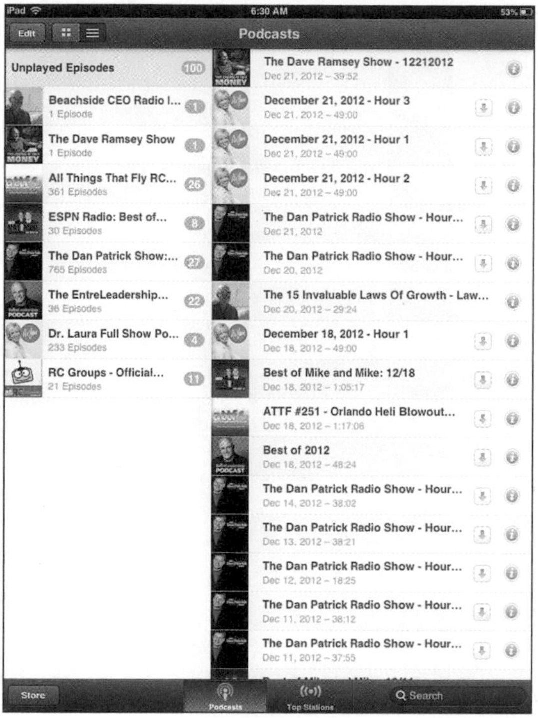

FIGURE 16.9

The List view is a more efficient way to browse your podcasts and to get to specific episodes (iPad shown here).

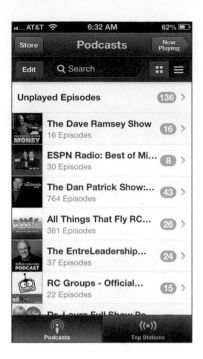

FIGURE 16.10

The List view on an iPhone/iPod touch looks a bit different, but works similarly.

On an iPad, on the right side of the window, you can browse all the episodes to which you haven't listened. If you tap a podcast on the left side of the window, you see episodes for only that podcast on the right side of the window.

On an iPhone/iPod touch, you can tap a podcast to view its episodes.

Deleting Podcasts

To remove a podcast from your library, tap the **Icon view** button and then tap the **Edit** button. Tap the **Remove** button (x) that appears on the podcast's icon. The podcast is deleted from your library. When you are finished deleting podcasts, tap **Done**.

Changing the Order of Podcasts

You can change the order in which podcasts are listed by doing the following:

1. Tap the **List view** button.

2. Tap **Edit**. List buttons appear for each podcast to the right of the podcast's name (see Figure 16.11).

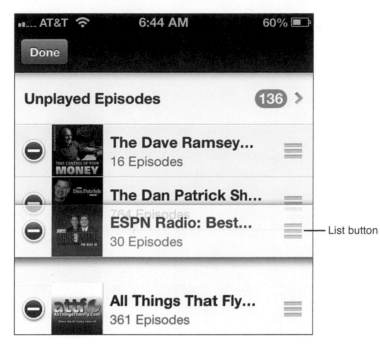

FIGURE 16.11

You can change the order in which podcasts are listed by dragging them up or down this screen.

  TIP   You can delete podcasts when you are in the Edit mode by tapping the **Unlock** button that appears to the left of their icons and then tapping **Delete**.

3. Drag the List button up or down the screen to change the order in which a podcast is listed.

4. Repeat step 3 until you've put all the podcasts where you want them.

5. Tap **Done**.

The order you set in the List view changes the Icon view, too.

  NOTE   You don't have to have Podcast syncing enabled for a device in iTunes for the podcasts to be in sync. As long as the podcast is subscribed to in iTunes and on the iOS device, the syncing process occurs via your Apple ID/iCloud account; when you switch devices, you pick up in a podcast right where you left off.

Listening to Audio Podcasts

The point of stocking your library with podcasts is so that you can enjoy them.
The Podcasts app has a lot of useful tools you can use to listen to (or watch) the
podcasts available in your library.

Finding Podcasts to Which You Want to Listen

Earlier, you learned how to browse your podcast library, which is one way to find
the podcast to which you want to listen.

In Icon view, tap the icon for the podcast you want to listen to; the episode list for
that podcast appears (see Figure 16.12.). List view on an iPhone/iPod touch works
in the same way; tap the podcast whose episodes you want to see and you move
to the episode list for that podcast.

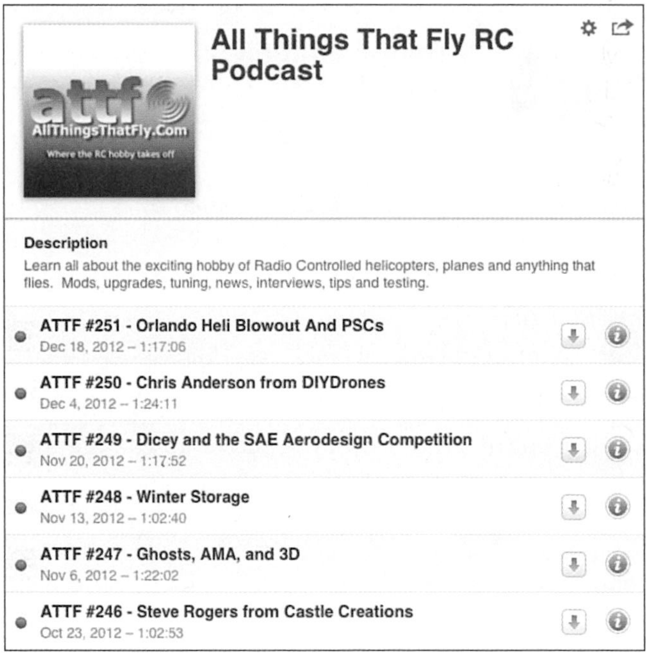

FIGURE 16.12

Here you see all the episodes for the All Things That Fly *podcast in this library.*

TIP In the List view on an iPad, you can tap a specific podcast to see only its episodes, or you can tap **Unplayed Episodes** to see all the unplayed episodes of all podcasts. This enables you to listen to episodes from any podcast all from one screen.

If you have a lot of podcasts, you can use the app's Search tool to find the podcasts to which you want to listen. Tap the Search bar (on an iPad, this is in the bottom-right corner of the screen; on an iPhone/iPod touch, it is in the top center, and you might have to swipe down the screen to move up on the screen to see it). Type the information for which you want to search, such as the title of the podcast. The search results appear as you type. Depending on your search term, you may see podcasts along with individual episodes that meet your search. Tap a podcast to see its episode list or tap an episode to listen to it.

Working with a Podcast's Episode List

You typically move to a podcast's episode list (see Figure 16.12) to choose an episode to which you want to listen. Episodes you haven't listened to are marked with a blue circle; as you listen, this circle "empties" to indicate how much of the episode you've heard.

On the episode list, you can do the following:

- **Browse episodes**—Swipe up or down the screen to browse all the episodes available to you.

- **Get information**—At the top of the episode list, you see the podcast's title and graphic. Below that is a description of the podcast (on an iPhone/iPod touch, you may have to tap **More** to see all the description). Under that, you see each episode. The title of each is shown in bold. Under that is the date on which the episode was released and the running time. To get specific information about an episode, tap its info button ("i" on iPad, the right-facing arrow on an iPhone/iPod touch). You see detailed information for the episode (see Figure 16.13).

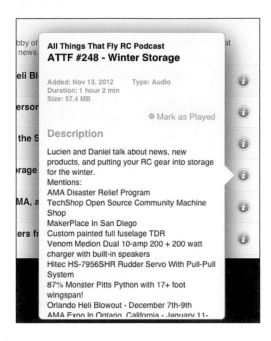

FIGURE 16.13

You can get detailed information for each episode of a podcast.

 TIP If you don't want to hear a particular episode of a podcast, tap the **Mark as Played** on its information window. That episode will be skipped if the app chooses an episode to play.

- **Share**—Tap the **Share** button to tell others about the podcast using Mail, Messages, Twitter, or Facebook. You also can copy a link to the podcast that you can paste into other documents.

- **Configure a podcast's settings**—Earlier in the chapter, you learned how to configure the Podcasts app to manage your podcasts, such as by automatically downloading episodes. You can override these global settings for a podcast to customize how the Podcasts app manages it and you can set some additional options for a podcast. On an iPad, tap the **Gear** button at the top of the episode list. On an iPhone/iPod touch, tap the right-facing arrow that appears at the top of the screen. You see the settings for the podcast.

  Slide the **Subscription** to ON to subscribe to the podcast, or slide it to OFF to stop subscribing to it. Assuming you have the global Auto-Downloads enabled, tap **Default (On)** and tap **OFF** if you no longer want new episodes to be downloaded automatically. Tap **Auto-Downloads to Keep** (this appears only if Auto-Downloads is enabled) to determine how automatically downloaded episodes are retained; for example, tap **All Unplayed Episodes** to have only episodes you haven't listened to kept on your device. In the Sort This Podcast section, tap **Newest First** or **Oldest First** to see the episodes listed in the order you choose. The same options are available to determine how the app plays episodes when it chooses an episode to play (more on this later). You can use the **Mark All As Played** or **Marked All As Unplayed** options to change the play status of all the podcast's episodes.

When you are done configuring the podcast, tap outside the window on an iPad, or tap **Episodes** on an iPhone/iPod touch.

- **Download episodes**—Any episodes not stored on your device are marked with the Download button (the downward-facing arrow). Tap this to download an episode to your device so that it will play without an Internet connection. If your device will be disconnected for a while, or if you don't allow podcasts to stream via a cellular network, it's a good idea to download the podcasts to which you want to listen before you disconnect from a Wi-Fi network.

- **Listen to an episode**—To listen to an episode, tap it. If it has been downloaded to your device, it starts playing immediately. If not, it starts to download, and when a sufficient amount has been downloaded, it starts to play. When you play an episode, the Now Playing screen appears.

Using the Podcast App's Now Playing Screen

While you are playing a podcast, there are lots of ways you can control it from the Now Playing screen (see Figure 16.14), as you see in the following list:

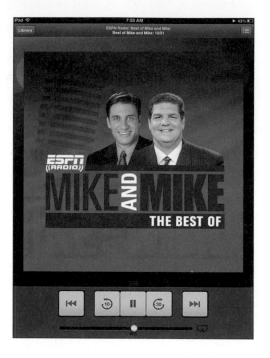

FIGURE 16.14

The Now Playing screen offers lots of ways to control your podcasts.

- **Change episodes**—Tap the **Previous** button (on the far left of the toolbar) or the **Next** button (on the far right of the toolbar) to jump to the previous or the next episode, respectively.

- **Repeat the last ten seconds**—Tap the **10** button to replay the last 10 seconds of the episode.

- **Skip ahead 30 seconds**—Tap the **30** button to jump ahead 30 seconds in the episode.

- **Play/Pause**—This button plays a paused episode or pauses one that is playing.

- **Change volume**—Drag the slider to increase or decrease the volume.

- **Change playback device**—Tap the **AirPlay** button to stream the episode to an AirPlay device, such as an Apple TV.

Swipe up on the Now Playing screen just above the toolbar, or double-tap this area to reveal even more controls (see Figure 16.15):

FIGURE 16.15

When you swipe up on the Podcast app's Now Playing screen, you see additional controls.

- **Share**—Tap the **Share** button to share information about the podcast.

- **Change playback speed**—Tap the **1x** button; the podcast plays at 1.5 times normal speed, tap again to play at twice the normal speed, tap again to play at three times normal speed, tap once more to play at one-half speed, and tap again to return to normal speed. The button changes to reflect the current playback speed.

- **Set the sleep timer**—Tap the **Sleep Timer** button (the clock icon); tap when you want the playback to stop and tap **Done**. When the timer expires, the podcast will stop playing. When the sleep timer is on, this button is marked with a green light.

- **Move forward or back**—Drag the playhead (the red line) to move forward or back in the episode.

 TIP You also can show or hide the additional controls by tapping once just above the toolbar at the bottom of the screen to display them or by tapping once just under the episode's title at the top of the screen to hide them.

To hide the additional controls again, swipe down on the area just below the podcast's name and episode information at the top of the screen.

TIP   You can work with your library (such as to look for new podcasts) while a podcast is playing. To move back to the Now Playing screen, tap the **Now Playing** button.

THE ABSOLUTE MINIMUM

In this chapter, you learned how to use the Podcasts app to listen to podcasts of all flavors.

- Podcasts are episodic audio or video programs. Podcasts exist on many, many topics. Most radio programs have a podcast version, for example.

- With the Podcasts app, you can find and subscribe to podcasts so that future episodes are downloaded to your iOS device automatically.

- You can store podcasts on your device by downloading them so you can listen to them at your convenience. You can also stream podcasts to your device so they play while they download.

- The Podcasts app offers lots of playback controls on the Now Playing screen. Swipe up on this screen to get to the more advanced controls, such as the playback speed button.

WATCHING VIDEO WITH THE VIDEOS APP

An iOS device is a great way to enjoy movies, TV shows, and other video content because they have very high quality displays and you can take your movies and TV shows with you wherever you go. You can load video content onto your device in a number of ways; these are explained in Chapter 13, "Downloading Content onto iPads, iPhones, or iPod touches," and Chapter 14, "Synchronizing iTunes Content with iOS Devices." Watching video on an iOS device is similar to listening to music (see Chapter 15, "Listening to Music with the Music App") because it is basically a two-step process: find the video you want to watch and use the app's playback controls to watch it. Before you start watching, take a few moments to tweak your device's video settings.

Configuring Video Settings

There are a few settings you use to configure various aspects of your iOS device's video functionality.

1. Tap **Settings** on the Home screen.

2. Tap **Videos**.

3. Tap **Start Playing**.

4. Tap **Where Left Off** to have the Videos app remember where you last were watching in a video so that it resumes at the same location when you play it again, or tap **From Beginning** to have the app always start playback from the beginning.

5. Tap **Videos**.

6. To enable or disable Closed Captioning on video, turn **Closed Captioning ON** or **OFF**, respectively.

7. To access shared video through iTunes' Home Sharing feature, tap the **Apple ID** field.

8. Enter the Apple ID and password that are being used to share content through Home Sharing in iTunes. When you are on the same network over which iTunes is sharing content, you can access any shared movies, TV shows, and other video on your iOS device.

9. Tap **Done**. You're ready to start enjoying video.

Selecting Video to Watch

The first step in watching video is to find and select the video that you want to watch. This is simpler than finding tunes in the Music app or podcasts in the Podcasts app; because video files are much larger, you typically don't have that many individual videos to watch on a device at the same time. You can usually find something to watch pretty quickly and easily by just browsing for it.

NOTE   Video files are large, which is something you need to keep in mind for several reasons. One is that they take a while to download, even if you are using a fast Wi-Fi connection or are adding them to your device via the sync process. Be sure you allow enough time to download a movie before disconnecting from the download source to complete the download, or you might not be able to watch the video when you want to. Another is that you need plenty of room on a device to store many video files on it. If your device has a relatively small amount of storage space, you must be selective about the video you have on the device to be sure you have the video you want to watch on it.

The Video app's library looks a bit different on an iPad than it does on an iPhone/ iPod touch, so read the following sections that apply to the devices you have.

TIP If you tap the **Store** button that appears on the Videos screen in the Videos app, you move into the iTunes app, where you can download additional movies, TV shows, and music videos (see Chapter 13 for details).

Selecting Video on an iPad

To get started, tap **Videos** on the Home screen. The Videos app launches, showing you the video content on your iPad. The Video app organizes your content by its type. Each type has its own tab at the top of the screen (see Figure 17.1). If you don't have a type of video, its tab won't appear (for example, if you don't have rented movies, you won't see the Rentals tab).

FIGURE 17.1

On an iPad, video content is organized on tabs.

NOTE If you don't have any videos stored on the device when you open the Video apps, you move directly to the iTunes app so that you can download video to watch.

Tap the tab for the type of content you want to watch. For example, to watch a movie that is stored in your movie library, tap **Movies**. You see the movies currently stored on the iPad. Swipe up and down the screen to browse your movies.

When you find a movie you are interested in, tap it. Its information screen appears (Figure 17.2). On the Info tab, you see a description of the movie, its release date, and other information about it. To see the chapters of the movie, tap the **Chapters** tab.

FIGURE 17.2

When you tap a movie's icon, you see its information page.

You can play the movie by tapping the **Play** button on the Info tab or by tapping the chapter that you want to view on the Chapters tab. Control the movie as described later in the section, "Watching Video."

TV shows are organized by season. When you move to the TV Shows tab, you see a thumbnail for each season of a show that is on the iPad. Tap a season to see the list of episodes it contains (see Figure 17.3). You see each episode's title, airdate, playing time, rating, and description; tap **More** to read all of an episode's description.

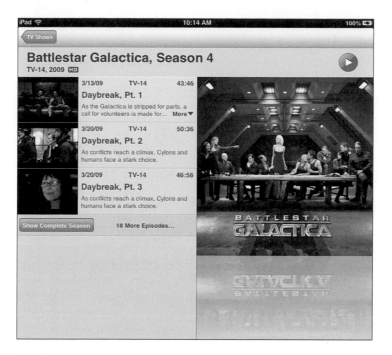

FIGURE 17.3

Here you see the episodes of season 4 of the series Battlestar Galactica *that are currently stored in the Videos app.*

If you downloaded the entire season from the iTunes Store, tap the **Show Complete Season** button. The episode list expands to show you all the episodes in that season. Tap **SD** to see the standard definition versions or **HD** to see the high definition versions (if the series has only one version, you won't see these buttons). Tap **Download** to download an episode to your iPad. Then you can watch it just like the others that are stored on your device.

TIP If you haven't downloaded an entire season from the iTunes Store, you see the **Get More Episodes** link. Tap this. You move into the iTunes app and onto the season's page. You can use the app's tools to download additional episodes from the season or the entire season (see Chapter 13 to learn how to use the iTunes app).

To play an episode, tap it. It starts to play. Control it as described in the "Watching Video" section.

Watching other types of video content is similar. Select the video you want to watch and tap its **Play** button. You can then control it using the information in the section, "Watching Video."

Video you haven't watched yet is marked with a gray dot; as you watch, the dot empties to indicate how much of the video you have watched. If you've just started the video, the dot might still be full, but the more you watch, the more empty it becomes.

 NOTE You probably won't need to search for video because your iPad can't hold that many movies and other video files due to their size. However, you can search if you want to. Scroll to the top of the Videos screen, tap the **Search** bar, and type in your search criterion. The content shown is limited to video that matches your search text.

Selecting Video on an iPhone/iPod touch

To get started, tap **Videos** on the Home screen. The Videos app launches, showing you the video content on your iPhone/iPod touch (see Figure 17.4).

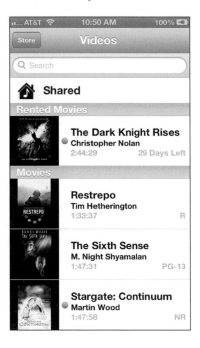

FIGURE 17.4

The Videos app on an iPhone/iPod touch presents your videos in various categories, such as Movies, TV Shows, and so on.

 NOTE If you don't have any videos stored on the device when you open the Video apps, you move directly to the iTunes app so that you can download video to watch.

Swipe up and down the screen to see all the video content, which is organized by type, such as Rented Movies, Movies, TV Shows, and Music Videos.

Video you haven't watched yet is marked with a blue dot; as you watch video, the blue dot empties to indicate how much of the video you have watched. If you've just started the video, the dot might still be full, but the more you watch, the more empty it becomes.

To get more information about a movie or TV show, tap and hold on it. An information bubble appears. For a movie, this shows the movie's title, director, and playing time.

To play a movie, music video, or episode of a TV show (when there is only one), tap it. The video begins to play; see the section, "Watching Video," to learn the tools you can use to control it.

If you have multiple episodes of a TV series, you see the name of the series and the number of episodes stored on the device, organized by season. (If you haven't watched at least one episode, the series is marked with the blue dot.) To watch an episode of a TV series when more than one episode is stored on your device, tap the season of the series you want to explore. You see the episodes of the series in that season that are stored on your iPhone/iPod touch (see Figure 17.5).

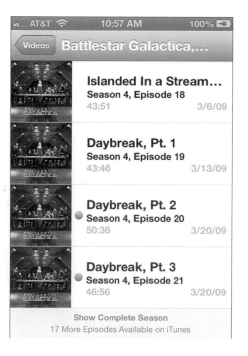

FIGURE 17.5

TV series are organized by season; tap a season to view and select the episodes it contains.

If you downloaded the entire season from the iTunes Store, tap **Show Complete Season** button. The episode list expands to show you all the episodes in that season. Tap **SD** to see the standard definition versions or **HD** to see the high definition versions (if the series has only one version, you won't see these buttons). Tap **Download** to download an episode to your iPhone/iPod touch. Then you can watch it just like the others that are stored on your device.

TIP If you haven't downloaded an entire season from the iTunes Store, you see the Get More Episodes link. Tap this. You move into the iTunes app and onto the season's page. You can use the app's tools to download additional episodes from the season or the entire season (see Chapter 13 to learn how to use the iTunes app).

To play an episode, tap it. Use the app's controls to manage the video as it plays (see "Watching Video" for the details).

NOTE You probably won't need to search for video because your iPhone/iPod touch can't hold that many movies and other video files because of their size. However, you can search if you want to. Scroll to the top of the Videos screen, tap the **Search** bar, and type in your search criterion. The content shown is limited to video that matches your search text.

Watching Video

When you tap a movie, episode of a TV show, or other video, the Videos app begins to play it. Video plays in either orientation, but you'll have the best experience if you hold your device in the landscape mode so that the video can fill the screen. The video controls appear on the screen initially; Figure 17.6 shows video playing on an iPad, and Figure 17.7 shows video playing on an iPhone (video on an iPod touch looks the same). After a few moments, the controls disappear so that all you see is the video. Tap the screen to display the controls again.

FIGURE 17.6

You can enjoy your favorite movies (one of mine is The Sixth Sense*) on your iPad.*

FIGURE 17.7

The Videos app does a great job playing TV series too, such as this show playing on an iPhone.

The Videos app provides the following controls:

- **Change volume**—Drag the volume slider (located at the bottom of the control bar) to the right to increase volume or drag to the left to decrease it.

- **Play/Pause**—This one works just like it does in the other apps, such as the Music app. Tap to play if a movie is paused, or tap to pause if a movie is playing.

- **Fast Forward or Rewind**—Tap and hold the Fast Forward or the Rewind buttons to move ahead or back in the video, respectively.

- **Move to the next or previous chapter**—Tap (but don't hold) the **Fast-Forward** or the **Rewind** buttons to move to the next chapter or back to the previous one, respectively. The video starts to play with that chapter.

- **Jump to a specific location**—Drag the playhead on the Timeline bar at the top of the screen to the right to move ahead or to the left to move backward. At the left end of this bar, you see the amount that has played, and on the right end, you see the remaining time.

- **Play a specific chapter**—To move to a specific chapter in the video on an iPhone/iPod touch, tap the **Chapter** button, which appears to the left of the Rewind button when available. (Not all video supports this feature; the controls appear only when video has chapters.) You move to the movie's Chapter Guide. Tap the chapter you want to watch or tap **Done** to return to the video at the same location. You move back to the viewing screen, and the video plays.

  To change chapters on an iPad, tap **Done**. Tap the **Chapters** tab. Then tap the chapter you want to watch. The video starts playing with the chapter you tapped.

- **Change scale**—If the aspect ratio of the video is not the same as the iOS device's screen, the video might not fill the screen and you will see black bars on the sides or at the top and bottom instead. If the video has a different aspect ratio than the device's screen, the Scale button appears just to the right of the remaining time. Tap the **Scale** button to scale the video to fit the screen or to show it in its native scale. This is a toggle setting, which switches between the two modes each time you tap it.

- **Change language**—Some video has soundtracks in different languages. To change the language for a movie or TV show, tap the **Language** button, which looks like a quote bubble. (Not all video supports this feature; the button appears only when you are watching content that does support it.) Tap the language you want to use. Tap **Done**. The video plays in the language you selected.

- **Stop watching**—When you are finished watching video, tap **Done**. The video stops playing and you return to the previous screen. It you enabled the Start Playing Where I Left Off feature described earlier, the Videos app remembers where you left off. So if you stop video and restart it at a later time, playback will resume where you left off, even if you've done a lot of other things since.

WATCHING RENTED MOVIES

Be aware that rented movies have two time limitations. One is that you can keep rented movies on your iOS device for 30 calendar days, starting from the time you downloaded the rented movies to your iOS device using the iTunes app or to your computer (not from the time when you synced the rented movies from your computer to your iOS device). The second limitation is that after you start playing rented movies, you have 24 hours (U.S.) or 48 hours (elsewhere) to finish watching it. (However, you can watch it as many times as you want within that 24- or 48-hour period.) When either of these time periods expires, the rented movie disappears from whatever device it is on.

As the expiration time nears, you see warnings on your iOS device or other device where the rented movie is stored. The time remaining for a rented movie (either since you downloaded it or since you started playing it, whichever is less) is shown next to the movie on the Rented Movies tab (iPad) or Rented Movies section (iPhone/iPod touch).

Another difference between rented movies and other kinds of content is that rented movies can exist on only one device. When you move rented movies from your computer to your iOS device, it disappears from the computer (unlike music or movies you own that remain in your iTunes Library where you can listen to or view that content). This also means that rented movies can be on only one iPhone, computer, iPod touch, or iPad at the same time. However, you can move rented movies back and forth among devices as much as you want. So you can start watching a movie on your iOS device and move it back to your computer to finish watching it (within the 24- or 48-hour viewing period).

Yet another difference is that if you rent a movie on an iPhone, iPod touch, iPad, or Apple TV, you can watch it only on the device on which you rented it.

NOTE   Video that is being shared from an iTunes library appears on the **Shared** tab on an iPad or in the **Shared** section on an iPhone/iPod touch. Tap this and then tap the iTunes Library whose video you want to watch. The video available in that library appears. You can select and play it just like video stored on your device (except that you must remain on the same network as the iTunes Library where the video is stored).

Using AirPlay to Stream Video onto Other Devices

You can use AirPlay and an Apple TV to display your iOS device's video on a TV (big screen or otherwise). As long as the iOS device and the Apple TV are on the same network, you can use the AirPlay button to select the Apple TV as the output device. As you learned in Chapter 15, you can also stream music and other audio to AirPlay devices, too.

 NOTE   AirPlay is Apple's technology that enables devices to stream audio and video to other devices. AirPlay is covered in detail in Chapter 9, "Streaming Music and Video Through an AirPlay Network."

To stream video to an AirPlay device, perform the following steps:

1. Open the **Videos** app and play the video you want to stream.

2. Tap the **AirPlay** button, which is the video icon with the upward-pointing triangle. A menu showing the devices available for streaming appears (see Figure 17.8).

FIGURE 17.8

Streaming video to a device is as easy as tapping it on this list.

3. Tap the device to which you want to stream the video. If you tapped an Apple TV, you see the AirPlay screen.

 NOTE On the AirPlay menu, when a device is marked with the video screen icon, you can watch the video on the device. If it is marked with the speaker icon, only the audio streams to the device.

4. Use the controls on the AirPlay screen to control how the video plays on the AirPlay device (see Figure 17.9). The video controls work the same as they do when you watch video on the device, except that the video appears on the AirPlay device (the iOS device is a remote control). You control the volume level using the volume controls associated with the device to which the Apple TV, such as an HDTV or home theater receiver, is connected to adjust the volume level.

FIGURE 17.9

You can manage streaming video using the Video app's controls.

To display the video on the iOS device again, tap the **AirPlay** button. Tap the **iOS device**. The video appears on the iOS device again.

Deleting Video

If you want to free up some of the iOS device's memory for other things, you can delete video directly from the iOS device. For example, you might want to download additional episodes of a TV series, but there may not be enough room to do so. You can delete video to free up enough storage space so that you can download additional content.

 NOTE Deleting video from an iOS device removes it only from the iOS device (except for rented movies, which exist only on the iOS device, so don't delete rented movies unless you've watched them as much as you want to). The video remains in your iTunes Library, even after the next sync. You can add video back to the iOS device again by including it in the sync settings. In fact, unless you remove the video content from the sync settings, it will be moved back onto your iOS device the next time you sync. You can download video you purchased from the iTunes Store whenever you want, so it doesn't hurt to delete that video from a device.

To delete movies or an entire season of a TV show from an iPad, perform the following steps:

1. Go to the tab containing the content you want to delete, such as the **Movies** tab.

2. Tap **Edit**.

3. Tap the **Delete** button (x) that appears on each video.

4. Tap **Delete** at the prompt. The video is deleted from the device.

5. Repeat steps 3 and 4 until you've deleted all the video you want to get rid of.

6. Tap **Done**.

To delete video from an iPhone/iPod touch or individual episodes of a TV show from an iPad, perform the following steps:

1. Move to the screen containing the video you want to delete.

2. Swipe left or right on the video you want to delete.

3. Tap **Delete** (see Figure 17.10).

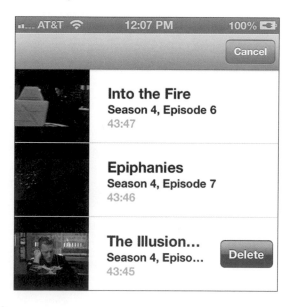

FIGURE 17.10

You can delete video content from a device to free up room for other things.

4. Tap **Delete** at the prompt. The content is deleted from the iOS device.

5. Repeat steps 1 through 4 to delete other video.

MUSIC VIDEOS AND ITUNES MATCH

If you use iTunes Match, music videos you haven't downloaded yet are marked with the iTunes match icon. Tap the video and it is downloaded to your iOS device; it starts to play when enough has been downloaded that it will stream smoothly.

THE ABSOLUTE MINIMUM

In this chapter, you learned about the Videos app that you can use to enjoy movies, TV shows, and music videos on your iOS device.

- You can use the Videos settings to specify whether video resumes playback where it left off or from the beginning; you can also enable or disable Closed Captioning.

- The first step in watching video is finding it. You can do this by browsing the various sources of video in the Videos app, which can include movies, TV shows, and so on. When you tap video on an iPad, you see its information screen. When you tap video on an iPhone/iPod touch, it plays.

- The Videos app offers playback controls that are pretty straightforward to use, especially if you've used other media apps on iOS devices, such as the Music app.

- To see video on a bigger screen, you can stream it to an Apple TV connected to a TV. You can control playback using the Video app's controls much like you use a remote control.

- You can delete video from an iOS device to free up space for other video or other kinds of content.

18

READING BOOKS WITH THE IBOOKS APP

Reading ebooks with the iBooks app offers many benefits over reading paper books. One is that you can carry an entire library of books with you so you are never without something to read, and if you don't happen to have a book you want to read in your iBooks Library, you can quickly get to the iBookstore to download new ones. Another advantage is that you also carry your own lighting with you because of iOS devices' bright screens; you can even read in the dark. Also, the iBooks app offers a lot more features than a paper book does; one of my favorites is the integrated dictionary that enables you to look up a word's definition with a couple of taps. After you've read a couple of books in iBooks, you may never want to go back to paper again.

NOTE The iBooks app is not installed by default. If it isn't installed on your devices, see Chapter 13, "Downloading Content onto iPads, iPhones, or iPod touches," for help downloading and installing apps.

Configuring iBooks Settings

Like most other apps you've learned about in this book, iBooks offers some settings you can use to configure some aspects of how it works. Here's how:

1. Tap the **Settings** app's icon to open it.

2. Tap **iBooks**. You see the iBooks settings (see Figure 18.1).

FIGURE 18.1

Use the iBooks settings to tweak the way iBooks works.

3. If you want text to evenly run from the left margin to the right margin (except for indented text and the end of paragraphs), set the **Full Justification** switch to ON. If you set this to OFF, the right side of paragraphs will be "jagged," meaning they display only as far to the right as needed to show the words in each sentence. Some people believe full justification is harder to read, so you should try both to see which you prefer.

4. To allow iBooks to automatically hyphenate words, set **Auto-hyphenation** to ON.

5. One way to advance pages in iBooks is to tap the right margin; if you want to be able to advance by tapping the left margin, too, set the **Both Margins Advance** switch to ON.

6. Later, you learn how to use bookmarks to mark places in books; to ensure your bookmarks are synced across your devices, set the **Sync Bookmarks** switch to ON. Frankly, I can't think of a reason why someone wouldn't want bookmarks to be in sync, but the OFF option is available if you need it.

7. Set the **Sync Collections** to ON to keep your collections, which are groups of books or PDF documents in your iBooks Library, in sync on all your devices. This ensures you have the same set of reading material available on each device. Again, I'm not sure when someone wouldn't want this, but you can disable it if you don't want your collections synced.

8. Set the **Show All Purchases** switch to ON to display all the books you've downloaded from the iBookstore in your iBooks Library, regardless of whether they are currently stored on the device. You can quickly download a book by tapping it. If you set this switch to OFF, only books currently stored on the device are displayed (you have to move into the iBookstore to download books you have purchased previously).

9. Turn the **Online Content** switch to ON if you want to allow iBooks to access online content that is embedded in some books.

10. If you want to see some of the sources of the programming code used in iBooks, tap **Acknowledgements**.

KEEPING YOUR BOOKS IN SYNC

When launching iBooks for the first time on an iOS device, any books you've downloaded from the iBookstore are downloaded to your device and you see a message saying that has been done. Tap **OK** to close the message. You're also prompted to allow it to sync your iBooks content (books, notes, and so on) across multiple devices (such as an iPod touch and iPad). If you tap Sync, the information is copied to your iCloud account. The next time you access iBooks with a different device that has the same account configured on it and syncing enabled, your iBooks data is updated. This ensures you have the same data available in iBooks no matter which device you happen to be using. So you can read a book on your iPod touch, and if you move to the same book in iBooks on an iPad, you'll pick up at the same page where you left off. You'll also see any notes you've created on other devices, and so on.

Downloading Books from the iBookstore

You can build your iBooks Library directly from within the iBooks app by downloading books from the iBookstore. (You can also download books from the iBookstore using iTunes on a computer, as explained in Chapter 3, "Building Your iTunes Library.") Like the iTunes app, you can browse or search for books. The method you use depends mostly on whether you have a specific idea of what you want (such as books from a particular author) or are just looking for a good read.

To get started, tap the **iBooks** app's icon. You move into your iBooks Library; if there aren't many books on its digital bookshelves, don't fret—you can remedy that situation quickly. Move into the iBookstore by tapping the **Store** button.

 NOTE If you see a book's pages instead of your iBooks Library, tap the **Library** button to move back into the iBooks Library (if you don't see that button, tap the screen and it appears).

You see the iBookstore; at the bottom and top of the screen, you see toolbars you can use to access content in different ways. The store looks a bit different on an iPad (see Figure 18.2) or an iPhone/iPod touch (see Figure 18.3), but you can download books similarly on both types of devices.

FIGURE 18.2

The iBookstore enables you to quickly find and download books for your iBooks Library's shelves.

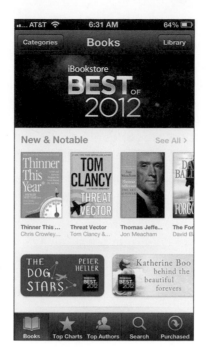

FIGURE 18.3

The iBookstore looks a little different on an iPhone/iPod touch, but it works just as well as it does on an iPad.

Here's a quick tour of some of the iBookstore's key features that enable you to find books, either by browsing or searching:

- At the top of the screen on an iPhone/iPod touch, you can tap **Categories** to browse books by category. On an iPad, you can tap **Fiction** or **Nonfiction** to browse books of those types, or tap the **More** button to see all categories of books that are available in the store. On other tabs, you can click the **All Categories** button to display the category list. When you open the list of categories, you can tap a category to browse the books it contains. This works in context of the other options. For example, when you tap **Top Authors** and then tap **Categories**, you can select a category in which you want to browse books from the top authors.

- Tap **Books** to browse books, which is the default tab you see when you first open iBooks. Like the iTunes app, you can browse books by tapping the graphics and text you see on the screen.

- Tap **NY Times** on an iPad or tap **Top Charts** and then tap **NY Times** on an iPhone/iPod touch to browse books on *The New York Times* bestsellers list.

- Tap **Top Charts** on an iPad or tap **Top Charts** and then tap **Books** on an iPhone/iPod to browse books by various "top" categories, such as Top Paid, Top Free, and so on.

- Tap **Top Authors** to browse books by author; tap **Top Paid** or **Top Free** to see books you have to buy or those you can download for free. You can browse the list or tap the index to jump to a specific author. If you tap **All Categories** (iPad) or **Categories** (iPhone/iPod touch) and tap a specific category, you can browse books by authors in that category.

- Tap **Search Store** (iPads) or **Search** (iPhone/iPod touch) to search for books by author, title, and so on by typing text into the Search bar.

- Tap **Purchased** to see and download any books you've downloaded previously from the iBookstore, whether on an iOS device or in iTunes. You can download these books from this screen. (As you learned in Chapter 13, you can configure iOS devices to automatically download any books you purchase on other devices. If you enabled the Show All Purchases option, you always see all the books you've downloaded in your library.)

The iBooks app makes it easy to find and download books into your library. The next section provides an example of browsing for books. If you know something specific about a book, such as the author, you can use the Search tool to get to books quickly; there is a section showing you how to search, too. When you've found a book you are interested in, you can add it to your library so that you can read it.

Browsing the iBookstore

Browsing the iBookstore is a great way to discover books you might not know about, but may enjoy reading, or books that you know something about, such as the author or category. Like the iTunes app, you can tap just about any graphic, button, or text to move to the object to which its link is connected. As you learned in the previous section, there are many options for browsing books in the store. The following steps show how to browse the books by author in a specific category; using the options is similar, so after you've browsed in one way, you can easily browse using any way you choose:

1. On the Home screen, tap **iBooks**. iBooks opens.

2. Tap **Store**.

3. Tap **Top Authors**.

4. Tap **Paid** (iPads) or **Top Paid** (iPhone/iPod touches) to browse books you have to pay for or **Free/Top Free** to browse free books.

5. Tap **All Categories** (iPads) or **Categories** (iPhone/iPod touches).

6. Swipe up and down the screen to browse the list of categories (see Figure 18.4).

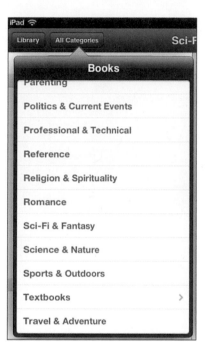

FIGURE 18.4

You can tap a category to browse books it contains.

7. Tap a category you want to browse, such as **Sci-Fi & Fantasy**. A list showing authors with books in that category appears.

 NOTE If a category has subcategories, when you tap it, you see a list of those subcategories. Tap the one of interest to you.

8. Swipe up and down the screen to browse the list of books, or tap the index to jump to a specific section of the list.

9. Tap an author. What you see depends on the number of books the author has. For example, if you tap an author containing only one book in the category, you see a screen showing the book with a link to see other books by the same author in different categories. If you tap an author with multiple books in the category, you see a list of books by that author (see Figure 18.5).

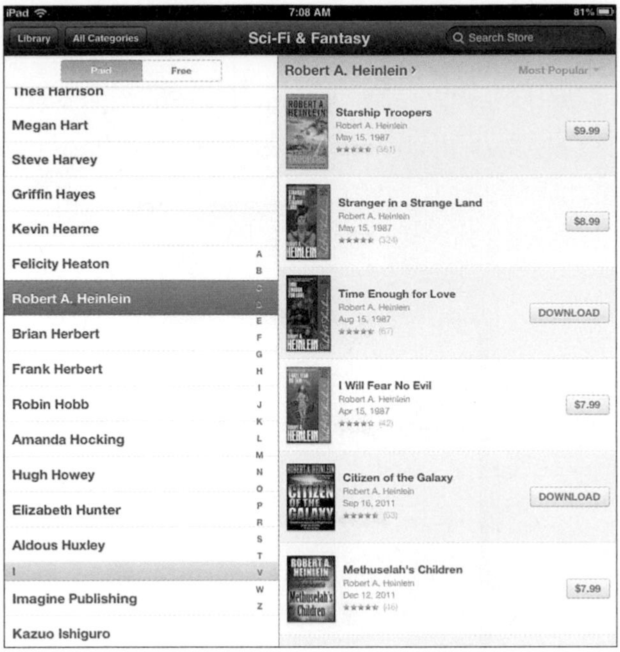

FIGURE 18.5

Here you see books in the Sci-Fi & Fantasy category by the great Robert A. Heinlein.

 NOTE Because of their larger screens, on iPads, you can see the author list and list of books for a specific author at the same time. On an iPhone/iPod touch, when you tap an author, the book list fills the screen. To get back to the author list, tap the Back button located in the upper-left corner of the screen (it is labeled with the name of the screen from which you came).

10. Swipe up and down the list of books.

11. Tap a book in which you are interested. The detail screen for that book appears. Here you see a description of the book, its user rating, and other information. You're ready to review the book, and if you want to add it to your library, download it. See the section "Downloading Books" for details of doing those tasks.

Searching the iBookstore

If you know something specific about a book you want, searching for it can be a faster and more direct route than browsing for it. Searching is straightforward, as you see in the following steps:

1. On the Home screen, tap **iBooks**. iBooks opens.

2. Tap **Store**.

3. On an iPhone/iPod touch, tap the **Search** button on the toolbar at the bottom of the screen, and then tap in the Search bar; on an iPad, tap in the Search Store bar at the top of the screen. The keyboard appears.

4. Type the criteria for which you want to search. This can be an author, part of a book's title, and so on. As you type, the app presents a list of results that match your criterion (see Figure 18.6).

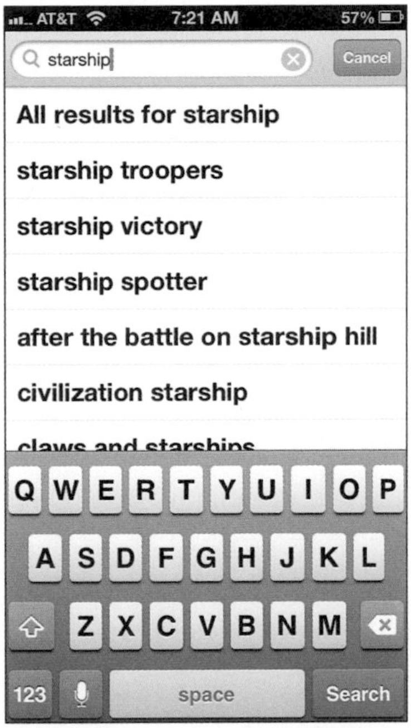

FIGURE 18.6

Here I've searched for books associated with the term "starship."

5. If something you see on the list is what you want to explore in more detail, tap it; its detail screen appears; skip to step 9.

6. To see all the results, tap **Search**. The keyboard closes, and you see the entire list of books that are related to your search term.

7. Swipe the list of results to browse it until you find the book that interests you.

8. Tap a book you want to explore.

9. Use the book's detail screen to see a description of the book, its user rating, and other information. If you want to add it to your library, download it. See the section, "Downloading Books," for details about doing those tasks.

 NOTE One area in which paper books and some other ebook readers beat an iOS device running iBooks is in bright sunlight. Because of the glossy display on iOS devices, you can get a lot of reflection in the screen, making reading difficult. You can try the different themes (explained later) to see if one works better for you in the sunlight or you may just have to shield the device from the direct sunlight.

Downloading Books

A book's detail screen provides lots of information about the book and enables you to download it to add it to your iBooks Library (see Figure 18.7). If you aren't sure you want to buy a book, you can download a sample to read for free and then buy and download the entire book later when you are sure.

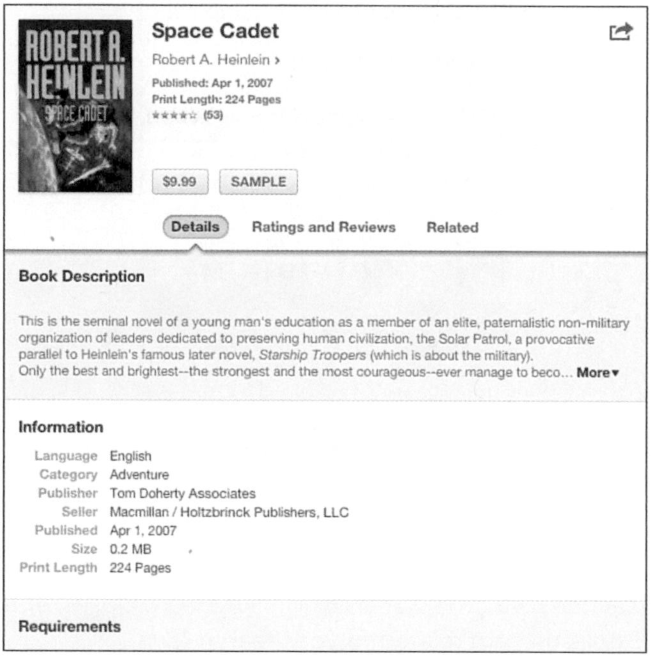

Space Cadet

Robert A. Heinlein ›

Published: Apr 1, 2007
Print Length: 224 Pages
★★★★☆ (53)

$9.99   SAMPLE

Details   Ratings and Reviews   Related

Book Description

This is the seminal novel of a young man's education as a member of an elite, paternalistic non-military organization of leaders dedicated to preserving human civilization, the Solar Patrol, a provocative parallel to Heinlein's famous later novel, *Starship Troopers* (which is about the military). Only the best and brightest--the strongest and the most courageous--ever manage to beco... **More▼**

Information

Language   English
Category   Adventure
Publisher   Tom Doherty Associates
Seller   Macmillan / Holtzbrinck Publishers, LLC
Published   Apr 1, 2007
Size   0.2 MB
Print Length   224 Pages

Requirements

FIGURE 18.7

Here you see the detail screen for the book Space Cadet.

On a book's detail screen, you can do the following:

- **Evaluate it**—At the top of the screen, you see the book's title, author, publication date, print length (which doesn't correlate to "pages" in iBooks, but it does give you a general idea of how long the book is), average rating, and number of reviews/ratings. Below that information on an iPad, or to the right on an iPhone/iPod touch, you see different buttons depending on the status of the book. If you haven't downloaded it, you see the book's price (or Free if it doesn't have a price) and the SAMPLE button. If you have previously downloaded the book, but it is not currently on your device, you can download it again by tapping **DOWNLOAD**. If the book has the DOWNLOADED status button, the book is already in your iBooks Library.

  On the **Details** tab, you see the book's description (tap **More** to see the entire description), information (such as language, published date, and so on), and requirements (including the version of iBooks that is required to read it).

  Tap **Ratings and Reviews** (iPad) or **Reviews** (iPhone/iPod touch) to see what other people think about the book (see Figure 18.8). At the top of the tab, you see the number of ratings and the relative amount of each "level" (which is indicated by the number of stars). Swipe up the screen to read the reviews, which are located toward the bottom of the window.

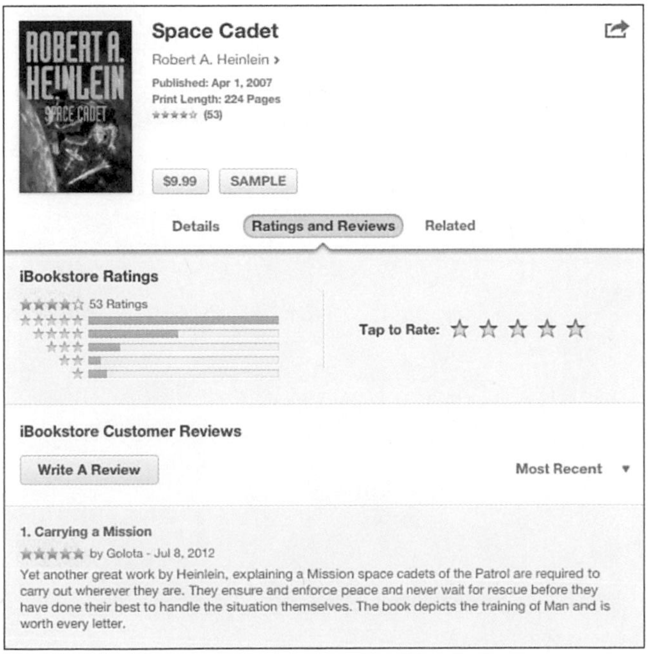

FIGURE 18.8

Most reviewers are quite positive about this book.

TIP You can rate a book by tapping one of the **Tap to Rate** stars (iPad). To add your own review, tap **Write a Review** and follow the onscreen instructions. (You must provide your Apple ID password to write a review.) On an iPhone/iPod touch, you can rate the book by tapping the stars at the top of the Write a Review screen.

- **See related books**—To view books related to the one you are evaluating, tap **Related**. You see other books by the same author, books other people who bought the current book also downloaded, and so on. You can tap a book on the Related tab to view its detail.

- **Share it**—Tap the **Share** button (located in the upper-right corner of the window). You can share a link to the book via email, message, tweet, Facebook posting, or by copying it and pasting it elsewhere.

- **Download a sample**—To try a book before you buy it, tap **SAMPLE**. The sample is downloaded and you move back to your library where you see the sample with the red Sample banner on its cover (see Figure 18.9). You can read the sample to see if you want to add the whole book (see "Reading Books in iBooks" for the details). If you decide you want the whole book, you can tap the **BUY** button that appears in iBooks when you are reading a sample. This takes you to a screen showing the price of the full book. Tap the **Price** button to start the purchase process (as described in the following bullet).

FIGURE 18.9

Samples you download are marked with the red Sample banner; full books you add to the library are marked with the blue New banner.

- **Buy a book**—To purchase and download a book, tap its **Price** button. The button becomes **BUY BOOK**. Tap that button to download the book. If prompted to do so, enter your Apple ID password and tap **OK**. You move back to your Library and see the book you added to it. Books you haven't read yet are marked with the blue New banner (see Figure 18.9). You're ready to read the book (see "Reading Books in iBooks" for the details).

TIP   You don't have to be on a book's detail screen to buy it. You can tap the Price button anywhere you see it to buy the book from that location, such as on the results of a search.

- **Download a free book**—Many books in the iBookstore are free. You can download these by tapping the **FREE** button and then tapping the **GET BOOK** button. If prompted, enter your Apple ID password and tap **OK**. The book is downloaded and added to your library, where you see it (also marked with the blue New banner).

NOTE   Use the iTunes & App Stores settings and iTunes preferences to ensure that books you download on any iOS device or computer are automatically downloaded to the others. See Chapter 2, "Working with the iTunes Store," and Chapter 13 for details.

Working with Your iBooks Library

As your book collection grows, it's important to know how to work with your iBooks Library so that you can easily find the books you want to read. You can also remove books from your library to free up storage space on your device.

Choosing a Book Collection

Your iBooks Library contains several default collections, which are Books. These are books you've added from any source; Purchased Books, which are books you've download from the iBookstore; or PDFs, which are documents you have added to your device either by downloading them directly or through the sync process. You can select a collection to work with the books or PDFs it contains. This is the first step in browsing or searching for books you want to read if the current collection doesn't contain them.

On an iPhone/iPod touch, tap the button in the center of the screen, which is labeled with the collection you are currently viewing, such as **Books** or **PDFs**. The Collections screen appears. Tap the Collection you want to view, such as **Purchased Books**. You move back to the bookshelf, which is populated with items from the collection you selected. (Later, you learn how to create your own collections.)

On an iPad, tap the **Collections** button. Then tap the collection you want to work with. You see the books in that collection on the bookshelf.

Browsing for Books

Like other areas, you can browse your bookshelf to find a book you want to read. You can browse by cover or by list.

Browsing for Books by Cover

To browse by cover, tap the **Cover** button, which contains four squares and is located in the upper-right corner of the screen. The bookshelf is organized to show covers of the items in the current collection (see Figure 18.10). Swipe up or down the screen to browse all the items in the collection. To read a book or PDF, tap its cover (the details of reading in iBooks are explained in the "Reading Books in iBooks" section, later in this chapter).

FIGURE 18.10

Browsing by cover is a lot like looking at a physical bookshelf.

Browsing for Books by List

To browse a collection using a list, tap the **List** button that is located next to the Cover button. The bookshelf changes into a list of the books in the current collection. At the bottom of the screen are four tabs you can tap to change how the list is sorted. **Bookshelf** (when you are viewing your Books or PDFs) or **Purchased** (when you are viewing your Purchased Books) matches the order of the books on the bookshelf. **Titles** sorts the list alphabetically by title. **Authors** sorts the list alphabetically by author. **Categories** organizes the contents by category; within the categories, the items are sorted alphabetically by title.

Tap the button for the sort option you want to use. Then swipe up and down the list to find the book you want to read (see Figure 18.11). To read a book or PDF, tap it (the details of reading in iBooks are explained in the "Reading Books in iBooks" section).

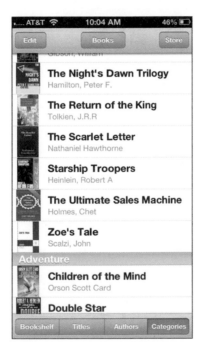

FIGURE 18.11

Browsing by list enables you to see more books on the same screen.

Searching for Books

Searching can be a way to get to a specific book more quickly than browsing for it, especially if a collection has lots of books in it. You can search from either the Cover or List view.

Swipe down the screen to get to the top where you find the Search bar. Tap in the Search bar and the keyboard appears. Type in the book's title or author. As you type, the search results shows books that match your criteria; the more specific your search term becomes, the narrower the results are. When you are done typing, tap **Search**. The keyboard closes and you see the books that meet your search term (see Figure 18.12). To read a book or PDF, tap it (the details of reading in iBooks are explained in the "Reading Books in iBooks" section).

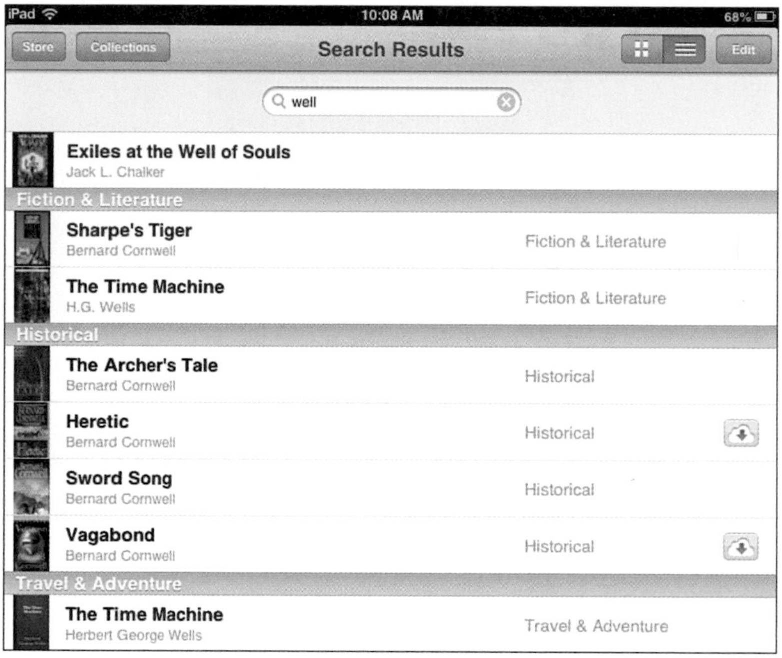

iPad
10:08 AM
68%
Store
Collections
Search Results
Edit
well
Exiles at the Well of Souls
Jack L. Chalker
Fiction & Literature
Sharpe's Tiger
Bernard Cornwell
Fiction & Literature
The Time Machine
H.G. Wells
Fiction & Literature
Historical
The Archer's Tale
Bernard Cornwell
Historical
Heretic
Bernard Cornwell
Historical
Sword Song
Bernard Cornwell
Historical
Vagabond
Bernard Cornwell
Historical
Travel & Adventure
The Time Machine
Herbert George Wells
Travel & Adventure

FIGURE 18.12

The search term "well" has resulted in books with the word "well" in their titles, along with authors whose name includes "well."

TIP If a book is marked with the Download button, you have purchased it from the iBookstore, but it is not currently stored on your device. Tap the button to download it again.

Creating Your Own Collections

As your library gets larger, you may want to organize books or PDFs into your own collections. For example, you might want to create a collection for a favorite author. Or you might want to place books on a specific topic in their own collection. Here's how to create a collection and add items to it:

1. Tap **Collections**.

2. Tap **New**.

3. Type a name for the new collection.

4. Tap **Done**.

5. Tap the collection containing the items you want to move into the collection you just created. That collection opens.

6. Browse or search for the books or PDFs you want to add to the new collection.

7. Tap **Edit**. Selection circles appear next to each book.

8. Tap the selection circles next to the items you want to place in the new collection.

9. Tap **Move** (see Figure 18.13).

FIGURE 18.13

Here I'm moving all my books by Robert A. Heinlein into a collection

10. Tap the collection into which you want to move the selected items. The items are moved into the collection on which you tapped, and you see it on the screen.

11. Move to the next collection containing items you want to add to the new collection.

12. Repeat steps 6 through 11 until you have added all the items to the new collection.

Managing Your Collections

You can change collections that you create in a number of ways:

- You can change the name of your collections by opening the Collections list and tapping **Edit**. Tap the current name and edit it as you see fit. Tap **Done** to save your changes.

- To change the order of the collections you create on the list (you can't change the order of the default collections), open the Collections list and tap **Edit**. Drag the collection name up or down using the List button on the right until your collections are in the order in which you want to see them. Tap **Done** to save your changes.

 CAUTION Before removing any item from your library, make sure you have another copy stored someplace else. If you downloaded the item from the iBookstore, you can always download it again. If the book came from your iTunes Library through the sync process, it remains there. If the book or PDF exists only on your iOS device, don't delete it unless you are sure you don't want to use it again.

- To delete a collection you've created, open the Collections list and tap **Edit**. Tap the Unlock button next to the collection's name. Tap **Delete**. If you want only the collection to be removed and its contents to remain in your Library, tap **Don't Remove**. If you want the collection and its contents to be removed, tap **Remove**. Tap **Done**.

Removing Books from the Library

You can remove books or PDFs from your library to free up space on your device—see the previous Caution before doing this. To remove an item from your library, open the collection containing the items you want to remove. Tap **Edit**. When you are using the List view, tap the selection circle next to each item you want to delete; when you are using the Icon view, tap the cover of the items you want to delete. Tap **Delete**. Tap how you want the selected books to be handled in the resulting prompt. For example, when you delete an item that you downloaded from the iBookstore, the options are **Delete This Copy** or **Delete From All Devices**. If the item is from another source, the only choice is **Delete**.

When you choose an option in the prompt, the selected items are deleted.

Reading Books in iBooks

iBooks offers many features that make reading digital books even better than reading the paper version. To read a book, tap it in the library. The book opens to the first page if you haven't read it before or to the page you left off if you have been reading it in a previous session. Although it might not be obvious when you first see it, the reading screen offers many useful features, including the following:

- **Turn the page**—To move to the next page, tap on the right side of the screen or swipe your finger to the left to flip the page. To move to a previous page, tap on the left side of the screen or swipe your finger to the right. (If you enabled the **Both Margins Advance** setting, tapping the left margin moves ahead too.)

> **NOTE** The iBooks app offers different ways to format the books you read, as you learn in this chapter. The information in this section is based on the White/Book theme. The other themes provide different screen layouts. Also, different types of books can display different types of controls. For example, when you read a children's book, thumbnails replace the page numbers.

- **Hide/Show controls**—Tap the center of the screen to show or hide the controls on the toolbar that appears at the top of the screen. These controls are as follows (from left to right): Library, which takes you back to your library; Table of Contents, which takes you to the table of contents and bookmarks, Formatting, which enables you to change the font and other formatting options; Search, which you can use to search the book's contents; and Bookmark, which enables you to set or remove a bookmark on the current page (see Figure 18.14).

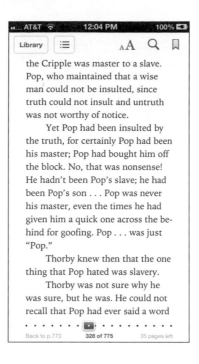

FIGURE 18.14

The toolbar at the top of the screen provides lots of useful functions.

At the bottom of the screen, you see the relative position of the current page (indicated by the box) to the total length of the book. At the bottom of the screen, you see the current "page" number and the total number. In the lower-right corner, you see the number of "pages" left in the current element, such as the chapter.

PAGE NUMBERS

The page numbers you see in iBooks are actually screen numbers. When you change the device's orientation, font, or another factor that causes iBooks to change the layout of a book's screens, the page location and total page count also change to reflect the current number of screens in the book and element (such as chapter).

- **Change Orientation**—When you rotate the device, the book is reformatted to match the current orientation and theme (themes are explained shortly).

- **Navigate with the Table of Contents**—Tap the **Table of Contents** button; then tap the **Contents** tab. Browse the book's table of contents by swiping up and down the screen. Tap the location to which you want to move; the book jumps to that chapter. To return to your previous location in the current book, tap **Resume** instead.

- **Change pages quickly**—Drag the location box at the bottom of the screen to quickly scroll ahead or back, respectively, in the book. As you drag, the chapter and page number of the box's current location appears in a pop-up box. When you release the box, you jump to its new location.

- **Set brightness**—Tap the **Formatting** button. The Formatting palette opens (see Figure 18.15). Drag the slider to change brightness. Tap outside the palette to close it.

- **Change font and size**—Tap the **Formatting** button. The Formatting palette opens. Tap the larger letter to increase or the smaller letter to decrease the size of the font displayed; as you change the size, iBooks resizes the book's font in the background. Tap the **Fonts** button; the list of available font types appears. Tap the font type you want to use; iBooks reformats the book with that style in the background.

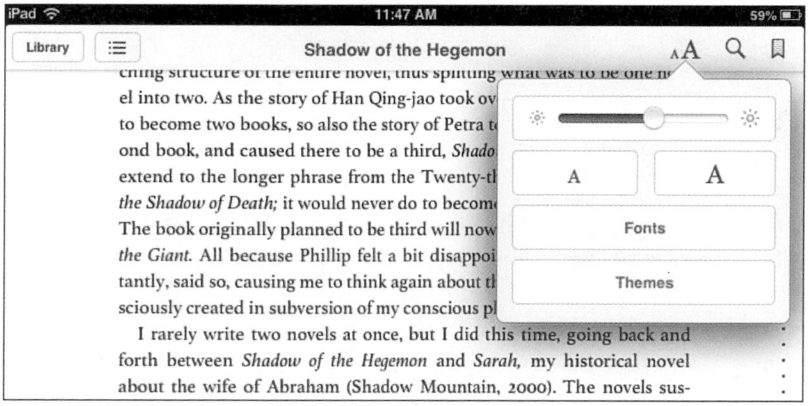

FIGURE 18.15

You can use the Formatting palette to change how books appear in the iBooks app.

- **Change theme**—Tap the **Formatting** button. The Formatting palette opens. On an iPhone/iPod touch, tap **Themes**. Tap **White** to use the default black text on a white background. Tap **Sepia** to apply Sepia tones to the book's pages, tap **Night** to change the layout to light text on a dark background (see Figure 18.16). Tap **Scroll** if you want the book to appear as a single, continuous block of text that you swipe up the screen to read, or tap **Book** to have the text appear on "pages." On an iPad, tap **Full Screen** to remove the page-like elements from the screen, such as the curved page edges. Tap outside of the palette to close it.

FIGURE 18.16

The Night theme enhances the nighttime reading experience.

- **Search—** Tap the **Search** button (the magnifying glass) to search for specific text in the book. Type the text for which you want to search. iBooks searches your books and presents matches to you. The results include instances in the current book, which are indicated by chapter and page number and those from other books, which are indicated by including references to those books. The more specific you make your search, the narrower the list of results will be. When you finish entering your search text, tap **Search** to close the keyboard to see the full list of results. Swipe up and down the screen to browse the results. Tap a result to move to it in the book; the search term is highlighted on the page.

  To return to the search results page, tap the **Search** button again. When the keyboard is hidden, you can tap the **Search Web** button to perform a web search or **Search Wikipedia** to search the Wikipedia website. To clear a search, tap the **Clear** button (x) in the Search bar. Click **Cancel** to close the search feature.

- **Navigate with bookmarks**—When you want to be able to return to a location in the book, tap the **Bookmark** button (the icon looks like a bookmark and is on the right end of the toolbar). The page is marked and a red bookmark appears on it in the upper-right corner of the page. You can mark as many pages with bookmarks as you like.

  To return to a bookmark, tap the **Table of Contents** button and then tap the **BOOKMARKS** tab. You see a list of all the bookmarks in the book; the chapter, page number, and day when the bookmark was created are shown. Tap a bookmark to return to its location.

  To remove a bookmark, move to its location and tap it; the bookmark will be deleted and disappears from the page.

- **Work with text**—Select some text on a page; you can double-tap a word to select it or use the selection markers to enclose the words you want to select (just like text in other apps, such as in an email message). When you lift your finger from the screen, a menu with the following commands appears:

  - Tap **Copy** (shown only for nonprotected works) to copy the selected text.

  - Tap **Define** to look up the selected text in a dictionary. (This is my favorite and most-used iBooks feature, especially when reading older books.)

  - Tap **Highlight** to highlight the selected text. The selection is highlighted with the current color. To change the highlighting, tap the highlighted section. On the results menu (see Figure 18.17), tap the color buttons on the far left to change the highlight color. Tap the circle with a slash through it to remove the highlight.

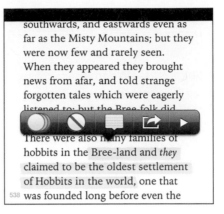

FIGURE 18.17

The iBooks highlighter never runs out of ink.

 TIP To select text without highlighting it, double-tap the first word you want to include, and then drag the selection markers to enclose the text you want to select.

- Tap **Notes** to add notes to the selected text. On the resulting screen, type the note you want to attach to the text, and tap **Done** (see Figure 18.18). When you return to the reading screen, the text is highlighted, and you see the note icon on the side of the screen. Tap this icon to read or edit the note. You also can navigate to specific notes in a book by moving to the Table of Contents tab, tapping the **NOTES** tab, and tapping the note to which you want to move.

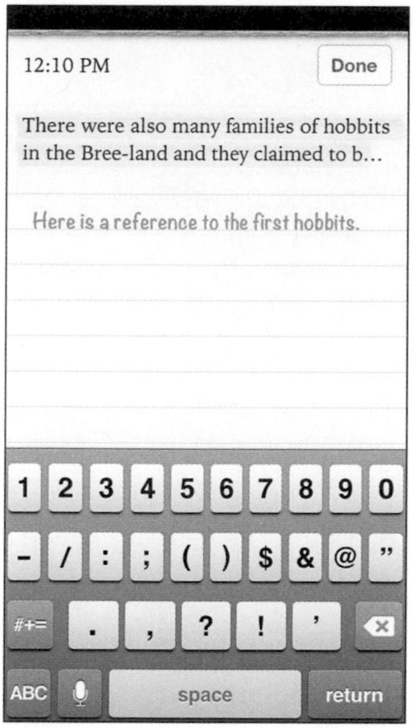
12:10 PM
Done
There were also many families of hobbits in the Bree-land and they claimed to b...
Here is a reference to the first hobbits.
1 2 3 4 5 6 7 8 9 0
- / : ; ( ) $ & @ "
#+= . , ? ! '
ABC
space
return

FIGURE 18.18

You can attach notes to text.

- Tap **Search** to perform a search for the selected text.
- Tap **Share** to include the selected text as an excerpt via Mail, Messages, Twitter, or Facebook.

NOTE The commands you see depend on what you have selected, so the specific menu you see when you select text changes based on what is selected

- **Read PDFs**—iBooks is also a great PDF reader for your iOS device. To read a PDF, open the Collections list and tap **PDFs**. When you return to the library, you see the PDFs stored in your library. Tap a PDF's cover to view it. It opens and you can use controls that are similar to those for reading books to view it.

ADDING PDFS TO YOUR LIBRARY

When you tap a PDF document in a different app, such as an attachment to an email message or a link on a web page, you are presented with the option to open it in iBooks. When you choose this option, the PDF is copied into your iBooks Library and added to the PDFs collection.

THE ABSOLUTE MINIMUM

In this chapter, you learned about the amazing iBooks app that you can use to read books and PDFs on your iOS device. Key topics included the following:

- You can configure a few iBooks settings, such as whether you want to be able to advance pages by tapping on both the left or right margins.

- The iBookstore is integrated into the iBooks app so you can easily add books to your library whenever you want. You can browse for books or search for them. You can download and read a sample of a book for free. When you are ready to download a full book and add it to your library, it requires only a few taps.

- You can browse or search in your library to find books you want to read. You can also work with various collections, such as the default Books or Purchased Books collections that come with iBooks or collections that you create.

- iBooks has lots of great features to make the most of your ebook reading experiences. You can rapidly navigate books, and you can change a variety of formatting options, including fonts and themes. You can also work with text, such as highlighting it, adding notes, getting definitions, and searching.

19

WORKING WITH PHOTOS AND VIDEO WITH THE CAMERA AND PHOTOS APPS

Photos and video are major features of iOS devices. You can use iOS devices to capture both photos and video using the Camera app. You can use the Photos app to view, edit, and organize your photos. When combined with Photo Stream, you can also put your photos on the cloud so that you can easily share them with others.

Photos are also useful in many other apps. For example, you can use the Mail app to email photos to others, the Messages app to transport them via messages, the Settings app to create custom wallpaper using your photos, and so on.

Setting Photo Preferences

There are a number of settings related to photos; these include Photo Stream, slideshow, and HDR (if available) settings. Here's how to set them:

1. On the Home screen, tap **Settings**.

2. Tap **Photos & Camera** (see Figure 19.1).

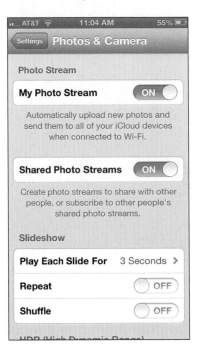

FIGURE 19.1

Here are the Photos & Camera settings for an iPhone 5.

3. To have your iOS device automatically download photos from and upload photos to your Photo Stream, set **Photo Stream** to ON; if you don't want photos to be downloaded or uploaded automatically, set it to OFF instead. (Configuring Photo Stream on an iOS device is explained in more detail in Chapter 11, "Putting Your Photos on the Cloud with Photo Stream.")

4. To share your Photo Streams with others and to subscribe to other people's Photo Streams, slide the **Shared Photo Streams** switch to ON (you learn how to share Photo Streams later in this chapter).

5. Tap **Play Each Slide For**, which impacts slideshows you view on your iOS device.

6. Tap the amount of time you want each slide in a slideshow to appear on the screen.

7. Tap **Photos & Camera**.

8. To make slideshows repeat until you stop them, set **Repeat** to ON. When it is ON, you have to stop slideshows manually. When the status is OFF, slideshows play through once and then stop.

9. To view photos in a random order in a slideshow, set **Shuffle** to ON. When its status is ON, photos appear in random order during slideshows. To have photos appear in the order they are in the selected source for the slideshow, set Shuffle to OFF.

10. If you use the HDR capability when you take photos and want only the HDR version to be saved, set **Keep Normal Photo** to OFF. If you want both the HDR version and the normal version to be saved, set Keep Normal Photo to ON.

HDR

The High Dynamic Range (HDR) feature causes an iOS device to take three shots of the image with each having a different exposure level. It then combines the three images into one higher quality image. When HDR is ON and you take a photo, you see two versions in the Photos app: one is the HDR version and the other is the standard version. (You can change this so only one version is saved using the settings described as in the previous steps.) The downside to using HDR is that the app works more slowly because it has to take three versions of each photo. It also doesn't work well when the light is low. However, as long as you don't need to take rapid-fire photos and are in a fairly bright environment, try leaving HDR set to ON for best image quality. (HDR is not available on all iOS devices.)

Using the Camera App to Take Photos and Video

iOS devices have cameras with a lens on both sides of the device (the front-side lens faces you when you are holding the device, and the back-side lens points away from you) that you can use to take photos and video. Different types of devices (such as an iPhone 5 versus an iPad mini) have different quality levels and features, but all iOS devices can capture photos and videos at some level. The iPhone 5 and iPod touch, fourth generation, are currently the devices with the highest-quality cameras with the most features. Other devices have cameras that you can use just as easily, although they may not support all the features described in this chapter.

NOTE   Because of the variety of photo capabilities on the various models and generations of iOS devices, it is impractical to cover all of them in a short chapter. Because they are the most capable and useful (because of their size and shape) devices for taking photos and video, this section is based on iPhone 5 and iPod touch, fourth generation, hardware. Other devices will have different capabilities, so you may see some differences in the book's text and figures and your device, but you can still follow along. For example, taking photos on an iPad mini is somewhat different, but you won't have any trouble adapting the information here for a different device.

Taking Photos

The Camera app enables you to take photos on your iOS device. All iOS devices can take standard photos. An iPhone 5 and iPod touch, fourth generation, can also take panoramic photos.

Taking Standard Photos

You can use the Camera app to capture photos, like so:

1. On the Home screen, tap **Camera**.

2. To capture a photo in landscape mode, rotate the iOS device so that it's horizontal; of course, you can use either orientation to take photos just as you can with any other camera.

TIP   An iOS device's camera is sensitive to movement, so if your hand moves while you are taking a photo, the photo is likely to be blurry. Sometimes, part of the image will be in focus and another part of it isn't, so be sure to check the view before you capture a photo. This is especially true when you zoom in. If you are getting blurry photos, the problem is probably your hand moving while you are taking them. Because the camera is digital, you can take as many photos as you need to get it right. Just keep tapping the **Camera** button. You'll want to delete the rejects (you learn how later) periodically so you don't waste room storing them or clutter up the Photos app.

3. Ensure the **Photo/Video** switch is set to Photo (see Figure 19.2).

Flash

Change Lens

Photo/Video

FIGURE 19.2

The Camera app enables you to take photos whenever you have your iOS device.

4. Tap the **Lens Change** button to switch the camera being used for the photo.
    When you change the lens, the image briefly freezes, and then you start
    seeing through the other lens. The front-side lens has fewer features than the
    back-side lens. For example, you can't zoom when using the front-side lens,
    nor does it use the flash. When you are using the front-side lens, some of the
    details in these steps won't apply, but the general process is the same.

5. By default, the flash will go off automatically as needed; if that's what you
    want, skip to step 7. If you want to manually turn the flash off or on, tap **Auto**.

6. Tap **On** to set the flash to fire or **Off** to prevent it from lighting up. The menu
    closes and you see the current setting for the flash.

7. Tap **Options**. (If you are using the front-side lens, you have to switch to the
    back-side lens to change the options.)

8. Set **Grid** to ON to see an alignment grid over the image.

9. Set **HDR** to ON if you want to capture images with the highest possible
    quality.

10. Tap **Done**.

11. Tap the screen where you want the image to be focused. The blue focus box appears where you tapped. This indicates where the focus and exposure will be set.

12. Unpinch on the image to zoom in. The Zoom slider appears. (You can't use zoom when taking photos with the front-side camera.)

13. Pinch or unpinch on the image, or to change the level of zoom drag the slider toward the + to zoom in or toward the − to zoom out.

14. Tap again where you want the focus and exposure to be set. The blue focus box indicates the current location on the image.

15. Continue using the zoom and focus controls along with moving the camera until the photo is properly framed (see Figure 19.3).

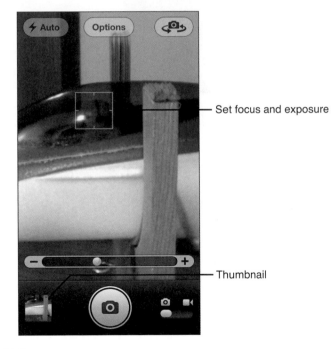

FIGURE 19.3

When you've framed and focused the image, you're ready to capture it.

16. Tap the **Camera** button on the screen or either **Volume** button on the side of the iOS device. The Camera app captures the photo, and the shutter closes briefly while the photo is recorded (you hear the shutter sound unless the device is muted). When the shutter opens again, you're ready to take the next

photo. The process takes longer when HDR is on because the camera has to save three versions of the image and blend them together.

17. To take more photos, repeat steps 4 through 16. To see the photo you most recently captured, tap the **Thumbnail** button, which shows the most recent photo you took. The photo appears on the screen with the Photo app's photo-viewing controls.

18. Use the app's tools to view the photo (see "Working with Photos Using the Photos App" later in this chapter for the details).

19. To delete a photo, tap the **Trashcan** and then tap **Delete Photo**. The app deletes the photo, and you see the next photo in the Photo Roll album.

20. Tap the **Camera** button. You move back into the Camera app, and you can take more photos.

LOCATION INFORMATION ON PHOTOS

If you allow it when you are prompted, the iOS uses its GPS system or network location to tag the location where photos and video were captured. Some applications can use this information to associate photos with specific places, such as iPhoto (where you can use this data to locate your photos on maps, find photos by their locations, and so on).

Taking Photos Quickly

Because it is likely to be with you constantly, an iOS device is a great camera of opportunity. You can use its Quick Access feature to take photos in a very short time when your iOS device is asleep/locked.

1. Press the **Home** button. The Lock screen appears.

 NOTE If you have a passcode set on your iOS device, you can use the Quick Access feature without entering your passcode. You can also view the photos you have taken since you started using Quick Access. To do anything else, you need to enter your passcode to unlock the device.

2. Swipe up on the **Camera** icon at the bottom of the screen (see Figure 19.4). The Camera app opens.

FIGURE 19.4

The Quick Access feature enables you to take photos more quickly than you can by unlocking the device and opening the Camera app.

3. Use the camera controls to frame and zoom the photo and set options as needed; these work the same as when you start with the Camera app as described in the previous steps.

4. Press either Volume button on the side of the iOS device or tap the **Camera** icon to take the photo.

Taking Panoramic Photos

The Camera app can take panoramic photos by capturing a series of images as you pan the camera across a screen and then "stitching" those images together into one panoramic image. To take a panoramic photo, perform the following steps:

1. Open the Camera app.

2. Tap **Options**.

 NOTE The Panorama mode works only when the iPhone/iPod touch is held in the Portrait orientation.

3. Tap **Panorama**. The app moves into Panorama mode (see Figure 19.5). On the screen, you see a dark box across the screen representing the entire image and a thumbnail showing the current frame.

FIGURE 19.5

You can use the Panorama mode to capture a large image.

4. Tap the **Camera** button. The app begins capturing images.

5. Slowly sweep the iOS device to the right while keeping the arrow centered on the line on the screen. This keeps the centerline consistent through all the images; the better you keep the arrow on the line, the better the photo will be.

6. When you've moved to the "end" of the image, tap **Done**. You move back to the starting point and the panoramic photo is created.

7. To capture another image, repeat steps 4 through 6.

8. When you are done, tap **Done**.

9. Preview the image by tapping the **Thumbnail** button.

Taking Video

You can capture video as easily as you can still images. Here's how.

1. Open the Camera app.

2. To capture video in landscape mode, rotate the device so that it's horizontal; you can use either orientation to take video just as you can with any other video camera.

3. Set the **Photo/Video** switch to **Video** (the video camera icon).

4. Choose which lens you want to use, configure the flash, and use focus controls to frame the starting image for the video, just like setting up a still image (see steps 4 through 15 in the "Taking Standard Photos" task). (You can't zoom, show the grid, or use HDR when taking video.)

5. To change the proportion of the video image to widescreen, double-tap the screen. Black bars appear at the top and bottom of the screen.

6. To start recording, tap the **Start/Stop** button (see Figure 19.6). The iOS device starts capturing video, and you hear the start/stop recording tone; you see a counter on the screen showing how long you've been recording.

FIGURE 19.6

The Camera app also enables you to take video.

7. To stop recording, tap the **Start/Stop** button again. You hear the stop recoding tone and the clip is saved in the Photos app.

8. To preview the video clip, tap the **Thumbnail** button.

9. Use the video tools to view or edit the clip (see "Working with Video Using the Photos App" later in this chapter for the details).

Working with Photos Using the Photos App

After you've loaded your iOS device with photos, you can use the Photos app to view them individually and as slideshows. You can also do some basic editing on your photos and use the photos for a number of tasks, such as setting the iOS device's wallpaper or emailing them.

 NOTE In Chapter 14, "Synchronizing iTunes Content with iOS Devices," you learn how to copy photos from a computer onto an iOS device so that you can view and work with them.

Viewing Photos Individually

The Photos app enables you to view your photos individually. When you open the Photos app, you see that photos are organized in various groupings, indicated by tabs at the top of the screen on an iPad and at the bottom on an iPhone/iPod touch.

The Photos app gets information about these groupings from the photo application from which the photos were synced or captured. If the application you use doesn't support one of these concepts or you don't add information to your photos, such as faces (which tags photos with a person's name/face), that grouping won't appear in the Photos app. Likewise, if you don't have photos associated with events, you won't see the Events tab.

The list of all possible tabs/categories follows:

- **Photos (iPad)/Photo Library (iPhone/iPod touch)**—The Photos tab on iPads and the Photo Library album on iPhones/iPod touches contain all the photos currently stored on the device (you don't see the Photo Library on an iPhone/iPod touch if you haven't synced photos from iTunes onto the device).

- **Camera Roll**—The Camera Roll album, which is located on the Albums tab, stores the photos that you've taken using the device's camera or that you've saved from email, messages, or other apps on the device.

- **Albums**—This tab shows photos organized by album. You can create albums in a photo application on a computer and then sync them to the iOS device, or, as you learn later in this chapter, you can create albums on your iOS device.

- **Photo Stream**—You can use this tab to access the photos stored on your Photo Stream. You can view photos and save them to your iOS device. Working with Photo Stream is covered in detail later in this chapter.

- **Events**—Events are collections of photos based on time (such as all the photos taken on the same day) or some other criteria, such as vacation.

- **Faces**—Some applications, such as iPhoto and Aperture, enable you to tag people in photos with names. You can use the Faces option in the Photos app to find photos to view based on the people in those photos.

- **Places**—When photos have been tagged with location information (either automatically through a camera with a GPS locator, such as when they were taken on an iOS device, or manually by adding the location in a photo application), you can find photos to view by selecting a location on the map.

You can open the Photos app and view photos individually by performing the following general steps:

1. Select the grouping of photos containing photos you want to view. You do this by tapping the corresponding tab. For example, if you want to look at the photos in a specific album, tap **Albums** (see Figure 19.7); if you want to looks at photos based on their location, tap **Places**. You see all the sources of photos in the grouping you selected.

2. Use the resulting screen to find the specific source you want to view. In most cases, such as Albums, Events, and Faces, you swipe up and down the screen to browse the available albums, events, and faces, respectively. Places works a bit differently, as described shortly.

FIGURE 19.7

Here I'm browsing the Albums available on this iPad mini.

3. Tap the source of photos you want to view, such as an album or event. You see thumbnails of all the photos in that source (except for Places, which is slightly different) as shown in Figure 19.8.

FIGURE 19.8

The screen shows thumbnails of the photos in the album called Boston Trip.

4. Tap the photo you want to view. It opens, and you see the photo viewing tools as shown in Figure 19.9.

FIGURE 19.9

Here I'm viewing a photo in the Boston Trip album.

The steps to view photos based on location are slightly different:

1. Tap **Places**. You see a map; each location that has photos associated with it is marked with a pushpin (see Figure 19.10).

FIGURE 19.10

The Places tab enables you to find photos based on where they were taken.

2. Drag on the map to move around until you see the area containing photos you want to view.

3. Double-tap or unpinch on an area on the map to zoom in. As you zoom in, the locations of the pushpins get more specific, so you may see several pushpins zoomed in where you saw only one when zoomed out.

4. Tap a pushpin. You see the number of photos associated with that location.

5. To browse the photos for a location, tap its Info button (the right-facing arrow). You see the photos taken at that location.

6. Browse and view the photos the same as you do from other sources.

When you are viewing a photo, you can use a number of tools:

*   **Move to the next or previous photo in the source**—Swipe to the left to view the next photo in the group (album, event, place, and so on). Swipe to the right to view the previous photo in the album.

*   **Jump to a specific photo (iPads)**—On iPads, you can use the thumbnail toolbar at the bottom of the screen to navigate through the photos you are viewing (refer to Figure 19.9). The thumbnail of the photo currently being

displayed is magnified and appears in the white box. You can drag the box until it is over the photo you want to view. You can also tap any photo's thumbnail to view it.

- **Change orientation**—Rotate the device to change the orientation of the photo so that it maximizes the display space of the screen. For example, if the photo is in landscape mode, rotate the device so it is also in landscape orientation.

- **Zoom in or out**—Unpinch or double-tap on the photo to zoom in. Pinch or double-tap on the photo to zoom out.

- **Scroll around**—When you are zoomed in, drag on the photo to scroll in it.

- **Display the photo on an AirPlay device**—Tap the **AirPlay** button and then tap the AirPlay device, such as an Apple TV, on which you want to display the photo. The button turns blue to indicate the photo is being streamed to the device. Use the Photo app's controls to change how the photo is displayed.

- **Share the photo**—Tap the **Action** button (the rectangle with an arrow coming out of it) to send the photo via email, message, Photo Stream, tweet, or Facebook posting. (Examples of some of these are provided later in this chapter.) You can also print photos, assign them to contacts, copy them, or use a photo as your device's wallpaper.

- **Show/hide tools**—After a few moments, the tools will automatically be hidden. Tap anywhere on the photo to show the toolbar. Tap again to hide the tools.

When you are done viewing the photos in the current source, tap the Back button located in the upper-left corner of the screen (it's labeled with the name of the screen from which you came).

Viewing Photos as a Slideshow

You can view photos in slideshows using the following steps:

1. Open the Photos app.

2. Choose the source of photos you want to view in a slideshow and browse the photos. You can start a slideshow from photos in any of the sources you see (such as Albums, Photo Stream, Events, Faces, or Places).

3. Tap the source of photos you want to view in a slideshow, such as a place. Thumbnails for the photos in the selected source appear.

4. On an iPad, tap the **Slideshow** button; on an iPhone/iPod touch, tap the photo you want to start the slideshow with in the selected source and then tap the **Play** button.

5. Tap **Transitions**.

6. Tap the transition you want to be used between photos in the slideshow.

7. If you want music to play during the slideshow, set the **Play Music** switch to ON.

8. Tap **Music**.

9. Use the Music app to find and tap the music you want to hear (see Chapter 15, "Listening to Music with the Music App," for details).

10. Tap **Start Slideshow** (see Figure 19.11). The slideshow begins to play, as does the music you selected.

FIGURE 19.11

Use the Slideshow Options tools to configure the slideshow.

The slideshow plays; each slide appears on the screen for the length of time you set using the Photos & Camera settings. The transition you selected is used to move between photos. If you set slideshows to repeat in Photos & Camera settings, the slideshow plays until you stop it; if not, it stops after each photo has been shown once.

11. To change the orientation of the slideshow, rotate the iOS device.

12. To stop the slideshow before it finishes, tap the screen. The photo tools appear, and the slideshow stops at the current photo.

13. Use the photo viewing tools to view the photos.

14. When you're done with the slideshow, tap the **Back** button, which is labeled with the source's name.

Editing Photos

You can use the Photos app to edit your photos. Follow these general steps to edit a photo:

1. View the photo you want to edit.

2. Tap **Edit**. The editing tools appear.

3. Use the editing tools to change the photo (see Figure 19.12); details for each tool are provided in subsequent steps.

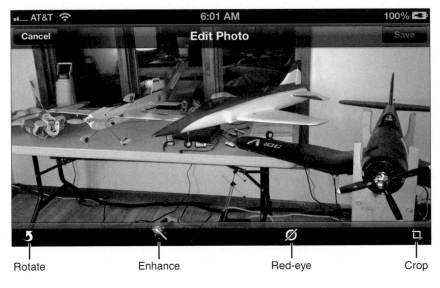

FIGURE 19.12

The Photos app enables you to edit your photos.

4. Tap **Save** to save the edited photo.

The following sections provide details for step 3 and assume steps 1, 2, and 4 are performed in addition to the steps included in the sections.

Rotating Photos

To rotate an image, edit it and tap the **Rotate** button. The image rotates 90 degrees each time you tap it until it returns to its original position. Tap **Save** when it is the orientation you want.

Enhancing Photos

To improve the quality of a photo, use the Enhance tool. Edit the photo and tap the **Enhance** button. The app attempts to improve the quality of the photo; you briefly see the Auto-Enhance On message. If you don't like the enhancements, tap the **Enhance** button again or tap **Cancel**. To save the enhanced image, tap **Save**.

 TIP On iPads, you can tap the **Undo** button to undo your last edit or the **Revert to Original** button to change the photo the way it was before you started editing it.

Removing Red-Eye

To remove red-eye, perform the following steps:

1. View the photo and move into edit mode.

2. Zoom in on the eyes from which you want to remove red-eye.

3. Tap the **Red-eye** button.

4. Tap each eye that has the red-eye problem (see Figure 19.13).

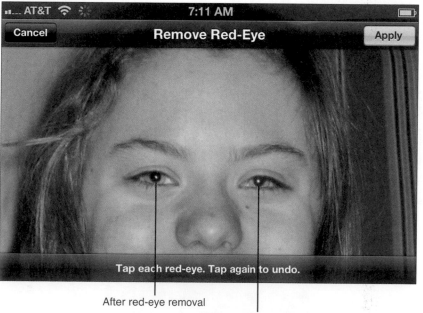

FIGURE 19.13

You can use the red-eye tool to remove the impact of using flash close to your subjects.

5. Tap **Apply**.

6. Tap **Save**.

Cropping an Image

To crop an image, do the following:

1. View the photo and move into edit mode.

2. Tap the **Crop** button.

3. To constrain the crop to specific proportions, tap **Constrain**; to crop without constraining, skip to step 5.

4. Tap the ratio to which you want to constrain the crop. The crop box is resized to be the proportion you selected.

5. Zoom or drag on the image and the crop box until the part of the image you want to keep is in the crop box (if you've constrained it, the crop box will automatically expand or contract in both directions). You can drag an edge of the box to change its size, and drag on the photo inside the box to change the box's location on the photo.

6. When the image you want is inside the crop box, tap **Crop** (see Figure 19.14). The image is cropped.

FIGURE 19.14

Use the cropping tool to remove unwanted parts of photos.

7. Tap **Save**.

EDITING PHOTOS YOU DIDN'T TAKE ON THE iOS DEVICE

You can edit any photo stored on your iOS device, whether you used the iOS device's camera to take it or not. When you edit and save a photo that wasn't taken with your iOS device, such as one you've imported from iPhoto, you are prompted to save the edited version to the Camera Roll. If you save it, you can sync your photos to move it to a computer or use Photo Stream to save it.

Organizing Photos in Albums

You can create photo albums and store photos in them. You can organize and store photos that you've taken on the device along with those from other sources, such as Photo Stream.

It is important to understand that when you place a photo in an album, the photo itself remains in the original source and a link to the photo is placed in the album. For example, it you take a photo on the device and then add it to an album, the original photo remains in the Camera Roll album.

This means whatever you do to the photo, such as editing it or deleting it, is done to the photo in each location. This is most important for photos you have taken with the device because when you delete a photo that is stored only on the device, it is deleted from all locations. It also impacts editing. If you crop a photo in one place, it is cropped in each location. (When you edit photos not captured on the device, you are prompted to save a copy, so this doesn't apply to the original.)

Creating Albums

To create a new album, perform the following steps:

1. Move to the Albums tab.

2. Tap the **Add** button (+).

3. Type the name of the album.

4. Tap **Save**. The new name appears on the list of albums, but it is gray at this point. You're prompted at the top of the screen to add photos to the new album.

5. To add a photo, tab the source, and then tap the photo you want to add to the album. Continue tapping photos you want to add. (You can add photos to the album later too, so you don't have to get them all now.) Each photo you tap displays a check mark in a circle.

6. Tap **Done**. The new album is created and the name of the album turns black in the Album list.

Adding Photos to Albums

You can add photos to existing albums by doing the following:

1. View the source of photos you want to add to an album, such as another album, a place, and so on.

2. Tap **Edit**. The screen becomes the Select Photos screen (if you have videos and photos, the screen's name is Select Items).

3. Tap the photos you want to place in an album. As you select photos, they are marked with a check mark, and the number you have selected appears at the top of the screen.

4. Tap **Add To**.

5. Tap **Add to Existing Album** (see Figure 19.15). You move to the Albums tab.

FIGURE 19.15

You can move photos to an existing album or create a new album for them.

   TIP   To place the photos in a new album, tap **Add to New Album**, name the new album, and tap **Save**.

6. Tap the album in which you want to place the photos (you can only choose albums created on the device). The photos are moved into the album and you return to the source you were working with.

Managing Albums

The following are a few more things you can do with albums:

- **Moving albums**—You can change the order in which albums appear on the Albums tab. On an iPad, tap and hold on the album you want to move; when its thumbnail enlarges, drag it to its new location. On an iPhone/iPod touch, tap **Edit** and the drag the album's **List** button (the horizontal lines) up or down the screen. When you've ordered the albums the way you want them, tap **Done**.

- **Renaming albums**—Tap **Edit**. Tap the name that you want to change. The keyboard appears. Make the changes to the album's name and then tap **Done** to close the keyboard. Tap **Done** to close the editing session. (You can only edit the names of albums that were created on the device).

- **Removing photos from albums**—Open the album. Tap **Edit**. Tap the photos you want to remove. Tap **Remove** and then tap **Remove from Album**.

- **Deleting albums**—When you delete an album, you remove only the album. The photos it contains remain on the device. On the Albums tab, tap **Edit**. On an iPad, tap the **Remove** button (x) that appears on the album and then tap **Delete**. On an iPhone/iPod touch, tap the **Unlock** button (the hyphen in a red circle) next to the album you want to delete and then tap **Delete**; tap **Delete Album**. Finally, tap **Done**.

Sharing Photos

There are lots of ways to share photos from the Photos app. These are Mail, Message, Photo Stream, Twitter, and Facebook. Each of these works similarly; an example using the Mail option will enable you to use any of the options, although the details will be a bit different:

1. Browse the source of photos you want to send in an email.

2. Tap **Edit**.

3. Select the photos you want to send by tapping them. When you tap a photo, it is marked with a check mark to show you that it is selected.

4. Tap **Share**.

5. Tap **Mail**. A new email message is created, and the photos are added as attachments.

6. Use the Mail app's tools to address the email, add a subject, type the body, and send it (see Figure 19.16).

FIGURE 19.16

Sending photos via email is a great way to share them.

 TIP You can share a photo by viewing it and then tapping the **Action** button. Tap the option you want to use such as **Mail** or **Message**.

7. If prompted to do so, tap the scale of the images you want to send. Choosing a smaller scale makes the files smaller but reduces the quality of the photos. You should generally try to keep the size of emails to 5MB or less to ensure the message makes it to the recipient (some email servers will block larger messages). After you send the email, you move back to the photos you were browsing.

SAVING PHOTOS SHARED WITH YOU

When a photo is shared with you, you can save it to your Camera Roll. For example, when you receive an email with photos attached, tap the **Action** button. Tap the **Save X Images** button, where X is the number of images attached to the message (if there is only one attachment, this is **Save Image**).

Using Your Photo Stream

With iCloud's Photo Stream, devices can automatically upload photos to the cloud. Other devices can automatically download photos from the cloud so you have your photos available on all your devices. Photo Stream has two sides: a sender and receiver. Your iOS device can be both. Photo applications, such as iPhoto and Aperture on a Mac, can also access your Photo Stream and download photos to your computer automatically. Windows PCs can also be configured to automatically download photos from your Photo Stream. (See Chapter 11 for configuring Photo Stream on iOS devices and on computers.)

You can also share your photo streams with others and view photos being shared with you.

THE CLOUD ISN'T FOREVER

New photos are stored on the cloud for only 30 days, so before that time expires, you need to move the photos into a location that stores them permanently. If you've taken them with your iOS device or other iOS device, they are stored in the Camera Roll album, and you can move them into a different album or onto a computer through a sync; these photos aren't deleted from the iOS device automatically. However, photos you are only viewing from the Photo Stream source on your iOS device will disappear from your iOS device after 30 days (when they leave the cloud). If you want to save them permanently on your iOS device, move them from the Photo Stream source into an album on your iOS device (as explained earlier). However, if you've configured the photo application you use on a computer to automatically download photos from the Photo Stream, the photos will be saved there automatically; you can move them back onto your iOS device through the photo sync process.

Viewing Photo Stream Photos

Viewing photos from the Photo Stream is just like viewing photos in albums or other sources. Tap the **Photo Stream** tab (see Figure 19.17). The My Photo Stream source contains all the photos stored in your Photo Stream; tap it to browse and view its photos.

FIGURE 19.17

The Photo Stream source contains all the photos on the cloud along with those you are sharing and photos being shared with you.

You also see photos you are sharing, which are annotated with "Shared by Me." Additionally, you see streams being shared with you, which are indicated by the "Shared by" caption. You can browse and view these sources too, though there are some additional options as you'll see shortly.

Sharing Photo Streams

To create a new, shared Photo Stream, do the following:

1. Move to a source of photos you want to share via Photo Stream.

2. Tap **Edit**.

3. Tap the photos you want to share.

4. Tap **Share**.

5. Tap **Photo Stream**; if you have not created a shared Photo Stream before, skip to step 7.

6. Tap **New Photo Stream**.

7. Enter the email addresses of the people with which you want to share the photos.

8. Give the photo stream a name.

9. To make the photos available to anyone in iCloud.com, set the **Public Website** switch to ON.

10. Tap **Next**.

11. Add commentary about the photo stream you are sharing.

12. Tap **Post**. The photo stream is shared and the people with whom you shared it receive a notification (see the following section).

To add photos to an existing, shared Photo Stream, perform the previous steps task, except in the step 6, tap a shared photo stream instead of creating a new one. Enter your commentary and post the new photos. The photos are added to your shared photo stream and the people with whom you are sharing it receive notifications that new photos have been added along with your commentary.

To create a new, empty photo stream, tap the **Add** (+) button on the Photo Stream screen. Enter the information to share the photo stream. You can then add photos to the new stream as described in the previous paragraph.

Working with Photo Streams Shared with You

You can work with photo streams people are sharing with you as follows:

1. Open the notification you receive (see Figure 19.18).

FIGURE 19.18

When someone shares a Photo Stream with you, you receive a notification like this.

2. Tap **Accept**. You move into the Photos app and see the photos in the photo stream being shared with you.

3. View the photos as with photos stored on your iOS device.

4. To see commentary about the photo, tap the **Quote** button (see Figure 19.19), which also indicates how many comments there are.

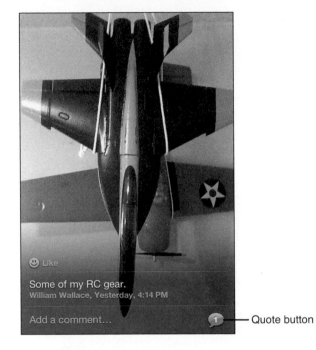

Quote button

FIGURE 19.19

You can add commentary to photos being shared with you.

5. Tap **Add a comment** to add your own commentary to the photo.

6. Tap **Like** to indicate you like the photo.

 TIP You can do most of the tasks with shared photos that you can with your own, such as emailing them, using them as wallpaper, and so on. To save a shared photo on your iOS device, tap the **Action** button and then tap **Save to Camera Roll**.

To unsubscribe from a photo stream on an iPad, open the **Photo Stream** tab and tap **Edit** and double tap the stream from which you want to unsubscribe. To unsubscribe from a photo stream on an iPhone/iPod touch, open the **Photo Stream** tab and tap its **Info** button (right-facing arrow). On the photo stream's screen, you see the owner of the stream along with other people sharing it. Tap **Unsubscribe** and confirm that is what you want to do. The shared photo stream is removed from your iOS device.

SAVING PHOTOS PERMANENTLY

An iOS device isn't really designed to be a permanent storage place for your photos. Its memory is relatively limited, and if you take enough photos (and store lots of other content on it, such as music and movies), you'll eventually run out of room and may not be able to take more photos. Plus, you can lose a device or it might get stolen. If you want to ensure you don't lose your photos, you need to store them in a more permanent location; for example, a photo application (such as iPhoto) on a computer.

If you are using Photo Stream on your iOS device and have set up automatic downloads to a computer (see Chapter 11), you don't need to worry about this because photos are automatically downloaded from your Photo Stream and either put in a folder or added to your photo application so they are stored permanently.

If you don't use Photo Stream, you should periodically import photos from your iOS device onto a computer. Most photo applications on Macs and Windows PCs can import pictures directly from an iOS device. In many cases, whenever you connect an iOS device to your computer and it has new photos on it, you are prompted to download them. You should make sure to do this regularly to protect your photos.

Deleting Photos

You can only delete photos and videos in the Camera Roll album or albums you have created (in which case, they are only removed from the album, not from your device). To delete photos or videos you've taken with iOS device's camera, captured as a screenshot, or downloaded from email or other sources, take the following steps.

TIP   To remove photos that are loaded onto an iOS device via syncing with a computer, you must change the sync settings so those photos are excluded and then re-sync the device. You also can delete photos from your Photo Stream, as you learn later in this chapter.

1. Open the **Camera Roll** source.

2. Tap **Edit**.

3. Tap the photos or videos you want to delete. Each item you select is marked with a check mark to show you it is selected.

4. Tap **Delete**.

5. Tap **Delete Photo** or **Delete Selected Photos**. The items you selected are deleted.

Working with Video Using the Photos App

The Photos app also enables you to view and edit video. The tools are similar to those for working with photos.

Watching Video

Watching videos you've captured with your iOS device works like so:

1. Open the **Camera Roll** source. Video clips have a camera icon and running time at the bottom of their thumbnails.

2. Tap the clip you want to watch.

3. Rotate the video to change its orientation if necessary.

4. Tap the **Play** button (see Figure 19.20). The video plays. After a few moments, the toolbars disappears.

Playhead

FIGURE 19.20

You can watch videos in the Photos app, too.

5. Tap the video. The toolbars reappear.

6. To pause the video, tap **Pause**.

7. To jump to a specific point in a clip, drag the **Playhead** to where you want to start playing it; if you hold your finger in one place for a period of time, the thumbnails expand so your placement of the playhead can be more precise. When you lift your finger, the playhead remains at its current location; if the clip is playing, it resumes playing from that point.

Editing Video

You can trim a video clip to remove unwanted parts. Here's how you do it:

1. View the video you want to edit.

2. Tap the screen to reveal the toolbar.

3. Drag the **left crop marker** to where you want the edited clip to start. If you hold your finger in one place for a period of time, the frames of video expand so your placement of the crop marker can be more precise. As soon as you move the crop marker, the part of the clip that is inside the selection is highlighted in the yellow box; the Trim button also appears.

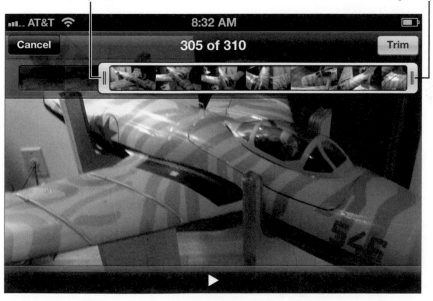

FIGURE 19.21

You can edit video by removing frames you don't want.

4. Drag the **right crop marker** to where you want the edited clip to end.

5. Tap **Trim**.

6. Tap **Trim Original** to edit the clip and replace the original version with the edited version or **Save as New Clip** to create a new clip containing only the frames between the crop markers. The frames outside the crop markers are removed from the clip. The clip is trimmed and replaces the original clip or a new clip is created depending on the option you selected.

Sharing Video

You can share videos you've taken on your iOS device by email, text message, or YouTube. (You must have a YouTube account to share videos via YouTube.) Sharing videos is similar to sharing photos. Move to the clip, tap the **Action** button, and tap Mail, Message, or YouTube.

THE ABSOLUTE MINIMUM

In this chapter, you learned how useful an iOS device can be for photos and video.

- Use the Photos & Camera settings to configure the related options, such as Photo Stream sharing, how long slides in a slideshow appear on screen, and so on.

- An iOS device, especially an iPhone or iPod touch, makes a great still photo and video camera because it captures high-quality images, has a number of nice features, and you are likely to have the device with you most of the time.

- You can use the Camera app to take photos or video using either the front or back lens.

- The Photos app offers features you can use to view photos individually and in slideshows with transitions and music. You can also edit photos, organize them in albums, and share them via Photo Stream.

- The Photos app also enables you to watch video clips you've captured and do some basic editing by trimming frames out of clips.

Index

W-X-Y-Z

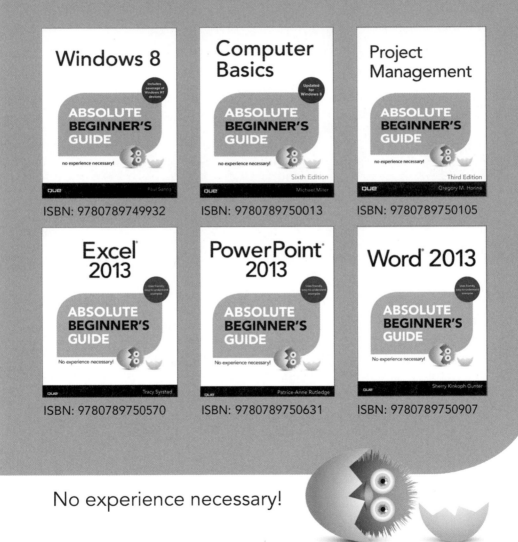

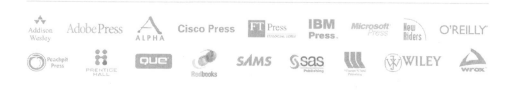

iTunes® and iCloud®
for iPhone®, iPad®, & iPod® touch

ABSOLUTE BEGINNER'S GUIDE

No experience necessary!

que   Brad Miser

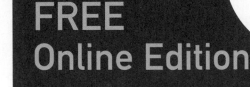

Safari® Books Online

FREE
Online Edition

Your purchase of *iTunes and iCloud for iPhone, iPad, & iPod touch Absolute Beginner's Guide* includes access to a free online edition for 45 days through the **Safari Books Online** subscription service. Nearly every Que book is available online through **Safari Books Online**, along with thousands of books and videos from publishers such as Addison-Wesley Professional, Cisco Press, Exam Cram, IBM Press, O'Reilly Media, Prentice Hall, Sams, and VMware Press.

Safari Books Online is a digital library providing searchable, on-demand access to thousands of technology, digital media, and professional development books and videos from leading publishers. With one monthly or yearly subscription price, you get unlimited access to learning tools and information on topics including mobile app and software development, tips and tricks on using your favorite gadgets, networking, project management, graphic design, and much more.

Addison Wesley   Adobe Press   ALPHA   Cisco Press   FT Press FINANCIAL TIMES   IBM Press   Microsoft Press   New Riders   O'REILLY

Peachpit Press   PRENTICE HALL   que   Redbooks   SAMS   SAS Publishing   vmware PRESS   WILEY   WROX